*G*lowing Comments from Corporate, Entrepreneurial, Sales, Marketing, Government, Educational, and other Leaders about . . .

NO EXCUSE!
JAY RIFENBARY

"We love your new book, *No Excuse!* We implemented your new philosophy company-wide and achieved a 30% increase in sales volume. You can take this book directly to the bottom line. There is "No Excuse!" for not reading it today."

-Kenneth J. Burgess Jr.
President, Morgan Hill, Inc.

"Jay Rifenbary has found the key to personal power, internal motivation, and individual excellence! This book gives a simple, practical blueprint for outstanding performance. Everyone needs to read it."

-Brian Tracy
Author of *Maximum Achievement*

"I read your book! Exciting! Filled with good stuff. Have quoted you in two speeches and two TV shows this week."

-Ty Boyd, CSP, CPAE
President, Boyd Enterprises, Inc.
Speaker and Consultant

"I am very impressed with the book *No Excuse!* You have gathered a wealth of knowledge and compiled it into a simple, clear, concise volume. I hope its circulation will spread far and wide."

-Robert A. Rohm, Ph.D.
President, Personality Insights, Inc.
Author of *Positive Personality Profiles*

"Well done...*No Excuse!* is a tough but caring view of the mission of our lives...read it and use the principles. I recommend it whole-heartedly."

-Larry Wilson, CPAE
Founder & CEO, Pecos River Learning Center
Author of *Stop Selling Start Partnering*
Co-author of *The One Minute Salesperson*

D1605721

"Jay Rifenbary has given the world a most generous gift. Anyone who reads this book and applies the "No Excuse!" philosophy daily can create the life they want and make a difference."

-Jack Canfield, CSP
President, Self-Esteem Seminars
Bestselling author of *Chicken Soup For The Soul*

"The philosophy and strategies that comprise *No Excuse!* are what is *sorely* missing from the public school curriculum. *No Excuse!* needs to be mandatory for school board members, administrators, teachers, senior high school and college students, and most importantly parents. The book is a breath of fresh air for our educational community."

-Dr. Edward Placke, Ed.D.
Director of Pupil Services
North Colonie Central School District

"You have no excuse for not reading *No Excuse!*...or for accomplishing all that you're capable of achieving as a result! Jay Rifenbary's "No Excuse!" Action Plans could positively change your life."

-Michael P. McKinley, CSP, CPAE
President, National Speakers Association

"Imagine you were in a life and death situation. Would anything matter other than getting to safety? Of course not! That's exactly the attitude that *No Excuse!* conveys. This book will cause every reader to 'snap-out-of-it' and get on to living. Jay Rifenbary has done an excellent job of showing all of us, youth and grown-ups alike, how to 'grow-up, get-over-it, and get-on-with-it.' I think you'll find this book exciting, and you'll feel that it's a very effective wake-up call. I certainly did."

-Jim Cathcart, CSP, CPAE
Speaker
Author of *Rethinking Yourself* and *The Acorn Principle*

"Never before in my lifetime has this society needed the philosophy contained in these pages more. In business, government, education, and religion the time is now to stand up and be totally accountable for our own actions. The antithesis has failed miserably in socialistic countries as well as in social programs in our great nation. It's time to stop expecting our government to coddle each of us from the cradle to the grave. It's time to be a "No Excuse!" person."

-J. Charles Plumb
Bestselling author of *I'm No Hero*
One of America's Top 10 Speakers
Former Vietnam POW

"Excuses are a dime a dozen. For every reason something can be done, there are a dozen reasons why it can't be done. *No Excuse!* gets you to focus on the one and not the dozen. It's a marvelous book that you will not only get a lot out of, but it's a book that will get a lot out of you. Buy it today. Read it tonight!"

-Morris E. Goodman
President, Miracle Man Productions
Author of *The Miracle Man*

"*No Excuse!* will have a tremendous impact on young and old alike. The philosophy and skills in this book need to be shared with coaches, players, business executives, managers, salespeople, employees' families, and anyone who is reaching for excellence in their life. Jay's inspirational thoughts and anecdotes will leave you feeling better about where you are today. By incorporating the "No Excuse!" philosophy into your life, you'll be able to accelerate to where you want to be tomorrow."

-Daniel E. "Rudy" Ruettiger
Motivational speaker and author of *Rudy's Rules*
Inspiration for the blockbuster movie *Rudy*

"Over-regulated, bureaucratic leadership has turned many employees and citizens into whining 'victims' that cry for 'level playing fields.' If our young, new managers and leaders follow Jay's "No Excuse!" philosophy, they will truly reinvent our organizations and allow society to evolve to its next level of greatness."

-Charles "Chic" Thompson
President, Creative Management Group
Author of *What a Great Idea!* and *Yes, But...*

"Tremendous! This book has it all, because all success begins and ends with the "No Excuse!" philosophy. Jay Rifenbary brings new life to this great truth because he lives it every day. It's never too early or too late to adopt the "No Excuse!" philosophy. This book is a living classic. It will be a life-changing experience for those who make this philosophy a way of life."

-Charlie "Tremendous" Jones
Bestselling author of *Life Is Tremendous*
Speaker and owner, Executive Books

"I found *No Excuse!* excellent due to the importance of its message. I can only wish you bestseller status for a long time and a 100% reader conversion. The conversion will make our world a much better and simpler place."

-Robert A. McCormick
President & Chief Executive Officer, Trustco Bank

"*No Excuse!* is succinct. Jay Rifenbary has given the tools to accept total responsibility for your life. When you act on the "No Excuse!" philosophy, you can have freedom and inner peace in all areas of your life."

-Miriam Burkart
Director, McGrane Self-Esteem Institute

"This book gives you the gifts of a "No Excuse!" life. Read it, apply its principles, and share it with your friends and business associates."

-Andy Andrews
Humorist and Motivational Speaker
Bestselling author of *Storms of Perfection*

"During my 70+ years of being on a constant excursion in life, searching for all the things my curiosity leads me to, I have concluded that the word *excuse* needs to be banished from our vocabulary. I believe this book will draw us closer to that point. It will have immense value to those who take advantage of your philosophy of overcoming obstacles. With this book you have done very well, exceeding all expectations. I hope to use it as a self-guide for myself and as a suggestion to others."

-Ida Crawford Stewart
Former VP, Estee Lauder

"Jay Rifenbary's work *No Excuse!* is a step-by-step program that will help parents and students achieve success in their daily lives. The pressures of scholastic life and the world of work can be so overwhelming that parents and students alike can struggle without a support system. *No Excuse!* is that support system. It brings to light such needed values as integrity, honesty, commitment, and most of all personal accountability. This work is extremely readable and filled with real-world examples. The book reveals Jay's commitment to the education of our youth, and through his teachings, his genuine concern for every individual's personal and professional development. I recommend the book without reservation for businesses, schools, and homes."

-Michael McCarthy, M.Ed.
High School Principal
Education Specialist, The George Washington University

"Many, many people came to me and were encouraged by your message. I heard, 'This is something I want to put into practice today,' and one of the fellows said, 'Wouldn't it have been nice if everybody had been here to hear this?' Exciting reading, enjoyably straightforward, emotionally challenging. *No Excuse!* needs to become a way of life, not only good reading."

-Warren Smith
President, Electro-Term, Inc.

Leaders Comments continued on page 334

A New Philosophy
for Overcoming Obstacles
& Achieving Excellence

JAY RIFENBARY
WITH MIKE & MARJIE MARKOWSKI

A Success Publishers Book
Published by Markowski International Publishers
Hummelstown, PA USA

with
Mike & Marjie Markowski

Published by
SUCCESS PUBLISHERS
Markowski International Publishers
1 Oakglade Circle
Hummelstown, PA 17036 USA

Success Publishers is an imprint and trademark
of Markowski International Publishers

Manufactured in the United States of America

Publisher's Cataloging in Publication
(Prepared by Quality Books, Inc.)

Rifenbary, Jay.
     No excuse! : a new philosophy for overcoming obstacles and achieving excellence./Jay Rifenbary with Mike & Marjie Markowski. – 1st ed.
     p. cm. – (Personal development series)
     Preassigned LCCN: 94-077875.
     ISBN 0-938716-23-9 (Cloth)
     ISBN 0-938716-22-0 (Paper)
     1. Success–Psychological aspects. 2. Self-realization. 3. Happiness–Psychological aspects. I. Markowski, Michael A. II. Markowski, Marjorie L. III. Title.
BF697.5.S8R54 1995   158'.1

                                             QBI94-2377

DEDICATION

To my beloved wife Noni and my children Nicole and Jared, for their patience, love, and understanding of their adventurous spouse and dad.

To my mother Dorothy, for her lifelong love, patience, and untiring desire to be the best parent possible, which she accomplished.

To my sister Deborah, for her expertise in language and life.

To my Uncle T.J., for the love and support he gave me in all that I strived for in my life.

To my dad George, for the spirit of what he was and what he gave.

Tribute: To all contributors of knowledge, hope, common sense, and love, and all those who strive to make a difference.

LETTER TO MY FATHER

Dear Dad,   January 1, 1995

This is the first letter I have ever written to you. As you know, I was only eleven when you died, but I never had a need to write to you until now. I am thirty-eight now, and a lot has happened in my life that I know you would be proud of.

I just want to tell you how much I have missed you and how much I have desired your encouraging and reassuring words. There were many times in my life that your being there would have meant the world to me. It certainly would have made life's trials more bearable.

That simple hug or touch a father shares with his son I will never feel again, yet I now have the wonderful opportunity to share that with my own children. It took many years for me to become satisfied with me and what I have to offer others around me. I know that while you were here you gave me everything you felt was best, with honesty and sincerity.

I truly love you and ask for your blessing. I ask for your spirit of strength for me and my family. Thank you for helping me find peace within myself and to feel the satisfaction of giving to other people.

Your beloved son,
Jay

Please Consider This A Personal Welcome

Dear Friend,

Welcome to what I have endeavored to make one of the most dynamic success programs ever developed. *No Excuse!* is the culmination of the knowledge and experience I have acquired over the years. I believe it will invigorate you to achieve new heights in your personal and professional life. You'll learn some of the finest success principles known to man. Forgiveness, Self-Esteem, and Attitude are just a few of the areas addressed.

The "No Excuse!" philosophy can help you unleash many of your hidden desires and talents and teach you how to utilize them to benefit yourself and others you want to help. The premise of "No Excuse!" centers around the concept of self-responsibility. We are each the decision-makers and managers of our personal and professional lives whether we realize it or not. Once you understand that you are the one who is in charge of your life, there will truly be "No Excuse!" for you not to achieve the success you want.

I believe people everywhere are "sick-and-tired" of irresponsible behavior and mediocrity. I also believe people are realizing more than ever the importance of the family unit and good interpersonal relationships. It's time for everyone to stop blaming and complaining, whining and moaning, and taking the stance of a victim. No one is entitled to a "free ride," and we all need to start living more self-responsibly.

The world is in desperate need of more leaders in the home, as well as in communities, corporations, and government. I believe the "No Excuse!" approach will help a lot of people grow and become all they can be. I am convinced *No Excuse!* is the right book at the right time; it's a book for 21st Century Leaders. I believe it's a book for everyone!

As soon as I adopted this philosophy, my life began to have greater meaning, purpose, and focus. Using these ideas I took charge and built my life in the way I desired, not at the expense of others but by helping others! I believe you'll find it's a wonderful feeling to have a positive influence on other people and their success. After all, isn't that what true success is all about?

"No Excuse!" gives you the foundation to develop the skills you need to achieve the success you have always wanted for yourself and other people you want to help. It's a sincere pleasure to share the philosophy with you. It is my wish that the impact it has had on my life benefits you even more.

Remember, there truly is "No Excuse!" for you not to achieve success in your life.

Wishing you unlimited success,

-Jay Rifenbary

A Personal Message From The Publishers

When we first saw Jay present his "No Excuse!" philosophy on national television, we promptly ordered his workbook and tape. We felt an immediate kinship with him, discovered he was looking for a publisher, and soon became good friends. After we watched him present several times and learned more about him, we fell in love with the "No Excuse!" approach to life. We then agreed to help him write and publish his book.

We studied his work intensely, devoured his tapes, researched, modified, supplemented, re-wrote and fine-tuned the manuscript to make it as easy to read, understand, assimilate, and apply as possible. We approached our work on *No Excuse!* with a love and passion that knows no bounds. We poured our hearts and souls into it!

Along with Jay, our objective was to make *No Excuse!* the finest success/motivational/inspirational book it could possibly be. Jay's integrated, holistic approach to living self-responsibly, with greater purpose both personally and professionally, is innovative and refreshing. It is our hope to reach people all over the world to help them live happier, more productive lives.

We wish you tremendous success as you apply the "No Excuse!" approach to your life. Through his teachings and by his example, Jay has taught us and thousands of others how to live happier, more fulfilling and purposeful lives. Meeting Jay has been one of the best things that has ever happened to us, and we are forever grateful. We hope you'll say that reading *No Excuse!* and applying its principles to your life is one of the best things you have ever done for yourself, your family, and your career or business.

As the owners of Markowski International Publishers, our mission is to help people all over the world grow and become all they can be through the written and spoken word. We want to make a difference in people's lives and help make the world a better place to live. We believe this is the best way we can serve.

May all your dreams come true,

-Mike and Marjie Markowski

CONTENTS

Acknowledgements

It's impossible to succeed alone. It takes the cooperative, interdependent effort of many people to accomplish anything worthwhile.

This work is a product of many fine people. It is a collection of thoughts, dreams, life experiences, and the wishes of many people for a better world. It is also a reflection, and an expression of the many wonderful people who have had a tremendous influence on my life achievements.

I am grateful for the inspiration and wisdom of many of the great teachers of motivation and success. I am also grateful for my many friends, relatives, classmates, teammates, coaches, teachers, professors, fellow soldiers, Airborne and Ranger instructors, commanders, managers and colleagues, for their positive support and guidance in all that I strived for. I am grateful for my experiences both at the Lawrenceville School in Lawrenceville, New Jersey, and the United States Military Academy at West Point, New York. Each provided a framework of challenges to grow and learn from and discover what made me *me*.

I am also grateful for my corporate sales and management experiences with Pfizer and HMSS. Each opened my eyes to a different world of how to conduct business and work with others. Finally, I am grateful for the many customers and business associates of my training and development center, retail operations, and other entrepreneurial endeavors. Thanks for your support and sharing my dream of helping others become successful, self-responsible, happy people.

It is important that I mention several specific people who, with their gifts of love, wisdom, understanding, and guidance helped make the dream of this book a reality. I feel a deep sense of gratitude:

To my wife Noni, for her constant love, continuing belief, and support of me through all the years of trial and error. It is easier to achieve when you're married to someone who lives the principles of love, compassion, patience, and empathy. She is my best friend and most helpful evaluator!

To my children Nicole and Jared, for their unconditional love and innocence, who never cease to amaze me just how great they are. You brighten every day!

To my mother Dorothy, for her devotion to her family, and the influence of her never-ending determination not to fail herself, her family, or her friends, and her constant saying to me, "You can do it!"

To my sister Deborah, for her perspective on life and how she inspired me to lighten-up when life got tough!

To the memory of my father, who gave me a positive example to live up to.

To my publishers Mike and Marjie Markowski, whose devotion to the completion of this work was surpassed only by their love for me and my family. Without their literary, publishing, and personal development talents and skills, the world would never have known the power of "No Excuse!" nor experience its lifelong benefits. They are more than publishers; they are teammates and friends in the quest to make this world a place where people recognize their responsibilities to themselves, others, and society.

To Ed and Dawn Placke, for their untiring friendship and love of my family.

To the employees of my first entrepreneurial endeavor. In particular Theodore Toppses, Michele Ippolito, Tracey Continelli, Timothy Gallagher, Sharon Randall, and Richard Sippel, for helping to make it a tremendous success.

To the staff of WMHT Educational Telecommunications. In particular, Dave Povero and Paul Hoagland for their production efforts in the making of the public television series.

To Anne Mulderry, Stephanie Brown, and Mary Scanlan for their literary efforts in providing a foundation to work from.

To Terry Goudie of the Nightingale-Conant Corporation, for her words of encouragement and support of my dreams.

And finally, to thank God for the gifts he has bestowed upon me, including my family, my health, the gift of expression, and the opportunity to make a positive difference in this world.

-Jay Rifenbary

A PERSONAL COMMITMENT TO EXCELLENCE

I am the sum total of the genetic endowment
with which I came into the world,
and of all the experiences which have
made up my life. Some of them have been good,
some bad, but all of them have been mine.
What I currently am is what I deserve to be.
My life, my reputation, my influence is the
mirror of the choices I have made. If I am not
everything I can be, it is because I haven't
chosen to be more.
I am determined not to live in my past, which
I cannot change, or to waste time waiting
for the future, which I cannot guarantee,
but to live in the emerging reality of the NOW,
which is all I have. I cannot do everything,
but I can do some things.
I certainly cannot do everything well, but I
can do some things well. I cannot guarantee I will
win, but I can promise I will not allow losing to
become a habit, and if I fail, it will not
be a failure of nerve.
So I will stand tall, feel deeply, think large,
and strive mightily, remembering what I
accomplish probably won't change the course
of human history, but what I attempt will create
the course of my personal history.
Toward making this declaration a reality,
I hereby commit myself!

JOHN COMPERE

PROLOGUE

"My lines are twisted."

I'm twelve hundred and fifty feet above the earth. My parachute hasn't snapped me out of my fall. I can't look up to see what's going on. My head is caught in a vise of tangled lines and my chin is hammered into my chest. Instinct and images recalled from training films tell me my parachute is trailing above me like a ribbon. The world around me appears chaotic and unconcerned about my dilemma. The drone of the plane above is gone. The sound of the wind and my awareness of the earth and sky is lost as I shut down and shut out. I can hear only my thoughts and feel my pounding heart.

I had only myself and my pack when our Airborne training unit boarded the C-130 "Hercules" transport plane for our *first* jump. As I stood in the belly of the plane, I felt all alone. All I had was on me and within me. Suddenly I was standing in the open door. I would be the first to fling a half-yearning, half-reluctant body out into space. "Go!" was the final word I heard from the Jump Master. The rush of wind, when it seems to pull you out the door, is the greatest thrill. All of a sudden you're suspended in mid-air, but only for an instant. As you start to fall, nature instantly measures your mass, and determines your destiny according to its laws.

My parachute was carefully packed...or was it? It's supposed to blossom and save me from falling to certain death. The laws of aerodynamics and physics are crucial. I knew this intuitively and through my education. They need to become allies. If not, my twisted lines will hold me hostage until I die!

"No excuse, Sir!" I thought back to my West Point training. No whining. No complaining. No blaming. Get on with it! Accept responsibility. I wanted to be Airborne, and was I ever. All I wanted now was a safe landing. I just wanted a chance to achieve what I desired in life. I wanted a successful military and business career; I wanted to be a loving husband and father; I wanted to be a leader who makes a difference in the lives of others. The future I dreamed about was instantly being tested by a courageous willingness to risk.

My survival was at stake. I had animal instinct and past experiences to rely on...my study of yesterday's pre-jump instructions...the academic, physical, emotional and spiritual discipline that got me into and through the United States Military Academy...my studies in nuclear physics, chosen because it was the toughest subject...my ninth-grade determination in swimming that formed championship proportions and drew me into poised, playful, social proficiency...my triumph in overcoming the humiliation I felt at having to repeat 7th grade...my mother's dauntless conviction that her only son, fatherless from age 11, would be a man of excellence. Finally, I had my father's heroic stature, his too frequent absences while he was alive, and his achingly illusive presence since his death.

"No excuse, Sir!" No! "Whose fault is this, anyway?"; "Did someone pack this parachute incorrectly?"; "Did someone...did I...slip-up in putting it on?"; "Who's going to be in trouble for this mistake?"

"No Excuse!" Cut through the garbage. *"My lines are twisted."* Do something!

"If The Lines Become Twisted...Bicycle!" All at once, my legs and brain remember. My feet are in heavy combat boots, never intended for flying or pedaling, but they must be put into motion. Miraculously...in action, the laws of physics are wonderful...the lines untwist. Like a newborn coming from the womb, whose lungs fill with that first breath of air, the parachute "explodes," forming a beautiful floating canopy. It jerks my freed head upward to behold the wonder. It gives me life and time to enjoy the glory of the world waiting for my touchdown.

If my mind drifted, even for an instant to make an excuse, it would have fatally distracted me from the enormity of my predicament. I would not have reacted fast enough to remedy the situation. Is this what we want when we jump into LIFE? Are we looking to explore new sensations...to push at the borders of our experience? Do we want to harness the forces that would control us? Do we want to grow and become better people? Do we want greater capacity for life and a deeper understanding of nature and other people?

Like an opened, gliding parachute, "No Excuse!" can help carry you over whatever thresholds you choose to cross. "No Excuse!" can help give your life a whole new meaning. "No Excuse!" can help you lead a successful, happy, fulfilling life of personal growth. "No Excuse!" can help you grow and become and make a difference. You can feel as if you are special and valuable...because you are.

RISK TO BE FREE

To laugh is to risk appearing a fool.
To weep is to risk appearing sentimental.
To reach out for another is to risk
exposing your true self.
To place your ideas, your dreams before
the crowd is to risk their loss.
To love is to risk not being loved in return.
To live is to risk dying. To hope
is to risk despair. To try is to risk failure.
But risks need to be taken because
the greatest hazard in life is to risk nothing.
The person who risks nothing does
nothing, has nothing, is nothing. He may avoid
suffering and sorrow, but he simply cannot
learn, feel, change, grow, love...live.
Chained by his beliefs, he is a slave; he has
forfeited freedom. Only a person who risks is free.

AUTHOR UNKNOWN

INTRODUCTION

"No Excuse!"
    The principles in *No Excuse!* have given me the understanding to reach heights I hadn't dreamed of. They can do the same for you when you put them in place and use them. They'll give you the tools to scale any mountain. At first they'll assist you like excited, new-found companions, met at the start of an adventure. With time and practice, they'll be your reliable, comforting friends, always ready to help you handle challenges. These principles can lead you to true wealth, which is so much more than just money. They can help you change untapped ambition into success.
    I have put together the "No Excuse!" principles based on my own experiences and observations, as well as those of Mike and Marjie Markowski. I have drawn particularly from my years at West Point and my Airborne/Ranger experiences. My years as a military officer, corporate executive, business owner, lecturer and motivational speaker, as well as a spouse and parent, have been invaluable in creating the "No Excuse!" philosophy.
    Fundamental to the philosophy is that people need the dignity of satisfying work to make their lives and the lives of others better. B.C. Forbes, founder of *Forbes Magazine* and author of several books, suggested that, "Whether we find pleasure in our work or whether we

find it a bore depends entirely upon our mental attitude toward it, not upon the task itself." *Whenever we combine labor and love, true success follows.* That's what the foundation of "No Excuse!" is all about. It can guide you to work smart at a life you love living.

We need to guard against drudgery and discouragement in everything we do. To be effective at this, we need to know that our work contributes to our well-being, as well as that of others. It is critical to your personal and professional development to understand that, *anything you let get in the way of applying yourself to your goals is only an excuse!*

"No Excuse!" is designed for people who want to make life better for themselves and others. They also need to be humble enough to be guided and encouraged to do so. "No Excuse!" is designed for people who want to lead fulfilled lives. It's for those who are willing to accept responsibility for their own success, as well as play a responsible role in the success of others. "No Excuse!" is designed for people who grow to understand and accept that success and failure are outcomes of their behavior. Failure is a lesson to prepare us to achieve the outcomes we want. It is a stepping stone.

For many, it's not easy to accept success. Many people see success only in the lives of others, which can cause them to develop apathetic, defeatist attitudes.

It's difficult to recognize our own success if we're caught in a web of negative thinking. "No Excuse!" means we accept responsibility for thinking positive. Dwelling on failure holds us back from having the results we want. Once we learn the lessons from our failures and mistakes, we can let go of them. "No Excuse!" is designed for people willing to eliminate the negative thinking that thwarts and overburdens their efforts. "No Excuse!" supports your efforts to identify, work toward, and achieve your dreams and goals.

The exercises in this book are meant to challenge you to explore your own thoughts, feelings, and perceptions. They are particularly meant to challenge your hidden thoughts so you can realize wisdom, strength, and goodness. More of your energies can then be used to serve others while achieving your dreams and goals.

What's your reward for this challenging work? How about getting rid of the fears of rejection and failure so you can move-on? Many of us carry around excess "baggage," full of excuses. They may always be there, ready to keep you in "safe" places when you fear failure and rejection. As you begin living a "No Excuse!" life, you'll have less room for excuses.

By using "No Excuse!" principles, you'll come to the day when *you can honestly say* "No Excuse!" because you won't need any. You'll eliminate that bad habit. You will have the opportunity to learn how to define success for yourself. You will learn from your own experiences that there is "No Excuse!" for you not to be successful.

When I devoted myself to developing and living out "No Excuse!", I made a personal and professional decision to walk away from what I thought was security. I would risk everything I had accumulated and have no one to blame, not even myself, if I failed. I had to realize that blaming myself would only be another way of defeating myself. This helped me remember my formal introduction to "No Excuse!"

I entered West Point in July of 1976. It's a place where the phrase "No excuse, Sir!" is uttered by cadets every day. It's one of the four answers a plebe (freshman) may give when addressed by an upperclassman. The others are "Yes, sir;" "No, sir;" and "Sir, I do not understand." In 1976, when I was 19, "No excuse, Sir!" meant no more to me than a way to end an uncomfortable one-sided conversation. I was too frightened and intimidated to understand why such rigid limitations were part of military training.

Thirteen years later, on a night in 1989, I had a powerful insight: *"No excuse, Sir!" was a basic statement that left nowhere to hide.* It had played a vital role in my development as a thinker and a doer. "No Excuse!" thinking was basic training. It was "Achievement 101." With every repetition, the "No Excuse!" response emphasized the benefits of "cleaning-the-slate" and "getting-on" with the search for solutions. There was no time to waste in unproductive excuse-making.

I was standing alone in my office, alone in the hush following a grand opening party for the business I had just started. For years I had dreamed of doing this, and I seized the moment. To get there, I had let go of a secure, flourishing career where I was methodically making my way to the top.

It was a difficult decision, about as hard as deciding not to make the military my career. I was driven by the desire for a different life. Fortunately, I was blessed with my wife's encouragement and support as I wrestled with decisions and made them.

I was happy about how I had gotten to where I was that night. But when the celebration was over and the hundreds of friends and supporters had gone, why did I stand there feeling so alone and frightened? When opening my own business was a dream come true, something most people only fantasize about, why did I feel so unaccomplished and unhappy?

I was filled with a rush of longing for my dad. I had never missed him so much; I never wanted his touch and approval as much as I did then. A yearning for what might have been surged through my heart. It was as though I was faltering on the edge of a cliff. I stood there until a peace came over me, as I sadly acknowledged it was time to let go of my father's death. It could not serve me as a reason or an excuse for making future decisions. It could never be an excuse for not attempting anything. His approval could not serve as motivation for attempting anything either. This would be true even if he were alive.

I realized that I was now an adult, moving-on to create the life I wanted for myself and my family. What I accomplished was achieved through honesty, sincerity, and commitment. It was also the result of vigorous effort in partnership with people I respected and loved.

In this moment I began my life as a self-responsible person. It's incredibly important to release the need for approval when we begin traveling on the road to fulfillment. I realized, for the first time, how crucial it is to create a life based on our own expectations. *In general, the real or imagined expectations of others simply don't matter.* Of course, if you are in a job situation, you may need to align some of your personal expectations with those of your boss. You'll want to be careful that your actions are in line with your value system and what you know to be right.

While feeling the great emptiness of my father's absence, I understood what was needed to begin a "No Excuse!" life. It required self-respect, self-responsibility, and self-acceptance to lead a full, mature life.

"No Excuse!" was born that night. It meant more freedom and power over my own destiny than I had ever known. Up to that point, all my achievements had only been on loan to me. Now I finally owned them and could benefit more fully from the lessons along the way.

I committed to moving-on. I felt secure in my ability to produce. I believed in the "Golden Rule" (Do unto others as you would have them do unto you.) and my ability to live and prosper by it. I was grateful for the love and support of significant people in my life. I was especially thankful for Noni, my loving wife, best friend, and business partner. Once I had made the decision, tremendous relief and exhilaration replaced the anxiety I'd been living with for so long. I had never quite experienced the power of the growth that occurs from responsibly crossing the threshold into new maturity and awareness.

Before we begin our "No Excuse!" journey toward greater achievement and personal fulfillment, here's a story I want to share with you.

Your Life Is In Your Hands

High on a hilltop overlooking a beautiful city, there lived a wise old man.   The local children were taught to seek his guidance and respect his teachings.

One day, two boys devised a plan to confuse the old man.   They caught a small bird and headed for the hilltop.   As they approached the seated figure, one of the boys held the little bird cupped in his hands.

"Wise old man," the boy said, "Can you tell me if the bird I have in my hands is dead or alive?"

The old man gazed silently at the two boys, and then said:
"If I tell you the bird locked in your hands is alive, you will close your hands and crush the life from it.   If I tell you the bird is dead, you will open your hands and it will fly away to freedom."

"Son, in your hands you hold the power of life and death.   In you resides the power to choose destruction and the end of a spirit and a song.   Or you can choose to free the bird so it has a future, with all its potential.   You are wise to know you can choose between life and death."

"If you allow my answer to determine whether the bird lives or dies, you will have given away your power.   You will have also given away your responsibility to make the correct choice, and to rejoice in your own strength and wisdom."

The boys came down that hill a bit wiser.   The old man, in respecting their desire to test themselves and his authority, proved to be a leader and a teacher.   He perceived their rebelliousness as an underlying desire to relinquish their self-responsibility.   By refusing to cooperate, he contributed to their self-awareness and growth.

We Are The Decision Makers

You and I need to be the decision makers in our own lives and careers.   It is also our responsibility to allow and encourage others to do the same.   We all have the power to choose, and our accumulated choices largely structure the lives we lead.   *Acknowledging we have choices is a first step toward accepting self-responsibility.*   Choosing to exercise our personal power by making choices is a challenge and joy in and of itself.

Children are exposed to society's expectations every day, through their parents/caretakers and other family members; in our churches and synagogues; through their peers and schools; and through movies, television, books, and music, to name a few influencing factors. Some of the expectations are positive and some are negative.

How often, if ever, are children taught that their first responsibility is to reflect on whether a certain direction is right for them? Did anyone ever tell you that? If so, when did you start doing it? Did you stop? Did anyone ever teach you how to think? Or were you, like many of us, taught to listen to parents and others without thinking for yourself?

This book will help you discover the power within yourself; the power to choose and act. It's a message meant to reach you where you think and feel, in your mind and in your heart, where it really counts. I hope "No Excuse!" will serve you, just as the wise man's words served the boys. I hope you will acknowledge your power and use it for the good of all. Did you know that when you use your power to obtain something truly in your best interest, as long as you aren't causing harm, that it is also in the best interest of others?

I believe you will use the principles explained here to make choices that are in your own and others' best interests. Your alternative would be to adopt the behavior patterns of many people; blindly follow the dictates of society and others, or blindly rebel against them. Either extreme is equally self-destructive and is not self-responsible. Just the fact that you are reading this book is a strong indicator that you are doing your best to make wise choices.

The outcomes we experience in our lives are largely dependent on our own choices and actions. The lessons I learned that night have been confirmed every day since. *Our actions, based on clear self-awareness and accompanied by self-responsibility, can create turning points in our lives.*

When you live a "No Excuse!" life, you will never again allow yourself to be pushed by circumstances or other people's desires that aren't in your best interest. You will clearly see where and when it is your opportunity and responsibility to make a decision. You will accept responsibility for the actions you take that contribute to your failures and successes. You will not blame anyone else for your failures, nor be self-centered in regard to your successes. You will always be aware of the part you played in both. You will rejoice in your successes and view your failures as learning experiences. When you live a "No Excuse!" life, you will be drawn toward your dreams.

The *THESAURUS Factor* and the *Staircase-of-Success*

The principles you find in this book constitute the treasury of my life. It is a treasury that increases every day and each time it is used. It contains truths that are essential to live a happy, fulfilled life. As you use these ideas, they will help you increase your understanding of life, thereby giving you the opportunity to increase your prosperity in all areas.

Why was the idea of "No Excuse!" and building a *Staircase-of-Success* developed? I wanted to organize the principles of success so that they are easy to understand and apply. I wanted to create a method anyone could use to make a difference in their lives and the lives of others.

Why are success principles so important? They're similar to the parts of a car. You could have the fastest car on the track, but if you neglect the fundamentals, you won't even finish the race. Things like gas, oil, and water, while simple, are vitally important.

You can be on the fast track of success, but if you neglect the fundamentals, you won't win. You need to concern yourself with things like honesty, integrity, purpose, desire, and letting go of the past. Do you ever think about these things? Most people are so concerned with the challenges of daily living, they rarely or never stop to think about these essential ingredients of success.

I wanted to find a synonym for success I felt would be appropriate to use as an acronym. I pulled out a thesaurus, but couldn't find a word I liked. Then I started thinking, "What does 'thesaurus' mean?" I went to a dictionary and found "thesaurus" means "a treasury of ideas; a treasury of knowledge."

So then I decided *THESAURUS* was a great word to describe the treasury of ideas on success that I wanted to share. And that's exactly what the *Staircase* is built on.   Your *Staircase-of-Success,* the *THESAURUS Factor*, takes each letter in the word *THESAURUS* and uses it as a step.

In Part I of this book, we'll cover the foundations of success: self-responsibility, purpose, and integrity. This will prepare you for your journey along the *Staircase-of-Success,* which is explained in-depth in Part II. Keep an open mind and have fun. It's going to be an exciting journey!

THE OPTIMIST'S CREED

Promise yourself:
To be so strong that nothing can disturb
your peace of mind.
To talk health, happiness, and prosperity
to every person you meet.
To make all your friends feel that there
is something in them.
To look at the sunny side of everything and
make your optimism come true.
To think only the best, to work only for the
best, and expect only the best.
To be just as enthusiastic about the success
of others as you are about your own.
To forget the mistakes of the past and press on
to the greater achievements of the future.
To wear a cheerful countenance at all times and
give every living creature you greet a smile.
To give so much time to the development of yourself
that you have no time to criticize others.
To be too large for worry, too noble for anger,
too strong for defeat, and too happy to
permit the presence of trouble.

AUTHOR UNKNOWN

Part One

Your Foundation for Success

THE MAN IN THE GLASS

When you get what you want in your struggle for self,
And the world makes you King For A Day;
Just go to a mirror and look at yourself,
And see what THAT man has to say.
For it isn't your father or mother or wife,
whose judgment upon you must pass;
The fellow whose verdict counts most in your life,
Is the one staring back from the glass.
Some people may think you're a straight-shootin'
chum, and call you a wonderful guy;
But the man in the glass says you're only a bum,
If you can't look him straight in the eye.
He's the fellow to please; never mind all the rest,
For he's with you clear up to the end;
And you've passed your most dangerous, difficult test,
If the man in the glass is your friend.
You may fool the whole world down the pathway
of life, and get pats on the back as you pass;
But your final reward will be heartaches and tears,
If you've cheated the man in the glass.

AUTHOR UNKNOWN

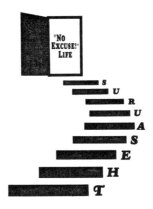

Chapter 1

SELF-RESPONSIBILITY
The Basis Of A "No Excuse!" Life

Attenn...TION!

At ease. You may have picked up this book to see what a successful life is all about and how to achieve it. In the simplest sense, the answers lie in the title: "No Excuse!" Once you become alert to the opportunity to make a productive decision, and are willing to take responsibility for it, the payoff can be a happy, fulfilling life.

I could tell you to go no further than that and be on your way. I could tell you to read no more, close this book, and start living the life you want. Well, it doesn't work quite like that.

As Ben Sweetland said, "Success is a journey, not a destination." It's also a learning process. Therefore, it is often helpful to learn about the experiences of someone else who has overcome obstacles that may be similar to yours. Perhaps some of the experiences I've had in learning to live a "No Excuse!" life can help motivate you toward living the life *you* want.

When I aspired to write this book, I had to get through all the roadblocks, all the really "good" excuses not to do it. I had to avoid distractions like raking the leaves, making more coffee, and the multitude of things I could do to avoid it. I had to imagine you starting here and getting inspired and instructed along the way.

What an important combination: inspiration and instruction. They're "tools" that can help you achieve more and live your dreams. Whatever your dreams and goals may be, inspiration and instruction are key components in beginning your journey toward the life you want.

Maybe you're not sure about what you want out of life. You might be emotionally reluctant to admit it. That's OK. Many people have been "beat-up" and "put-down" so many times that they've given up on their dreams. My suggestion is to do whatever it takes to, "*Snap-out-of-it!*" You can do it!

I've set and achieved some extraordinary goals using "No Excuse!" I'm not saying this to brag. I just want you to know that you too can do the same, using the ideas in this book. When everyone feels free enough and is encouraged enough to achieve their goals, this will be a better world. So I've taken the challenge and set the goal to let others know that it feels good to be self-responsible.

I encourage and challenge you to make the commitment *now* to "do-whatever-it-takes" to live your dreams. The time is now! The missing link may simply be that nobody ever told you how exhilarating it is to assume responsibility for your own life, dreams, and goals.

With this part of the book, you'll start mastering the basics of "No Excuse!" You'll build self-confidence as you develop a life-plan to guide you. You'll envision the success you have always wanted. As you later move through the steps of the Thesaurus, your *Staircase-of-Success,* you'll learn everything you need to accomplish your goals. Best of all, you'll experience more control over your life than ever before. This will lead to reduced stress and a gratifying sense of accomplishment.

Of course, it's likely that you're going to need to make some changes. As you might expect from a book called "No Excuse!", *if you want your life to change, you need to make some changes in your life.* After all, a definition of insanity is: "Doing the same thing and expecting a *different* result!" If you're waiting for your life to change, guess what? It waits! It is highly unlikely that someone will come to your door and offer you an exciting life.

Applying the principles in this book will give you the opportunity to eliminate the negative thinking that has formed seemingly insurmountable obstacles. You can start believing your dreams are attainable.

As you apply "No Excuse!" and discover you can reach your dreams and goals, you'll realize that you can be happy, successful, and fulfilled in all areas of your life. You can grow and become whatever you want to be. All you need to do is assume self-responsibility and take appropriate action.

If you have a healthy desire to be successful, then you're ready for "No Excuse!" living. You're then ready to make the most of yourself and your opportunities. If your patterns of personal management are crippled by ignorance and self-doubt, I suggest you prepare to let them go. From now on, you'll have the opportunity to live your life with new understanding.

Before we get to the *THESAURUS Factor* in Part II of this book, let's put the cornerstone of your new "No Excuse!" life in place. Let's begin with the fundamentals. Consider starting to build your success by making self-responsibility one of your greatest strengths.

From Roadblocks To Enrichment

Responsible parents want their children to have a healthy respect for life. Yet the warnings, advice, and encouragement we receive as children sometimes defeat that intent.   In some   instances, the message gets so serious that happy feelings seem wrong and inappropriate.   "Good" begins to be frightening.   Do we believe being responsible isn't any fun? Have you ever felt that way? "No Excuse!" can help you change your mind. Living responsibly can be *great* fun! Few things will lift your mood and strengthen your confidence as much. The pleasure of self-responsibility expands dramatically as you live it.

Does that mean it's easy? No, not necessarily. But it *is* simple. Clearing a space for a self-responsible act can be challenging. Once you've done it, however, it gets easier. Euphoria creates energy. Your determination grows with every experience of mature, decisive action. Whether it leads to success or failure, a self-responsible act increases your power to move-on. You are gathering momentum toward the life you want.

This book includes mental exercises that will challenge your thinking and cause you to explore your inner feelings. It will help you identify the obstacles that have stopped you from achieving your goals. Maybe you let inexperience or a difficult experience hold you back.   Perhaps, for the first time, you'll understand what happened and why.

Look for other things, too.   Most of all, watch for signs of the strength, courage, wisdom, and inner beauty you already possess.

These are the foundation blocks for you to build your future on. A greater understanding of the excellent qualities you have to offer is part of what's in the pot at the end of the rainbow! What about the baggage you're carrying as you travel toward it? Every time you rid yourself of an excuse, your load gets lighter. You have more room for the useful things you need for the journey. Every time you work to remove a roadblock, every time you see an excuse and allow it to evaporate, the qualities you value are enhanced. Your life is enriched.

"No Excuse!" will teach you to recognize your fears, yet not let them stop you. You'll use them as a resource to point the way to your heart's desire; the direction in which your greatest successes lie. *Whenever you sense a fear of failure or rejection, realize that you are getting closer to your heart's desire.* Let it be a sign to you that opportunity is near, and it's time for you to call on the inspiration and instruction of "No Excuse!" Challenge the cloudy and often deceptive nature of the excuses that seem to "protect" you from failure and rejection, at the cost of success and triumph. Get ready to cross new thresholds with a greater sense of who you are and what you are capable of doing.

My decision to leave the corporate life to launch a business is one example of how adding challenges brought unexpected growth. I carefully calculated the costs and benefits. At that time, I couldn't imagine how the "No Excuse!" philosophy would emerge. I gained a greater understanding of something that had always troubled me: Why some people reach for and attain fullness of life, while most don't. Most people make excuses!

Getting Your Wheels Turning

Do you remember the times you surprised yourself, and perhaps others, by taking charge of a risky situation and bringing it to a successful resolution? I hope you have such memories like that, because those experiences help you develop a confident maturity. Recall a moment from your past when you felt exhilarated by success; a moment when you achieved a goal. I suggest you stop here and don't go on until you do. Dwell on that memory. How sweet it is!

The memory from your past performance plays an important part in how you mold "No Excuse!" for your own needs. I'll prompt it by recalling one of my own experiences. I believe it's an almost universal memory for Americans who grew up in the Twentieth Century:

You are sitting on a hard triangular seat, but it's not on your trusty tricycle. You're up on a two-wheeler, wobbly, legs dangling. Your feet are slipping from the pedals, toeing the ground right and left to keep you from tipping over.

A parent's hand grabs the seat, balancing you until you're moving fast enough. Remember how they kept pace with your fledgling efforts? They were more confident than you that you could do it.

Remember the exhilaration you felt when you could finally ride and control the bike? The laws of physics formed a network of support. They enabled you to succeed at something that had seemed scary before.

Let's go back to why you wanted to ride a two-wheeler. Remember how great your tricycle was? When you were on it, you didn't even have to think about it. You could go backward and forward or turn, and not fall! Why were you choosing a wobbly bicycle over a stable tricycle?

Did you outgrow the tricycle? Had your knees started hitting the handlebars? Had you begun compensating with an awkward "legs-akimbo" style of riding? Try to remember. What told you it was time to move-on to a new challenge? Were there people helping you explore options and consider alternatives? A larger tricycle? A pedal car? How come the right decisions, the right size bicycle, the level terrain, the guiding hand that knew *just* when to let go, were provided for you?

Pedal Power

Before we examine these questions, and explore how the physical, mental, and spiritual components of life work together to help you overcome each obstacle, it's time for some sheer pleasure. *Feel it.* Feel it happening. *Your face parts the air...the wind whispers, gently passing by your ears...your arms and hands loosely guide your direction, confident and comfortable on the ringed ridges of handlebar guards...your feet press the pedals, pumping and coasting in natural rhythms of motion...you're excited and free!*

This is the feeling that "No Excuse!" gives you. It is exhilarating and freeing. It's the feeling of honest personal power; the power to choose and act. Self-responsibility is the key.

We could also examine the moment when you mastered your tricycle. It's important to recapture a moment of self-responsibility. Recall the pedals responding to your legs. Recall the forces of nature brought into play by your ability to coordinate your effort. Recall pushing the pedals and turning the big front wheel.

Pushing pedals! Turning a wheel! Going from stop to start! Did you go backward or forward your first time? It doesn't matter. You were in motion, turning at will. Your mind communicated the idea of "moving-your-steering-wheel-to-change-your-direction" into your arms and hands in a moment of almost miraculous coordination.

Would you like to experience that feeling of mastery again and again? Well, you can! The choices you make as an adult living a "No Excuse!" life can be more thrilling and fulfilling than any childhood challenge ever was.

Be The Hero In Your Own Life

Were you taught that "life-is-a-struggle"? This perception causes a lot of unhappiness. To "struggle" implies you are in a negative, no-win state. This dim view of life acts as a self-fulfilling prophecy and leads to negative results. It's an attitude of defeat. This is not to say that life isn't challenging. Without challenges your life would be boring; you would experience little, if any, personal growth. Challenges test you and help you stretch to new levels of achievement. As you incorporate "No Excuse!" into your life, I believe you'll find that doing it without a struggle mentality is more effective, not to mention just plain easier and a lot more fun.

Strive for the excitement and joy self-responsibility brings when you accomplish a goal. If you are reluctant to leave the comfort zone of hiding in shadowy fears, fine! It's your decision when to step out. The choice is yours.

It's a wonderful feeling when you understand and accept that outcomes depend on actions. This is the "cause-and-effect" principle. Even if you choose to stay in the shadows of your fears, and you accept responsibility for it, you have reached a level of awareness that most people will never know.

You can be a hero in your own life story. Whether or not this is apparent to anyone else is irrelevant. It is only important that you have reached this fundamental realization; essential for any meaningful accomplishment. Although your decision-making process can be influenced by others and the environment, it is ultimately *your* decision to act or not. *The actions you take largely determine how you live your life.*

A Knight To Remember

The Knight in Rusty Armor is a favorite story of mine that I'd like you to have as a traveling companion on your "No Excuse!" journey. In the opening pages of Robert Fisher's symbolic book, we meet a knight at the top of his career. No other knight had rescued more damsels in distress. No other knight had slain more dragons or ridden off in as many directions looking for the latest crusade. This knight was also famous for his armor. Its brilliance told the world (and reassured him, too) that he was *the* example of a good, kind, and loving knight. That's what he wanted to be, and that's what he happily thought he was.

His wife Juliet and son Christopher, however, were not so happy about him. It seems the armor never came off anymore; a knight needs to be ever-ready for battle, and never let his fans, or his guard down. Christopher didn't know what his father really looked like, or felt like, and Juliet couldn't remember. She had experienced enough of a life reduced to rigid and unfeeling embraces. She delivered an ultimatum: the armor gets hung in a closet, and the knight spends more time with her and Christopher, or else....

Was Juliet the damsel he once rescued? The knight pondered his predicament. He began to suspect getting the armor off would be a problem. He woke up to the fact, thanks to his wife, that he had lost himself in his own foundry-wear. What he didn't know, and she didn't either, was how he could get it off. When even the best efforts of his bully blacksmith failed, the knight started out on a journey for help.

First, he made the trip to bid farewell to a king he had worked for in the past. The king wasn't available, so the knight spoke to his jester about his dilemma. The man scoffed at the knight's notion that his situation was unique. "We all get trapped in our own defenses from time to time," he assured him, and he gave him the magic word. Merlin was the "can opener" the knight needed.

In the lonely woods, the knight eventually met Merlin. Finally, he was too weakened by his wandering to run from the truth. However, Merlin's direct observations didn't sit well with the knight. "Perhaps you have always taken the truth to be an insult," Merlin responded to the knight's indignation.

The knight's rehabilitation began. In the company of a squirrel and pigeon, who supported and cheered him, he would travel on the Path of Truth. He would enter three castles along the way: the Castle of Silence, the Castle of Knowledge, and the Castle of Will and Daring. He would leave each of them remarkably changed within and without.

His armor would gradually fall off. Each life-changing experience was accompanied by torrents of tears that rusted the armor in critical places. Each insightful moment was followed by a piece of rusted armor falling from the knight's face, head, arms, and hands. Increasingly less burdened, the knight was better able to climb the steep mountain slopes toward his goal.

The lesson the knight learns from the animals is *acceptance*. "When you learn to *accept* instead of *expect*, you'll have fewer disappointments," Rebecca the pigeon tells the knight, as he stands at the door of the Castle of Silence. At the Castle of Knowledge, the knight learned the difference between expectations and ambition. Merlin then reappeared and said, "Ambition that comes from the mind can get you nice castles and fine horses. However, only ambition that comes from the heart can bring happiness."

"Ambition from the heart is pure. It competes with no one and harms no one. In fact, it works in such a way that it serves others at the same time."

With each successful lesson learned, the knight found himself again on the Path of Truth. Each time he was encumbered by less and less of his armor. His insights, which were lessons in self-knowledge, continued to bring tears of recognition, remorse, and relief...as chunks of armor continued to rust and fall from him.

At the third and final castle, only his breastplate remained as the unlikely trio faced the dragon guarding the Castle of Will and Daring. The knight advanced bravely toward the dragon, because he believed that fear and doubt were illusions. As the knight's fear and doubt grew less and less, the dragon grew smaller and smaller, and finally disappeared.

Once again on the Path of Truth, he was within sight of the mountaintop. Hand over hand he pulled himself toward his final goal. He clung fiercely to the rocky surface, only to learn that his last challenge would be...*to let go*. He fell into the abyss of his own past. He recognized fully, for the first time, the responsibility he bore for his own life. He realized the necessity of shedding judgements that others are to blame for his mistakes and failures.

Faster and faster he dropped, giddy as his mind descended into his heart. Then, for the first time, he saw his life clearly; without judgment and without excuses. In that instant he accepted full responsibility for his life, for the influence that he allowed other people to have on it, and for the events that he had permitted to shape it.

From this moment on, he would no longer blame his mistakes and misfortunes on anyone or anything outside himself. The recognition that he was the cause, not the effect, gave him a new feeling of power.

He began to "fall" *upward*, as if the force of gravity was reversed, and found himself standing on the mountaintop. His tears of gratitude for life and the lessons he learned, brought him to his knees. The tears were extraordinarily hot because they came so fully from his heart. They melted the last of his armor, the breastplate.

The brilliant splendor once lent him by the armor has not been diminished. Now, because he is healed, he shines with an inner radiance more beautiful than reflected glory.

Like the knight, we can all get trapped in our own armor at times. But once we learn to shed society's expectations and realize the importance of our own expectations, we too can have our place in the sun.

"Brains In Your Head And Feet In Your Shoes"

In Dr. Suess's final published work before his death, *Oh, The Places You'll Go*, he wrote, "You have brains in your head, you have feet in your shoes, you can steer yourself any direction you choose."

When we follow the teachings of Dr. Suess's small verse and act on our decisions with honesty, integrity, and selflessness, the world will be our oyster. Every day we would witness new pearls.

You possess the unique talents and resources that will help you put yourself on the *Staircase-of-Success*. Of course, it is necessary that you first learn to take full responsibility for the decisions you make, unless you have already done so. The following list of questions will help you open your eyes to the excuse-making that may exist in your own life today.   HOW GOOD ARE YOU AT MAKING EXCUSES? *Read these questions out loud so you can hear your own voice.* This will make it easier for you to be truthful with yourself.

- Do I say, "The dog ate it"?
- Do I blame tardiness on an alarm that "didn't-go-off"?
- Do I use the words can't," or "couldn't," when actually I "won't" or "wouldn't" is the truth?
- Do I procrastinate and leave a mountain of work unfinished because "after all, I'm only human"?

- Do I avoid trying new activities because I'm "too old," "too young," or "too tired"?
- Do I accept defeat, convinced that "nice guys finish last"?
- Do I excuse myself from blame for a wrongdoing because "I was only following orders"?
- Do I fail to return phone calls because I "lose" the telephone numbers?
- Do I overeat because "I simply can't help myself"?
- Do I cheat on exams because "everyone else does"?
- Do I blame my career stagnation on my boss or the economy?
- Do I neglect my family because I "can't find the time"?
- Do I say, "I don't have time," to avoid doing the necessary tasks to become more successful in my life?
- Do I say, "It's not my cup of tea," when I am objecting to an idea, instead of stating the real reason?
- Do I say, "I don't have the money," when it's not true?
- Do I say, "It's in the mail," when it's not?
- Do I say, "I'd do it, but," when I'm about to offer an excuse?

If you answered these questions honestly and, like many people, said "yes" to some of them, you are well on your way to eliminating excuses from your life. You are on the road to living a life of self-responsibility.

What are some of the decisions you are preparing to make this week, month, or year? Which will have the most impact on your personal life and professional career? Are those decisions personal, financial, educational, familial, or spiritual? Are you willing to make the decisions necessary and take action to move forward? Are you willing to accept responsibility for the outcomes of those decisions?

Be courageous. Write a list of the decisions you will soon be making that will impact your life and the lives of people around you. This heightens your awareness of the excuses you may have frequently used to either avoid facing decisions or taking responsibility for the results.

1. _____

2. _____

3. _____

4. _____

5. ————————————————————————————————

6. ————————————————————————————————

7. ————————————————————————————————

8. ————————————————————————————————

9. ————————————————————————————————

10. ———————————————————————————————

Take A Brave New Look At Your Thinking

Benjamin Franklin once said, "He who is good at making excuses is seldom good at anything else." So how do we eliminate excuses? The first step toward becoming good at anything, is to realize you may own a storehouse of self-imposed burdens. They're called excuses!

What if you see the need for self-responsibility one moment, then see yourself slip back into an old excuse the next? It's better to see it all happening than be "blind", or pretend to be blind, to what's going on. Opportunities for courage are everywhere, and your brave moments will accumulate as you practice "No Excuse!" You'll become aware of your own excuse-making. A part of you will start peeking out from under the blindfold you've made for yourself and say, "Uh-oh, I did it again." Every time you say that to yourself, it's a self-responsible moment.

It can feel as good as the wind parting in front of your face on your first "all-by-yourself" bicycle ride. Remember, being alone is part of the glory. If it feels a bit lonely, that's OK. It's going to be challenging and rewarding.

So out with the old way of thinking and in with the new. Excuses can have a root in reality, and at one time every excuse may have been a real reason. For example, at one point it was true that you couldn't ride that bicycle because you weren't big enough, old enough, or skilled enough. When old reality turns into a permanent excuse, trouble sets in. "I'll never be big enough or old enough"; "I'll never be able to ride a two-wheeler, I'm one of those people born not knowing how to." Sure you are...you and everybody else! *Whenever you find yourself looking for an excuse, you'll need to change your thinking.* That's what this book is all about.

How To Keep Excuses In Check

We all live largely by behavior patterns and habits. They are practical solutions to our need to have ready responses to everyday situations. They are necessary and, for the most part, serve us well. In certain circumstances, however, our logic can falter. We may fall back on excuses to explain a failure or justify a fault.

Keep these things in mind:

- Initially, the challenges of "No Excuse!" are just that...challenges. Relinquishing excuses requires effort.
- What's true for you is true for me. We all face problems that have a certain degree of sameness. We all need reasons to live, people to love, work to do, and joy to share. We all have sorrow and disappointment to bear.
- We're all better off when we're on the path of self-responsibility and action. Most of us are immobilized by the habits of blaming and excuse-making, to one degree or another.

Will you grow rich with "No Excuse!" living? Yes. "Rich" may or may not include more money. That depends on you. "No Excuse!" living will:

- enrich your life.
- enrich the lives of the people you love.
- enrich the lives of the people you work with.
- give you the elements to create the success you want for yourself and your family.
- begin with a self-responsible act: accept that time is what you're born with, and life is, for the most part, what you make it.

A Lesson In Human Behavior

How you live your life is largely determined by how much you are willing to accept responsibility for shaping it. For too many people, time is what they are given...period. They never design a life. They look at what they have and what someone else has and make a judgement. Either they say, "I don't have it so bad, I've got more than the other guy." Or they say, "That other guy is so lucky. If I had what he's got, I'd be all set." Whichever determination comes up, their evaluation of their own life is based on another person's acquisitions and accomplishments. With "No Excuse!" living, you are freed from the bind of comparison. All you are concerned with is how to get started and stay on the path to the life you want.

Some people tend to get caught in the status quo of their circumstances. It's important to remember that life is meant to be more than the nine-to-five...or whatever routine or rut we may have created. *The challenges and stresses we encounter every day are not normally caused by nature. Most of them are the result of the unmet expectations that arise from our thinking.* Most of them are not original, but are the result of what we've been taught by our elders, observation, or experience. In most cases, your thinking determines your life. The good news is, *you can change your life by changing your thinking.*

Few young people reach adolescence without discovering that "a good excuse" will probably help them out of a tough spot. However, we are not born with this thinking. It's learned behavior. Most often it is learned by example and tested by experience. The more tough spots a kid gets into, the more excuse-making could become a habit.

What happens here? If a child's inappropriate behavior is not corrected, the opportunity for him to explore other behaviors may be lost. More importantly, the young person's insights into the part he or she actually plays in creating the tough situation becomes clouded. The truths of self-responsibility actually become hidden or lost to that individual. What kind of energy or motivation would a person have left to correct non-productive behavior, if the constant strain of coming up with a good excuse was always the first priority?

Three Little Words Changed My Life

I arrived at West Point in July, 1976, for seven weeks of basic training. We called it "Beast Barracks." By then, I had learned the value of having a good excuse. Whenever circumstances warranted, and I wanted someone or something to blame for an unwanted result, I thought a good excuse would benefit me. I guess I was pretty average in that regard, much like my fellow plebes. Then too, we were all achievers, or we wouldn't be at West Point. Even so, we were all going to be amazed at how difficult it was to be deprived of the opportunity to excuse our way out of a situation.

<u>Excuse-making was forbidden.</u> We weren't allowed to give the upperclassmen reasons for our mistake(s) or failure(s), regardless of whether we were involved individually or collectively. Because of this rule, we were frequently going to hear ourselves and other plebes say three little but powerful words: "No excuse, Sir!" Here's the full paragraph given to excuses in *Bugle Notes*, the Fourth Class System handbook:

Cadets cultivate the habit of not offering excuses. There is no place in the military profession for an excuse for failure. Extenuating circumstances may be explained and submitted, but, even if accepted, such explanations are never considered excuses.

BUGLE NOTES: *"Cultivating The Soldierly Habit"*

The idea of self-responsibility was enforced right from the start of the West Point experience. This excerpt from *Bugle Notes* illustrates its importance:

The first seven weeks of a cadet's life at West Point are devoted to intensive military training. During this period the entering class of cadets are equipped and given the preliminary training necessary before they join the Corps. Here, entering civilians undergo the stressful socialization process which produces a well-disciplined, motivated class, prepared for acceptance into the Corps of Cadets as fourth classmen. It consists of training characterized by clear, careful, thorough instruction of individuals; exactness of execution; strict but just discipline; immediate response to correction; development of willing compliance to directives, careful physical hardening, and begins the process of cultivation of the soldierly habit. The new cadet's waking hours are completely controlled. Every activity is carefully supervised. Attention to detail and flawless appearance become second nature to him.

BUGLE NOTES, 1976-1980, p. 53-54

At the successful conclusion of Cadet Basic Training, I was accepted into the Corps of Cadets as a fourth classman. The Fourth Class System is administered by the upperclasses and supervised by the Commandant of Cadets. This system is in place to achieve very specific objectives. One is to teach the customs, traditions, and heritage of the United States Military Academy to new arrivals. The system is also meant to generate a controlled, stressful, military environment. Cadets who cannot function under stress, or who cannot otherwise meet the standards of the military profession, are identified.

Completion of Cadet Basic Training coincides with the return of the three upper classes during the last week in August. For the first time, the upperclassmen have an opportunity to observe the new Fourth Class as they stride confidently to the stirring notes of "The Official West Point March."

This is a moment of high exhilaration. Inevitably, thoughts turn to the men of honor who passed this way before. Foremost on my mind on the day I joined the ranks of "The Long Grey Line," was General Douglas MacArthur.

Bugle Notes, the handbook quoted from earlier, is the plebe's "bible." It contains everything he needs to know for survival in the world of West Point. *Bugle Notes* is essential, because survival is truly a plebe's major concern.

Cadets without the capability or desire to perform to the standards of the Academy simply leave. Sometimes, they are there one day and gone the next. So it's only natural to look for inspiration from the remarkable people who persevered and made it.

Words To Live By From A Leader's Leader

General MacArthur was one of West Point's finest sons. The inspirational speech he gave as he accepted the Thayer Award in May, 1962, was reprinted in the plebe's handbook. In his speech, he pointed to the motto "Duty, Honor, Country," inscribed on the Military Academy's Crest:

> *...Those three hallowed words...make you strong enough to know when you are weak, and brave enough to face yourself when you are afraid.... They teach you to be proud and unbending in honest failure, but humble and gentle in success; not to substitute words for actions, nor to seek the path of comfort, but to face the stress and spur of difficulty and challenge; to learn to stand up in the storm but to have compassion on those who fall; to master yourself before you seek to master others.... They create in your heart the sense of wonder, the unfailing hope of what is next, and the joy and inspiration of life. They teach you in this way to be an officer and a gentleman.*
>
> *BUGLE NOTES, p. 31-32*

In my first days at West Point, I was too frightened and intimidated to understand that "No excuse, Sir!" was a response required to encourage plebes to be strong and self-responsible. This fact became clear to me, later on.

"No excuse, Sir!" I can still hear the trembling quality of those words. It was scary trying them out under the stern and unrelenting, often glaring, gaze of a questioning upperclassman. Gradually, "No excuse, Sir!" came out stronger, even assertively. What had seemed a natural inclination to find excuses, gave way to a new pattern of thinking: Cut through to a simple statement of fact and address the situation. Whether or not reasons are given or even known, consequences need to be dealt with when something's done incorrectly or left undone.

The Story of My Success

With each passing year, I have reaped lessons from my West Point training, and I expect that to continue for the rest of my life. Military training was designed to encourage healthy self-reflection.

In fact, the need to examine personal behavior was emphasized. I developed the habit of correcting patterns that were not producing desired results.

The lesson of the "No excuse, Sir!" response soon became clear...healthy self-reflection does not lead to excuse-making. To this day, when I find myself dwelling on past achievements or failures, I think of the words "No excuse, Sir!". This snaps me out of self-congratulatory or self-pitying traps.

Saying "No Excuse!" will help you to be stronger, particularly when you've taken a leap into the unknown, and find your belief in yourself faltering. Critical times are like the moment a trapeze artist hangs in midair. Will his timing be right as he releases his hold on one bar and waits for another to swing into his grip? I've felt that way many times; on the edge. How about you?

My arrival at West Point was one of those times of uncertainty. I felt like I was hanging in midair. Every new arrival had overcome some obstacles just to be admitted. We all had other options, yet we chose this one and we were now facing the consequences.

In entirely different circumstances, thirteen years later, I felt equally challenged. By 1989, I had experienced a successful career at West Point, in the military, and in corporate America. Those years had been full of challenges and achievement. Nothing, however, matched the thrill I felt while standing in the office area of my own business for the first time.

I was alone. The grand opening party was over; the crowd of supporters and well-wishers had departed; my wife had taken the children home. I was enjoying the calm solitude as I walked through the store preparing to lock-up and go home. I appraised, with pleasure, the retail operation my desire and efforts had put in place. I had a resource center for personal and professional enrichment. I was elated. And suddenly, I was scared.

"No excuse, Sir!" The words were in my mind. I had risked everything in this venture and there would be no excuse if it failed. For the first time it hit me; I wanted my father to be with me so very much.

I had not experienced this strong a feeling since his death. It had so suddenly interrupted the life of this vital, active man, that we didn't even have a chance to say goodbye. He was an established dentist and an accomplished amateur golfer. We (my father, mother, sister and I) lived in the small city of Kingston, New York, where he had been born and raised. He was gone in one shocking moment.

His heart stopped beating one sunny day on the patio of our home, while he was sitting with my sister and her friend.

The day he was buried was sunny as well. I can still see myself as an 11-year-old boy. There I was, standing by my mother's side, saying over and over to myself, "I will survive, I will survive."

From that moment on, I looked to my father's memory for strength and encouragement. He had shown me how he felt life was meant to be lived. I wanted to fulfill his expectations for his only son. But they had never been spoken, so they could only be imagined. I developed unrealistic expectations of myself as a substitute for his. I exaggerated the demands he might have placed on me. I tried to live up to my memory of him, which was distorted by my longing.

I wanted to please him and my mother. She has always been an encourager in my life, consistently supporting me and my efforts. Beginning with my six-weeks-premature birth with collapsed lungs, and those first days of "hanging-on-for-dear-life," she led me into a strong and healthy manhood. However unrealistic my expectations of myself had been, she had spurred me on to achieve some ambitious goals. They might not have been realized without my single-minded determination to keep my father's death from being an obstacle to my becoming a man of whom he'd be proud.

As I stood in the offices of my new business that night, I continued to reflect on my thoughts and feelings. I had deliberately separated myself from the hierarchical, paternalistic organizations where I had achieved success. I now felt as if I was face-to-face with my father's memory, in a way I had never experienced before. I had never before acknowledged or sensed so fully, my longing for his presence and approval.

"No excuse, Sir!" I was speaking to him, as well as myself. Something profoundly lonely had me in its grip. His death had deprived me of his loving presence, but had also been the catalyst for my will to succeed.

At that moment, I knew I was letting go of the hold I had allowed the past to have on me. I accepted that not even my father's death could be used as an excuse. It couldn't keep me from moving-on.

I knew I was ready to stand alone. I realized that my expectations, and not his, would be enough to keep me going toward my dreams and goals. I no longer needed to please him or anyone. I also knew I no longer needed his approval; all I needed was my own. In this moment of open longing and new understanding, I accepted that I was alone, and it was OK.

I had the memory of my father's love for me. I was also aware that we both had met success through honesty, sincerity and commitment.

"They Conquer Who Believe They Can."

It is vitally important to create your life based on your own expectations and not the expectations of others around you. All of us have the ability to accept or not accept who and what we are. Think about it. How often do we try to mold ourselves to someone else's expectations to please them? If we do, we will probably suffer, in silence or denial, the tragedy of not accepting ourselves and what we choose to do. Owning your life means having the courage to face up to such truths. It means risking, and maybe even taking a relationship "to-the-edge" to assert yourself. You're likely to generate more respect from others as well.

Becoming self-responsible is a process. As you practice "No Excuse!," your self-responsible experiences accumulate and can then positively contribute to structuring a life that is more reflective of who you are. You can become a whole person incrementally. If you believe you are "whole" already, you are further along than many. (Balanced and developed in the seven key areas of life–to be explained more later.) You grow with every mature decision and the understanding that you alone accept responsibility for your actions.

You may have noticed that your need for recognition from others was inversely proportional to how much you are at peace with yourself. To a point, it may be appropriate to seek advice from or model your behavior after a few select people whom you respect; people whose lives are worthy of emulating. It is human nature to desire acceptance from others. However, it is wise to be selective. Focus only on those people who have your best interests at heart, whose value system is admirable to you, and who love and support you. Then there are times when it is important to stand apart from even these people. It's essential to examine your life and discover whether you like where you're headed. Do you need to change your course in some areas of your life? Are you receiving the outcomes you want?

You'll find that practicing "No Excuse!" principles can enhance your feelings of self-worth, self-love, and self-esteem. You'll also have an opportunity to learn to let go of people you may be using as protection from the fear of rejection. You'll learn how to create new relationships and live life on your own terms. *As you "let go" of beloved people and stop hiding behind them, you and they will experience a freedom to love each other beyond anything you've ever known.*

You will experience life more fully when you realize that *you* determine your future. With "No Excuse!" thinking, you no longer blame events or other people for your shortcomings, failures, or timidity. You will have the opportunity to lay the foundation for a future of living life to the fullest.

You may want to ask the questions that anyone on a new path might ask: Am I ready for this? Am I self-responsible enough? Am I capable of dealing with success? Am I capable of dealing with failure? Am I prepared to accept the impact my new-found self-responsibility will have on my family and friends? Am I willing to take responsibility for my actions when things don't go my way? Am I willing to stop weaving an intricate tale of "inescapable" coincidences to tell the world how everything conspired against me? Am I willing to say "No Excuse!"?

Long ago, I knew a man who took responsibility for his actions; he didn't make excuses. For example, if he was late for dinner, he would say to his wife, "My dear, I didn't leave the office on time." Even when I was a youngster, I liked that fellow. I now believe his words had an early influence on the "No Excuse!" approach to life. He accepted full responsibility and wasted no time inventing excuses. Excuses would have been useless and wouldn't have helped the situation.

A Labor Of Love

As you accept responsibility for your actions, you will likely live life with a lighter heart. Knowing you have deliberately decided not to blame others for your actions, you will feel stronger, less alone and less frightened of the consequences. The fear of rejection and failure, that once crippled or handicapped your efforts, will diminish. You are taking charge.   The likelihood that you'll let fear control or paralyze your actions will be reduced. Your sense of self-responsibility can develop as you grow personally and as your life becomes more expansive.

As my business grew, it became clearer I was headed toward another career decision. I began to realize what I loved to do most, which you need to do whenever you consider changing careers. Throughout my life I've always been sociable. I'm eager to communicate with others. My enthusiasm often carried me into new situations where I quickly became acquainted with new groups of people. I particularly enjoyed public speaking while I was in school, in the military, and during my years as a businessman. I learned how important it was for organizations to utilize outside resources to help them meet their motivational and training needs.

The information provided by a "third party" is often considered more credible and is more readily received. I decided my niche would be that "third party." I started corporate training, speaking to small groups and large organizations. My objective was to help them better understand the relationship between self-responsibility and personal and professional success, thus increasing their productivity.

My retail store was full of inspirational and motivational materials. I read all of it voraciously and gained new insights into their valuable messages. I devoured the works of Dale Carnegie, Norman Vincent Peale, Napoleon Hill, W. Clement Stone, and Earl Nightingale, to name a few giants of the past. I also studied the books of such modern day authors as Harvey Mackay, Dr. Susan Jeffers, Stephen Covey, Dr. Robert Schuller, Larry Wilson, Tom Peters, M. Scott Peck, and more.

Self-responsibility is a critical part of all their messages. Nonetheless, many individuals have difficulty putting it into practice. Developing self-responsibility, to the degree necessary to attain notable personal and professional success, requires great courage, maturity, and the support of like-minded people.

I felt confident I could structure an approach to "No Excuse!" that would give people practical guidelines to living self-responsibly. I knew this approach could help people counteract personal and professional stagnation and mediocrity. It dawned on me I was the person to do it, because my life had been lived the "No Excuse!" way. My objective is for these insights to benefit you. That would be very rewarding for me.

Nothing has given me more pleasure and satisfaction than bringing "No Excuse!" into reality. It's for groups of three or four in boardrooms. It's for large corporations and small. It's for traditional sales and marketing organizations and network marketing groups. It's for government employees. It's for you and your family, friends, coworkers, business associates, and acquaintances. And finally, it's for anyone who will read this book.

I have the hard evidence that proves people have made their lives easier and more productive by using these principles. People with unsuspected potential have discovered themselves through "No Excuse!" They harnessed their emotion, ambition, and talents to benefit others, their organization, and, of course, themselves.

It is up to you to change your life. Through "No Excuse!", you will have resources and mechanisms to help you make positive changes. You will have a chance to relate differently to the people around you, and be a positive influence on their lives. It can spark in you a new zest for living, a new zest for accomplishing dreams you once thought were impossible.

Good Work

Now that you have completed this chapter, I hope you are aware that you are not at the mercy of circumstances. You are the master of your own destiny, if you choose to be. Congratulations! *You have been empowered to take charge of your life, if you haven't done so already.*

At this point it is likely that you have one foot firmly planted in the "No Excuse!" grounds of success. Step by step, you'll learn how to be committed to yourself and your personal action plan, which will lead you to accomplishing your life's goals. I believe you'll discover that as you gain a clearer sense of purpose, you will be better able to direct your energies precisely where they belong. With your new focus, you'll be able to achieve your success with an ease and swiftness you never dreamed possible.

Now that you have had an opportunity to equip yourself with a new sense of self-responsibility, are you ready for the next part of your success training? You'll discover why you might want to channel your newfound energies in a certain direction and how to do so. The time is ripe for you to arrive at your own resolve.

"No Excuse!" Action Plan For "Self-Responsibility"

1. Do whatever it takes to live your dreams.   Accept no excuses from yourself or anybody else.

2. If you want your life to change, change your thinking and actions toward what you want. Think something and do something that you haven't thought or done before, and you'll get something you never got before.

3. Watch for signs of the strength, courage, wisdom, and inner beauty you already possess. Recognize your excellent qualities and improve on the others.

4. Watch for the fears of failure and rejection. They indicate when you're near your heart's desire. They are signs that an opportunity to grow is near.

5. Be the hero in your own life. Let go of the perception that life is a struggle and you'll start achieving more. Let go of the excess "baggage" you may have been carrying around.

6. Write a list of excuses you have used in the past. Vow to never use them again, then throw the list away.

7. Write a list of the decisions you will soon be making that will impact your life and the lives of people around you. This heightens your awareness of excuses you may have used to either avoid facing decisions, or to avoid taking responsibility for the results.

8. Recognize you may have "outgrown" some honest reasons for not doing something. If you use them now, they're just excuses. When an old reality turns into a permanent excuse, trouble sets in. Whenever you find yourself looking for an excuse, change your thinking.

9. Create your life based on your own expectations and not those of others. Own your life by having the courage to accept yourself and what you want to do. This may take risking a relationship, but you're likely to generate more respect from others.

10. Let go of people you may be using as protection from the fear of rejection; stop hiding behind them. You and they will then experience a freedom to love each other beyond anything you've ever known.

11. Accept full responsibility for your actions, and it's likely you'll find your heart will be lighter. Decide not to blame anyone for your actions, and you'll feel stronger, less alone and less afraid of the consequences.

COMMITMENT

*Until one is committed, there is hesitancy, the chance
to draw back, always ineffective, concerning
all acts of initiative (and creation).
There is one elementary truth, the ignorance of which
kills countless ideas and splendid plans:
that the moment one definitely commits
oneself, the providence moves, too.
All sorts of things occur to help one that would never
otherwise have occurred.
A whole stream of events issues from the decision,
raising in one's favor all manner of
unforeseen incidents and meetings and
material assistance which no man could have
dreamed would have come his way.
Whatever you can do, or dream you can begin it.
Boldness has genius, power and magic in it.
Begin it now.*

GOETHE

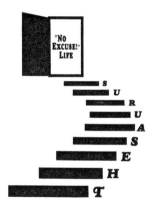

Chapter 2

THE POWER OF PURPOSE
Your Definition Of Success

Patton On Purpose

Before you can begin thinking about becoming a success, it is necessary for you to define what success is for you. You need to know what you want to reach for, and believe you can attain it.

Take the example of General George S. Patton. Even as a boy of barely seven, young George had his purpose as clearly defined as the edge of a toy saber. It was, pure and simple, to become a Brigadier General. He was so committed to this that, like any model soldier, he stood at attention and saluted his father every morning.

As Patton grew through his teen years, he continued to "do his damnedest always" to achieve his purpose in life as only he could define it. He avidly read stories of the great military men of history. He studied Persian, Greek, and Roman Generals, battle formations, and medieval wars. His class reports featured themes of fame, glory, and heroism.

Self-responsible to a fault, Patton learned early on that prizes in life were earned through persistent effort. It was sheer hard work that helped him overcome dyslexia and graduate from West Point.

Likewise, through the course of his historic rise to fame, culminating in his promotion to full General of the United States Army, he rode on no one's coattails. It was his honest, all-out effort that saw him to his end purpose every time.

As a plebe at West Point, he scribbled in his personal notebook the credo that would eventually help him achieve his greatest purpose, his Generalship:

Do everything with all the snap and power you possess.... When ordered to do a thing, carry out the spirit as well as the letter. Do all you can do, not only all you have to do.

Everyone who knew George Patton, or who has read about his life, has their own different opinion of him. However, I believe they would all agree that Patton was, above all, a man of purpose. He reached out and embraced history. In this sense, he fulfilled the destiny about which he often talked:

You have to turn around and know who (destiny) is when she taps you on the shoulder, because she will. It happens to every man, but damned few times in his life. Then you must decide to follow where she points. You have to be single-minded, drive only for the one thing on which you have decided....

> SOLDIER OF DESTINY: A BIOGRAPHY OF GEORGE S. PATTON
> Charles Peifer, Jr.

Having a purpose is more important than having talent in creating and shaping your life. Patton's example proves it. You can "move mountains" with great resolve if you apply yourself persistently and consistently. That's why having a purpose, or a mission, is essential.

What are your goals, anyway? What do you aspire to? What is your dream? Think of who you are today. Imagine yourself at your personal and professional best. Imagine feeling good about yourself in relation to your family and friends, neighbors, and co-workers or business associates.

What is your idea of success? A nurturing home life? A fabulous career? A prosperous business? Financial and time freedom? The happiest and best relationships with the people you love and care about? Strong bonds with those you need to support you in your quest for success? To make a difference in the lives of others, it is important to let your vision of who you are and what you want out of life guide you to your goals.

This chapter takes you on a journey that will help you define your purpose. Once you do, you will have taken a major step toward the future you choose. You will have acknowledged the possibility of being the person you would like to be. You'll be started on the path of living a life of accomplishing your dreams and goals.

In addition to your commitment to self-responsible living, having a purpose is essential to start you on the *Staircase-of-Success*. As you move through the treasury of principles in Part II, you'll have an opportunity to learn how to order your values. You'll discover how to examine expectations, set the standards by which you'll play the game of life, and respect yourself and others more. You'll learn to communicate with people in more meaningful ways, to develop the fulfilling and loving relationships you have probably always wanted. You'll gain a sense of contribution, of knowing you've made a difference in other people's lives.

You'll also learn (or be reminded) that *the most important human relationship you'll ever have is the one you have with yourself.* You'll have an opportunity to make changes in your life that will be in your best interest. Nonetheless, they will require self-discipline. You'll need the right mental attitude to sustain you on your new path.

"No Excuse!" will share with you how to nurture a sense of optimism, and change negative thinking patterns into positive ones. You'll adopt cheerfulness, optimism, persistence, and integrity as your new personal by-laws if you haven't already done so. You'll have the chance to see how helpful these qualities can be in achieving your goals.

The Strategy That Wins Wars

In any military situation, the commanding officer relies on a course of action; a "general plan." This plan anticipates a favorable outcome and maps out a strategy of operations for all combined forces. The memoirs of Marshal Ferdinand Foch (Supreme Commander of Allied Armies in WWI) speak to the importance of the plan:

> *...Even if one of these actions should come to a standstill or one group of these forces be particularly tried, the commander of the whole must unflinchingly stand by his general plan, at the same time stimulating or sustaining the failing action, but never admitting that it can be wholly renounced or that its weakness can cause the relinquishment or even any change of that plan.*
>
> MILITARY MEN
> Ward Just

The general plan, or purpose, is the strategy that helps win wars. Wars aren't won without plans. It's one of those things that gives an advantage to the aggressor. It's also one of the reasons that even a peaceable nation needs to have a plan of defense.

On a smaller, more personal scale, consider the general plan as your personal strategy for reaching your dreams and goals. As you gain new insights and outlooks through "No Excuse!", you'll be able to develop and adopt a plan of your own. It's important that you do. *Defining your own purpose in life is one of the most significant steps you can take in achieving success.*

Defining Your Purpose

Why do you think you are here on this earth? Your answer is your first step to being able to answer the question, "What is your purpose?" A child can legitimately answer, "To be loved." An adult could best answer, "To love."

Self-responsibility includes making choices about how you will use your energies. Who will you love? Who will you help? Which cause(s) will you support and fight for? When you reach the point where you are indeed working for who and what you believe in, you will more deeply understand what American author Joseph Campbell meant when he said, "Man is not in search of the meaning of life, but what it means to be alive."

Most of us want to feel what it means to be alive. When we are living a life guided by our self-defined purpose (rather than that defined by other people), we are likely to be better able to enjoy each passing day. Despite its challenges, we will probably be more grateful for life and eager to make the most of it. *Having a purpose helps self-responsible people be enthusiastic about life.*

Do you believe a grim demeanor is the sign of someone who is living self-responsibly? If your answer is "yes," you may want to reconsider. Yes, there are gloomy people who are very responsible. However, these are generally people fulfilling responsibilities imposed by others (e.g., boss, parents, spouse, or commanding officer). *Living with purpose is one of life's greatest joys.* If you have the courage to search your soul, you will find your purpose.

How many people live life as if Opportunity were Death knocking on the door? Those who ignore opportunities, and fail to define and work toward their purpose, usually fall into a slow, spiritual stagnation. Purpose naturally leads to prudent risk-taking, which wards off stagnation and boredom.

When you take charge of your decisions, and accept full responsibility for the outcomes, prudent risk-taking is easy. You can begin looking for a direction to move in. This helps you recognize your purpose. As your purpose evolves, it will guide your investment of energies and resources, and help you choose between attractive alternatives.

Self-responsible living brings an individual to a state of well-equipped readiness. You can compare it to a healthy, well-trained, willing soldier. When he is sent out on armed maneuvers, he is expected to make decisions regarding the use of the energies and resources at his disposal. Without a clearly defined purpose, he might wait, idly and anxiously, for someone else to take action. Or he might spend energy and ammunition on fruitless and dangerous displays of aimless action, shooting at shadows. In either case, a soldier handicapped by the lack of a clear purpose, no matter how self-responsible, is apt to be a danger to himself and his comrades. He will offer little or no aid to the cause.

How Purpose Pays Off

You are the ultimate decision maker in your own life only when you choose to be. Events and other people's purposes will direct you if you're not in charge of yourself.

It's pleasant to lay on a raft and float on a placid lake under a sunny sky. It's peaceful to let nature rule the day's events, without a care in the world. But some people never learn about the thrill of life with a rudder, a sail, an oar, or an engine. They repeatedly set themselves up in situations sure to lead to panic and the need to be rescued. They behave as if they are helpless, even when survival is at stake.

We all need to "float" at times to refresh and rejuvenate ourselves. However, the most vibrant people I know have equipped themselves for the challenges they are sure to meet. They look forward to the thrill of dealing with them head-on.

Self-responsible living means knowing how to enjoy life and being prepared for the situations it presents. "No Excuse!" living isn't reactive. There's no room to make excuses that prevent you from taking charge of which direction to steer your ship. Your purpose helps you decide which direction to take so you can pursue your dreams and goals.

Lack of self-responsibility can cripple your life. You can never be alone! You always need someone to blame in case things go wrong. With self-responsible living, you can be alone or join forces with self-responsible partners. As you grow, you will come to recognize other self-responsible people. You're more likely to choose them for friends, partners, and supporters, and avoid associations with companions who refuse to be self-responsible.

As you apply "No Excuse!", your sense of self-responsibility will grow. You'll feel an almost indomitable strength at the heart of self-responsibility and purpose. It will prevail through obstacles which attempt to thwart its development. You can count on it. It's inside you. Feel it. Look back on your life. It's likely you'll find evidence of your strength.

The desire for self-responsibility and purpose exists, at some level, in every human heart. It can grow stronger every time we get encouragement. It can strengthen when we focus our energies on what we really want. Self-responsibility grows strong when we seek and take advantage of new opportunities to learn and grow. Purpose intensifies when new dreams and goals are developed and pursued on a regular basis.

Your Best Preparation For A Full Life

As I reviewed my life's experiences, it became obvious how the principles of self-responsibility and fulfillment of purpose were at work long before I recognized them. The goals I chose to pursue were rigorous and challenging. The odds were against me, but I focused and did whatever it took to achieve them.

From a growth and motivational perspective, the role and career changes I made were important because of the experience gained. You may agree that this is true for you too. "One-thing-leads-to-another" throughout life. This is part of the reason for the transitions, certainly in my academic career. Have you noticed how your experiences are often linked to one another? Satisfaction with a job well done, however, eventually leads to dissatisfaction. Repeating a challenge you've overcome can get boring. When that happened to me, I looked for new horizons.

As you live self-responsibly, you'll find the need to scrutinize and exercise integrity. Honestly focus on who you are and what you are capable of accomplishing.

In order to fulfill your purpose, you need to develop the ability to select and focus on singular goals. Your scrutiny and integrity are essential as you shift to a combination of inward and outward focus. Your choice of goals needs to reflect and agree with your value system and your understanding of what you have to offer the world. *Knowing your purpose, while being true enough to yourself to work toward it, is the best way to prepare for a life full of worthwhile accomplishments.*

When you experience and recognize your success, working "on purpose" becomes more and more rewarding. It also becomes a habit. Here are some questions to consider as you reflect on the decisions you have made in your life:

- Has the opportunity to accomplish something meaningful ever come along and you ignored it?
- Did you evaluate timing and your priorities as you decided what activities to pursue?
- How alert have you been to indications that it is time to change directions in your life?

Most people give little or no thought to these questions. Many live day-to-day in a "survival" mode. They focus on maintenance activities like going to work, paying bills, and taking care of the house and yard. They concern themselves with keeping the children clothed, fed, and driven to their activities. These areas are often necessary, but exclusive focus on them can keep us from our purpose. We need to be aware of what else is going on and how we can best contribute.

Remember, *you get what you focus on.* If you are focusing only on doing minimal maintenance chores to "get by and through" each day, that's all you'll get: a life of gray mediocrity with little or no fulfillment. You would be living unconsciously; pushed by circumstances rather than pulled by your dreams and goals. If you are one of these people, this book could help you shift to a conscious, purposeful, and self-responsible life. You'll be better able to achieve cherished, but often buried, dreams and goals.

Your Dreams And Goals

Right now, may I suggest that you take some quiet time to get in touch with your dreams and goals? Many are probably tucked away in your subconscious mind because you didn't believe you could accomplish them. Perhaps you didn't believe you deserved them. It's OK if you don't totally believe that you can live the life you want. Just believe a little bit for now.

Take some time now to list 10 or more dreams and goals, big and little. Assume time and money are not obstacles; and you can become, do, and have anything you want. You may just want 20 minutes a day of uninterrupted time to read a book. Or you may want something as grand as a mansion or to give a million dollars to your favorite cause. It is what *you* want that matters. Go ahead, respect yourself enough to fill in the following blanks with your dreams and goals. Believe you deserve them.

1. _____

2. _____

3. _____

4. _____

5. _____

6. _____

7. _____

8. _____

9. _____

10. _____

For many years I considered a career as a consultant and professional speaker. My business brought me into contact daily with people searching for ways to develop their talents. I was impressed, over and over again, at how willing people are to consider ways to develop themselves personally. These people helped me discover my new-found purpose.

"Ten-Percent Living"

William James, a professor of psychology at Harvard in the first half of the 20th Century, observed that the average person develops only ten percent of his latent mental ability.

Why do most people average out at only "ten-percent living"? Why are most people discouraged from exploring more of their potential? You'll often hear of musicians and entertainers born into a family with little experience or interest in those fields. Or you may find an athlete born into a family with no desire to encourage a youngster's participation in sports. These situations are quite common.

If your talents were not nurtured during your early years, you have this additional challenge to overcome. The first step for you is to acknowledge and accept this fact. You can then make a decision to seek support and guidance elsewhere, as you explore and develop your neglected talents. You may have years of stagnation to overcome before you uncover those desires that lie dormant inside you.

Then you may be someone whose innate talents are stored away, or buried in "safe" places because of verbal abuse, usually in the form of ridicule. It is easier to ignore ridicule when you realize these unkind, unhappy people often resort to it to try to bring others down to their level of incompetence. "Misery loves company" is the rule that prevails whether they realize it or not. Every day I met people in my bookstore who wanted to discover the 90% of themselves where their unrealized talents, dreams, and goals live.

Putting Purpose Into Practice

For me, there is nothing as inspiring as meeting others striving for a full life. The customers inspired me. With each passing day, it became more apparent that self-responsibility was the key attribute for the success they sought. With increasing clarity I saw how critical "No Excuse!" living had been, and is, for me. As I introduced "No Excuse!", it became apparent how valuable this concept was to people aspiring to a better life. I saw immediate and long-term positive results in their lives.

That simple phrase "No Excuse!", from my West Point years, became the pivotal point of a practical approach to achieving success in all areas of life. Day after day, I saw the approach at work in the lives of people who accepted what I had to offer. I kept meeting people who were eager and willing to put it into practice in their own lives.

These folks quickly understood the idea of self-responsibility. They curtailed their old habitual retreats into excuse-making. They recognized that *fear always lies at the heart of excuse-making*. They uncovered their own fears and faced them and did what needed to be done to overcome them.

First, they learned to say "No Excuse!" to themselves. In a stressful situation, as shadows of excuses began forming in their minds, the words "No Excuse!" would come to rescue them. It was like the Unites States Cavalry taking the day, scattering the weak near-truths and falsehoods.

I saw how saying this simple phrase encouraged them to face the world. It became even more obvious when they exercised this new power as they encountered others. The excuses they once spoke were gone. Instead, they could honestly evaluate the reality of the situation. They grew personally through the process of facing and telling the truth. The results were honest, productive responses that served the best interests of everyone.

When the reality of a situation seems so overwhelming that you feel it can't be addressed, do you seek refuge in an excuse? You're only kidding yourself if you don't admit that excuse-making is rooted in fear. In fact, *making excuses leads to more fear.* Maybe someone will discover the truth. *Letting go of excuses diffuses situations. Where self-responsible living replaces excuse-making, purposeful, positive action replaces fear!* Here's a story that illustrates this truth.

Look Who's In The Driver's Seat

A couple (let's call them John and Mary), who had taken "No Excuse!" training, later told me how it helped them in a way they could not have imagined. They had an opportunity to enjoy a week vacation on the West Coast. Both looked forward to their first experience of the Pacific Ocean and the California coastline. The couple planned a trip that would begin in beautiful San Francisco, then take them south to the towns and beaches of Carmel and Monterey. It would end with a drive down the dramatic coastline highway to Big Sur, and a night in the Redwood Forest.

The time came and all went as planned. San Francisco was cosmopolitan, architecturally interesting, and distinctively hilly and balmy. Monterey brought a chapter of our economic and immigrant history alive. Carmel was as delightful as they expected. Our travelers fell in step with each other as they strolled the sand, lanes, and byways of that charming artists' community.

John and Mary's "No Excuse!" approach to vacation planning was paying off. It had seen them through some ups and downs, such as lodging challenges and delays. They kept alert to their need to be self-responsible. There would be no blame and no excuses if things didn't go as planned. They'd only seek the best possible outcome regardless of the circumstances. They kept their purpose in focus: to enjoy each other's company and the pleasures of the vacation.

In high spirits, John and Mary started the drive to Big Sur. They did not anticipate Mary would be terrified of the precarious road conditions. They traveled a two-lane highway that was only partially guard-railed from a sheer cliff, hundreds of feet above the sea.

The road was a man-made ledge, wedged into the face of the towering cliffs along the Pacific Coast. It wound almost exactly parallel to, but at a great height above the sea. The road curved inward and outward, following the natural contours of the cliff. At times, the car seemed momentarily on a trajectory to the far western reaches of the sky. A moment of relief came when it curved back away from the sea, tires hugging the "safety" of the yellow line.

Once they started on the road to Big Sur, there were few opportunities to turn back. There may have been only two or three outcroppings of land that would have allowed a car to be turned around. Mary's fear was not yet full-blown when they met these opportunities. There was no turning back. There was only the necessity to continue onward.

Mary's fear turned to panic and outgrew all her attempts to restrain it. She became a danger to John and herself. She also became a danger to the occasional cars they met going in the opposite direction. Her body became "stiff-and-straight-as-a-pencil," as she later described to me. Her arms would uncontrollably flail at her husband as he tried to maintain control of the car. He tried not to be distracted by her frightening loss of self-control.

Mary fought to contain her fear with varying degrees of success. John fought to stay focused on the task of following the road to their destination. Their "frightful" journey came to a finish when they reached the end of the cliff drive. They found comfort in the broad expanses of the parking areas at the entrance to the national park at Big Sur. They had reservations at the motel for the night.

Mary was drained of much of her energy and embarrassed by her lack of self-control. She was also concerned about the danger she had put her loved-one through. John was exhausted too. He could see clearly that it was in their best interest to make a new *plan*.

John and Mary were greatly concerned that their only choice was to face the journey again, retracing their path on the trip home. John felt it would be helpful to Mary if she drove the car back. This could give her more of a sense of purpose, and something other than the road conditions to focus on. Courageously, she agreed to drive.

The more purpose a "No Excuse!" person has, the more able they are to perceive, accept and fulfill their responsibilities to themselves and others. John had a purpose that exceeded having a safe, enjoyable time. He also took his responsibilities as a partner seriously.

John was other-centered enough to formulate a plan. He resolved the challenges of the situation without sacrificing Mary's right to share in the achievement of their purpose. He invited her to assume more responsibility, which increased their chances of a safe return. John enhanced her self-esteem in a way that lecturing, threatening, or blaming her never could have. In addition, his plan was successful. Mary was relatively calm on the return trip. They arrived safely and much relieved to have met and overcome the challenge of traveling the treacherous road.

John and Mary often share their experience with laughing pleasure. They point to it as an example of "No Excuse!" living.

Reaching For More Than You Ever Dreamed Possible

When I first began sharing "No Excuse!" with others, it became clear that most of them didn't recognize how their lack of self-responsibility negatively affected themselves and others. We looked back at their past behavior, and they learned to recognize how excuse-making had crept into their thinking. Their task was to identify every instance as it occurred, and persistently eliminate their excuse-making with "No Excuse!"

It was marvelous to see how the results came so quickly to those who used "No Excuse!" Again and again, self-confidence grew in the people who were willing to rid themselves of excuses, and take responsibility for the results of their action or inaction.

As they continued to live "No Excuse!", they reached for more and developed a higher purpose. The increased energy they experienced by living a "No Excuse!" life made it possible for them to see the options that existed in ways they had never imagined. With new courage and resolve, they began building a record of success.

Before I talk to the employees of a business or members of an organization, I get acquainted with its culture. This enables me to fine tune my presentation. My mouth fairly waters whenever I encounter a blamer, whiner, or complainer. I know I've got something that will help them break away from the endless cycle of unproductive behavior they've gotten themselves locked into.

I know that every blamer, whiner, or complainer impacted by "No Excuse!" becomes more effective on the job. He becomes a source of productive energy for the organization. It's exhilarating to help people open up and understand their excuse-making behavior. It's exciting to see how the simple message of "No Excuse!" works. I love to help people prepare to find their own way to the top of any mountain they choose to climb.

For you, the exhilaration and great pleasure right now is in *choosing* the mountain you wish to scale; in picking your purpose. "No Excuse!" will not fulfill its promise to you if it doesn't help you reconsider or discover your purpose. This can be done gradually. Your self-awareness can increase at an acceptable pace for personal growth, replacing old paradigms with new ones. It's valuable to evaluate your life as you live it. The more you discover about yourself and your purpose, the easier it will be for you to determine if you are on-track in the areas that are important to you.

Nature helps us when the changing seasons remind us that time is passing. This helps us focus on the changing patterns of our own existence. The yearly calendar gives us boundaries we can use to complete one task and begin another.

For many, the new year means new beginnings. This explains New Year's resolutions, doesn't it? This is a time when we may choose to admit that there are areas of our lives we wish to change. This is an excellent time to develop or strengthen the belief that we are capable of making changes that will enrich our lives.

A Tale Of Two Purposes

The intent of sharing the following two stories is to show you how having a purpose can be a powerful force in your life. In the first, a well-known movie producer turned motivational speaker identifies and articulates purpose early in life. In the second, a child in a fable shares a secret of life with the ages.

THE BOY WHO WOULD PLAY FOOTBALL AND INSPIRE A MOVIE

Once upon a time, a boy named Daniel "Rudy" Ruettiger had the dream of playing football for Notre Dame. He was the third of 14 children and grew up in the working class town of Joliet, Illinois. After high school, he worked at a power plant, joined the Navy, then returned to the plant.

When a friend was killed at the plant in an industrial accident, Rudy re-examined his life and began pursuing his dream. He wanted to play football at Notre Dame. All the while, he was being put down by friends and relatives. They would say, "Who do you think you are?"

His high school grades weren't good enough to get into Notre Dame, but he managed to get admitted to Holy Cross Junior College to "prove" himself. Despite suffering from a mild case of dyslexia, Rudy studied hard and earned good grades. He tried to get into Notre Dame three times and kept getting rejected. But, he persisted until he was finally accepted. He also managed to beat the odds by winning a position on the scout team. Even though Rudy was only 5 feet, 6 inches tall, he was a giant in his thinking and doing!

Through his dogged determination, Rudy won the respect of his teammates and coaches. He had spirit; his persistence won the prize. Then his ultimate dream came true. He was sent onto the field to play the last few minutes of the last home game of his senior year. His final victory came when he tackled the Georgia Tech quarterback. The crowd roared, and his teammates carried him triumphantly off the field on their shoulders. Rudy was their hero.

Rudy received his Bachelor's degree in 1976. Sixteen years went by, during which he accomplished little. Then in 1992, he began living another dream: involvement with the production of the movie "Rudy," which became a box office hit!

Rudy now has a career in motivational speaking. He is an excellent example of the power of a dream and perseverance in achieving it. His vision is to help others grow so they can realize their full potential.

THE GIRL WHO WOULD BE HAPPY

As a young girl, Mona had been left orphaned and unprotected. She moved sadly through her days. One day, on a lonely walk through a meadow, she saw a butterfly struggling to release itself from a thornbush. Mona carefully released the butterfly from its captivity. Her freeing touch caused the butterfly to turn into a beautiful fairy.

"In return for your kindness," the good fairy said, "I will grant you any wish." Mona thought for a moment and said softly, "I want to be happy!" The fairy leaned forward, whispered into the girl's ear, and flew off.

Mona developed into a beautiful woman and eventually grew to be old. She had left the sadness of her childhood in the field where she had met and aided the fairy. After that, Mona's years were marked by serene happiness. As the end of her life drew near, friends and admirers came to comfort her, and to say good-bye to this remarkable woman.

Mona's last gift to her friends was the story of her encounter with the fairy. She shared with them the words the fairy had whispered in her ear. As Mona spoke, her eyes shone with the joys of a lifetime of treasuring the fairy's message: "Everyone, no matter how secure they seem, no matter how old or young, rich or poor, has need of you."

Because she believed that, Mona had become a woman of purpose. *Happiness is a by-product of successfully working toward and fulfilling purpose.* The expansiveness of Mona's purpose had given her a reason to live, and a long and happy life. Living with a purpose does that for us. Self-defined purpose does it best.

You Can Create Your Own Tale Of A Purpose

Mona needed to know she was of value in an often inconsiderate world. However, her true value did not need to be proven at all. It already existed in her very being as a child of her Creator. First, she learned how to give and grow at the same time. Then she recognized the need in others and responded with a caring attitude.

It is important to respect yourself enough to define your own purpose. You may need to re-shape it as you move along. Each time you do, welcome the challenge as a life-giving, life-enhancing opportunity.

Welcome heroes and mentors into your life. You can stride along with them as you find your own pace. Look for generous ones who can see the fine qualities shining in you, just waiting to be brought out. You'll want to find a mentor who will affirm and support your desires for personal achievement, and who can help you believe in yourself. You'll want your mentor to assist you in finding your purpose. You'll need them to help you find the best path to follow to fulfill that purpose, and realize your dreams and goals.

The Principles of Success

The ideas and concepts presented in this book have their origins in the great books. When you apply "No Excuse!" to your own life, you will be living by *the* acknowledged principles of success, such as self-esteem, enthusiasm, attitude, forgiveness, goal setting, and more. These will be both the roots and the fruits of your tree of "on purpose" self-responsibility.

What will motivate you to be successful? Is it external factors that will motivate you to achieve, or your own internal drive? Both play important roles. Growth depends on external nourishment. However, your purpose will define the shape and direction your growth takes.

Your purpose is the essence of what you believe about yourself and what you can achieve. Given proper "nourishment," you alone will determine the limits of what you can do. A healthy purpose will help you reach your full potential.

Motivation Is From The Inside Out

Does external motivation have a place in your life? Yes! You may want to sit quietly...reading, writing, and studying. However, if what you're studying is inspiring, it may motivate you to get up and take action. Also, if you have just experienced an exciting seminar, you could be moved to take what you've learned and put it into practice.

In the military, external motivation is a way of life. The consequences of not complying with regulations are swift and harsh, sometimes punishing. In corporate life, money is often the external motivator used to accomplish a task. This, coupled with the prestige of being listed high in the monthly ranking report, often encourages people to do things. Who would want to be last? The regulations and rankings didn't really drive me. They weren't my purpose. However, I had implicitly committed myself and my energies to them when I joined the organizations that established them as goals. Those purposes were what someone else chose. Your employment with an organization implies you will help them achieve *their* dreams and goals.

Within most organizational structures, there are elements to stimulate both internal and external motivation. You can shine brightly in the organization as you learn to develop and benefit from their chosen motivators.

You may find, in situations you've chosen, there are external motivators that demand the impossible from you. They may even be directly opposed to your values and inclinations. You may or may not choose to continue with the organization, depending on how seriously their thinking differs from yours. You may choose to discuss the matter with someone in a higher position who oversees you, to reach a new agreement. You can create strong, internal motivators to help you achieve challenging goals. As you live self-responsibly, the strength to develop internal motivators will come. It'll help you overcome obstacles and may even empower you to move-on.

In 1981 I attended the U.S. Army's Ranger School Training Course at Fort Benning, Georgia. This experience provided one of those challenges where survival depends solely on how much you believe in yourself and your abilities. As a result of the physical and emotional hardships, you discover just how powerful internal motivation can be. There are moments when *everything* depends on your personal, internal reasons for persevering.

I began my career at West Point with what I felt was the right mental attitude. I made it my mission to demonstrate excellence, confidence, and selflessness. They became my internal motivators. I was on the alert for opportunities to exercise these qualities, not for anyone else's approval, but for my own personal satisfaction.

On Ranger School graduation day, fewer than half of those who started with me made it through the course. There are quitters in every arena. The Ranger Training School experience, though, was a true testing ground for one's internal motivators. Many of the students did not have a strong enough desire to finish. They weren't motivated enough internally to withstand the rigors of the external motivators.

Desire is the key ingredient. If it's weak, it can lead to a person quitting before the completion of a worthy goal. Success or failure in the course was decided by each person's ability or inability to mold the external motivators to support their internal goals. *Ability can be developed when the desire is strong enough.*

There are many positive external motivators that can influence our performance and desire to excel. Incentives and awards are used successfully in many organizations. However, positive external motivators will only have short-term benefits if they don't support your life's dreams and goals as well as your personal definition of purpose. *You can have all the plaques and bonus points that exist, but they'll have little or no meaning to you if their achievement does not support who and what you are and want to be.*

Most of us know unhappy people who are generally perceived as being successful. Be assured, it's only a limited success. Their success is often not based on their purpose or value system. They may be solely reacting to external motivators. They may be blaming their unhappiness on others. They may be living a lie; being untrue to themselves and others.

My Ranger Training didn't culminate on graduation day. The greatest moment was a time of crisis when I had to balance intense internal and external motivators. It was much like preventing a team of horses from bolting! That story is next.

What Happened When I Reached The End Of My Rope

In my mind I can see the "movie" reel of my Ranger Training days unwind. It is an indelible memory. I'm sure you would understand that, if you are at all acquainted with the rigors of Ranger Training or something similar.

The code word for my "moment-of-truth" in Ranger Training was "Far-Side." It had nothing to do with Gary Larson's comics. However, they did share a certain believability. It was a detached awareness that the experience of extreme circumstances offered; an opportunity to leap beyond what I believed was the outer limits of my endurance. This was similar to the humor of Larson's weird inversions of animal and human behavior. It depended on a momentary leap beyond possibility. The Ranger experience proved that dedication to high purpose can motivate anyone to achieve beyond what they had previously set as their outermost limits.

First, let's cover some background on the Rangers. The U.S. Army Rangers trace their lineage back to Rogers' Rangers. Major Robert Rogers formed nine companies of American colonists to defend British interests during the French and Indian Wars of the mid-18th century. Their battles were fought in what is now northern New York, New England, and the adjoining Canadian provinces.

Traditional European lines of march and attack had brought the "red coats" of the regular British forces to death and defeat. *Rogers' 19 Standing Orders* like, "If somebody's trailing you, make a circle, come back on your own tracks, and ambush the folks that aim to ambush you," helped make his raw American colonists into a real fighting force. They were capable of anticipating and responding to the particular demands of the enemy and the terrain they faced. Because of their success, Rogers' Rangers entered the annals of military history. To this day, *Rogers' 19 Standing Orders* are taught in military academies throughout the Western world.

Ranger groups are traditionally volunteers that were disbanded when wars ended. The history of U.S. Ranger groups originates from Rogers' men, to Morgan's Riflemen in the Revolutionary War. It was Darby's Rangers in World War II who spearheaded the amphibious assaults in North Africa and Sicily. They also performed with equal valor on the beaches of Normandy. In fact, it was on bloody Omaha Beach that the Rangers got the motto that has stayed with them ever since. When the order was given for Darby's Rangers to break through the wall of defending German machine guns, artillery and trenches, the words they heard were: "Lead the way, Rangers!"

Today, the goal of every group of Rangers is to be a band of leaders, each self-sufficient to the highest degree. Every Ranger is dedicated to accomplishing the mission of the group, while adhering to the highest standards. A volunteer Ranger is required to undergo and survive some of the most mentally and physically demanding training in the world.

When I completed my Armor Officer Basic Training (tanks) and Motor Officer Course (maintenance), I qualified for Ranger School. I thought I knew what to expect. I knew deprivation of sleep and food would be built into the program. Beyond that, it was coupled with physical training and classroom work more strenuous than I ever could have imagined. Meeting the standard was an exhilarating experience.   Each time I overcame an obstacle, I experienced personal satisfaction and enhanced self-esteem.

The Ranger Course, which is conducted by the Infantry School's Ranger Training Brigade, is the Army's premier leadership course. The soldiers who graduate from it are tough, competent, and confident.   They can lead units into combat and surmount all obstacles necessary to accomplish their mission.

This is how Rangers are described in the course book:

> *The Ranger Course identifies and further develops leaders who are physically and mentally tough, self-disciplined, highly motivated and committed, who enforce high standards and are able to think, act, and react effectively in stressful situations that approach (and possibly exceed) that found in combat.*
>
> INFANTRY, *"Training Notes: The Ranger Course"*
> *May-June, 1991, p. 37*

Unfortunately, many of the soldiers who begin the course fail to complete it. I never for a moment felt this would happen to me, until the following incident occurred.

Those of us in my class who had successfully completed the "Benning Phase" of Ranger training, conducted at Fort Benning, Georgia, and the "Mountain Phase," held in Georgia's Chattahoochee National Forest, were transported to Florida for the final phase. It consisted of days of waterborne training, night jumps, swamp infiltrations, and military operations on urban terrain. We arrived in late February of 1981 to experience the severest stretch of cold weather the people in Florida had encountered in many a winter.

I always felt good about my swimming ability. Through swimming, I was introduced to competitive sports. It was the first time I was recognized because of physical excellence, and this caused my peers to respect me. I don't think I was cocky about my capabilities, but admittedly, the 'waterborne' aspect of Ranger training sounded somewhat comfortable. When I thought of what I had already been through and accomplished at West Point, and in the first phases of Ranger training, I believed the worst was behind me. I had no idea how my sense of purpose was going to be put to the test.

"An expedient stream crossing" called for a "Far-Side" lifeguard; and Rifenbary, the all-American swimmer, was given the duty. I hefted the ends of a sixty-foot and eight-foot rope to my shoulder. They would be the guide line and safety line for those following me. I entered the bone-chilling water and fought my way against a strong current to the reedy banks of the opposite shore. There I secured the sixty-foot rope to a tree. I then took the eight-foot rope and swam back to the middle of the crossing, where I was to remain treading water and be prepared to save a fellow student in the event they fell into the river. My orders directed me to be the lifeguard at the middle of the crossing. I rigidly stretched one arm to take the weight off the safety rope, as it threatened to leave my grasp and whip down the river like a snake. I used the other hand to grasp a reed for whatever support it could supply.

I had to do this until my companions made it from shore to shore. I remained in the water as they clung to the sixty-foot rope, traveling one-by-one, hand-over-hand, with full battle-packs hanging like shells of upended turtles.

I knew and felt the signs of hypothermia, but I used every mind trick I knew to convince myself that the symptoms didn't exist. My convulsive shaking attracted the attention of the Ranger instructor, who "encouraged" me with jeers and ridicule. The cramping in my limbs became so severe, I asked to be relieved. Finally, the order was given to haul me out of the water.

At that point, another instructor came to where I sat. I was still shaking uncontrollably.

"Wanna go home?" he sassed.

Another instructor joined in.

"Wanna go home to *Mommy*?"

I thought the enlisted men at my side were like stone. Hear no evil, see no evil, speak no evil. I stayed silent. I knew what was at stake. *I had a decision to make.*

I knew that in the first phase, the Benning Phase, a medical drop had been used as an honorable way out of the course for most of those who had left. That was one way out. Then, of course, I could always voluntarily quit. That would be entered on the record as "lack of motivation." The harassment of the instructors kept on for ten minutes. One was at each ear, bending in low to shout insults and taunts.

I answered, finally, "No, I don't want to go home, Sir."

The order came: "Then get back into the water."

For the first time, I considered standing up and walking away. But something inside me stubbornly refused to let my tormentors decide whether or not I would be a Ranger.

I stood up and somehow found the strength to re-enter the water and to hold my post. I stayed until the blessed moment when the last classmate completed his crossing and pulled me out. A couple of men then wrapped me in blankets and prepared a fire to warm me before we began a 12-mile road march.

The triumph was that I didn't allow the privilege of fulfilling my purpose to be taken from me. I revisit the memory to recall my victory, despite the pain it vividly brings back.

I was deprived of food. Imagine eating only four meals in ten days. I was deprived of sleep. We averaged one or two hours a night. I was also deprived of dignity. Imagine enduring the verbal assault of tormenting instructors. But I was not deprived of purpose! My purpose was to be a Ranger. If I was going to reconsider that decision, it wasn't going to be because someone might take pleasure in my failure.

I was not trying to meet the standards of those instructors. I was meeting my own standards when I re-entered the water. I was thinking to myself, "I may leave the Rangers tomorrow because of this experience, but the decision to leave will belong to me, not to my tormentors." And that's what got me through this experience. I have three traumatized toes to prove I braved that moment of decision. I also have a depth of understanding of what allows a human being to go beyond what he believes are his limits of endurance to achieve high purpose.

What Does It Mean To Be Alive?

Purpose gives meaning and value to our lives. It provides us with a reason to become the person we are meant to be. Most importantly, it offers us the opportunity to contribute to others. It is well known senior citizens often live longer when they have a house pet or plant to care for. They have another reason to be alive. Those who retire from their professions without future plans or direction, sometimes have shorter life spans than those who do.

Purpose establishes, in your own heart and mind, that others need you and your talents. Countless studies have demonstrated the negative impact depression and a lack of self-esteem have on physical health. *Establishing a purpose can assist you in maintaining a healthier lifestyle.* Always conclude that you have something more to offer. You may want to communicate to others that you have a certain ability or talent. Then pursue the opportunities available to you to give what you would enjoy giving the most. For example, if you love spending time with children, you may want to seek an opportunity to work or volunteer at a local children's hospital.

Purpose enables us to enjoy more of life's pleasures. It's the greatest when our purpose becomes our pleasure. If my purpose is to motivate others to achieve success, then no other career is going to give me as much satisfaction as doing that. Therefore, it is not practical for me to spend a great deal of time fixing automobile engines. It's not where my talents lie; it's not what I've defined as a purpose; it's not what would give me optimal pleasure; and it's not what would enable me to make a difference.

What Is Your Main Purpose In Life?

It is important, both to you and others, to honestly admit to yourself what your main purpose in life really is, or what you would like it to be. Here are six steps that can assist you in defining your purpose. You can also discover whether your work and outside activities are helping you fulfill your purpose.

I.   WHAT PURPOSES ARE PROVIDED BY YOUR LIFE'S WORK?

1. _____

2. _____

3. _____

4. _____

5. _____

6. _____

7. _____

II. WHAT PURPOSE DOES YOUR EMPLOYER EXPECT YOU TO FULFILL? OR, IF YOU ARE SELF-EMPLOYED, WHAT PURPOSES DO YOU EXPECT YOURSELF TO FULFILL THROUGH YOUR BUSINESS? (Examples--represent the highest standards of the firm to the public; maintain the teamwork attitude of the workplace; justly conform to the firm's best financial interests.)

1. _____

2. _____

3. _____

4. _____

5. _____

6. _____

7. _____

III. WHAT PERSONAL ATTRIBUTES WILL SHAPE MY PURPOSE?

1. What do I do well? What skills do I possess that clearly reflect my talents?

_____

_____

_____

_____

_____

_____

2. What would I love to do? What would I do if I didn't need to earn money?

_____

_____

_____

_____

_____

_____

3. What do others appreciate about me?

_____

_____

_____

_____

_____

_____

4. What areas am I weak in? Are any of these skills necessary
    for accomplishing what I would love to do?

_____

_____

_____

5. What do others not appreciate about me? Are any of these
    skills necessary for accomplishing what I would love to do?

_____

_____

_____

6. What is my attitude like? Do people want to be around
    me?

_____

_____

_____

7. What do I want out of life? What does it mean for me to be alive?

_____

_____

_____

_____

_____

_____

_____

_____

IV. WHAT OTHER ACTIVITIES ARE YOU INVOLVED IN OUTSIDE OF YOUR WORK WHERE YOU ARE ABLE TO USE YOUR TALENTS TO DO WHAT YOU LOVE TO DO?

1. _____

2. _____

3. _____

4. _____

5. _____

6. _____

7. _____

V. IF YOU HAVE DISCOVERED THAT NEITHER YOUR WORK ACTIVITIES NOR THOSE OUTSIDE WORK HELP YOU TO FULFILL YOUR PURPOSE, WHAT COULD YOU DO TO MOVE IN THIS DIRECTION?

1. _____

2. _____

3. _____

4. _____

5. _____

6. _____

7. _____

VI. WHAT STEPS ARE YOU WILLING TO TAKE?

1. _____

2. _____

3. _____

4. _____

5. _____

6. _____

7. _____

By answering these questions, you'll be better equipped to determine the true fundamentals for your purpose in life. What do you think it is? If you feel that you don't know, use your imagination. Pretend that you know and write down what your heart speaks.

My purpose in life is:

_____

_____

_____

You've Done It

Good for you! Let yourself come away from this section feeling exuberant. Yes, the possibilities you once only imagined are now becoming real.

The key to your success is defining your own purpose, which you've just had an opportunity to do! Your personal action plan may be beginning to unfold. It is likely that you know the general direction you need to take to lead you through the life lessons that await you in Part II of this book. I believe you'll find it will be a fantastic voyage through a treasury of timeless principles. You may come to think of them as best friends, always there for you. They can exert a positive influence on your life and help keep you on course.

With the strength of self-responsibility as your support, and a well-defined purpose as your guide, your preparations for embarking on the *Staircase-of-Success* are likely to be virtually complete. Next, we'll take a closer look at what it means to be successful, both in a personal and a broad sense, and establish the guidelines of fair play.

"No Excuse!" Action Plan For "The Power of Purpose"

1. Establish your purpose, mission, or dream in life. It's more important than talent in creating and shaping your life. You can move "mountains" when you know where you're going. Otherwise, you're like a ship without a rudder, bound to drift aimlessly. It'll help you be enthusiastic about life.

2. Become what you choose to be; do what you choose to do. Events and other people's purposes will direct you if you're not in charge of yourself.

3. Make a list of twenty or more things you'd like to accomplish. Believe you deserve them. This will open up your mind and excite you with the possibilities that exist for you. The more purposes you have, the more you are able to perceive, accept, and fulfill your responsibilities to yourself and others.

4. Let go of excuses, and situations will be diffused. Where self-responsible living replaces excuse-making, purpose and positive action replace fear.

5. Once you've established your purpose, you'll become happy by successfully working toward and fulfilling your purpose. Purpose is a key ingredient to happiness.

6. Develop a strong desire for your purpose. It'll make up for any ability you may lack; you'll figure out "how" along the way. The stronger your desire, the greater your chances for success.

7. Find out what motivates you, deep down inside. While external factors can trigger your motivation, it's what's really in your heart that will sustain you.

8. Establish your purpose and you can maintain a healthier lifestyle. Feelings of a lack of self-esteem and depression negatively impact health. Purpose establishes that others need you and your talents.

"Life is too short to spend time doing anything except what you are passionate about."

GEORGE MATELJAN

If I had my life to live over, I'd dare to make more mistakes next time; I'd relax, I would limber up. I would be sillier than I have been this trip. I would take fewer things seriously. I would take more chances. I would take more trips. I would climb more mountains and swim more rivers. I would eat more ice cream and less beans. I would perhaps have more actual troubles, but I'd have fewer imaginary ones. You see, I'm one of those people who lives sensibly and sanely hour-after-hour, day-after-day. Oh, I've had my moments, and if I had it to do again, I'd have more of them; in fact, I'd try to have nothing else. Just moments, one after another, instead of living so many years ahead of each day. I've been one of those persons who never goes anywhere without a thermometer, a hot water bottle, a rain coat, and a parachute. If I had it to do over again, I would travel lighter than I have. If I had my life to live over, I would start barefoot earlier in the Spring and stay that way later in the Fall. I would go to more dances. I would ride more merry-go-rounds. I would pick more daisies.

NADINE STAIR (WRITTEN AT AGE 85)

"If a man does not keep pace with his companions, perhaps it is because he hears a different drummer. Let him step to the music he hears, however measured or far away."

THOREAU

DARE GREATLY...

*It is not the critic who counts; nor the man
who points out how the strong
man stumbled, or where the doer of deeds
could have done better.
The credit belongs to the man who is actually in
the arena; whose face is marred by dust and
sweat and blood; who strives valiantly;
who errs and comes short again and again;
who knows the great enthusiasms, great devotions,
and spends himself in a worthy cause;
who at the best knows in the end the triumph of
high achievement; and who at the worst, if he fails,
at least fails while daring greatly;
so that his place shall never be with those cold and
timid souls who know neither victory nor defeat.*

THEODORE ROOSEVELT

Chapter 3

INTEGRITY
Your Cornerstone Of Success

The Definition of Success

Anyone who is living self-responsibly and with purpose could now ask, "What does success mean to me?" Well, there's more to it than just defining your purpose.

With "No Excuse!", you'll recognize and appreciate the difference between success and purpose. Your purpose is defined by you, after careful evaluation of why you are here on this earth. The path to accomplishing your purpose is traveled by pursuing the goals you set for yourself; the journey *is* the success! Success means different things to different people. Success is also determined by *how* you go about getting what you want every day of your life. *Success comes by being consistently committed to your dreams and goals, and taking the actions which lead to fulfilling your purpose.*

For people practicing "No Excuse!", success is not found at the end of the rainbow. It's the way we behave as we journey through life that determines what our lives are all about. Success is the way we treat ourselves and others. Success is the love, self-esteem, and respect in general that we direct inwardly and outwardly as we work every day for a better tomorrow.

Some say successful people are those who get what they want. This is only partially correct; there's more to success than that. The task at hand is to determine what that "more" is. So roll up your sleeves while we work towards some answers.

Might Makes Right?

When a war "machine" rolls over its enemies, one of the joys of victory is the privilege of writing the first version that tells the story of its success. Posterity re-examines the victor only when the ghosts of the vanquished emerge from the fog of the past. They gather like shadows under triumphal arches, demanding a second hearing. It is the second writing of history that often echoes through the ages.

Homer told the story of the Greek victory over the Trojans. The world will always honor the defeated Trojans. Why? He draws a portrait of their integrity. Perhaps the greatest message of the *Iliad* is just this: *Victory alone does not define success.*

Integrity is necessary for us to find true success in victory or defeat. It's what's missing in so many people who are considered successful. However, as history reveals, the leader of the Allied Forces in the 1991 Persian Gulf War was a man of integrity.

The General's Conviction

General H. Norman Schwarzkopf's moral courage was obvious to everyone he commanded. He and his troops were sent to recapture Kuwait and destroy the regional threat of Iraq's dictator, Saddam Hussein.

Schwartzkopf was a new kind of leader. He was down to earth, blunt, clear, idealistic, and swiftly effective. He was a leader born of his own convictions, rather than molded by traditional standards. He was admired by his troops as an officer who led by passionate example. He rewarded others generously by giving them real responsibility. He addressed junior officers' mistakes with direct, clear, corrective discipline, followed by warm personal encouragement.

Schwartzkopf acted solely on what he believed in. He led "from-the-heart." As a result, he achieved an overwhelming victory over Iraq's forces, the world's fourth-largest army. The loss of his own soldiers was minimal (263 out of 541,000 troops), a figure unprecedented in the annals of military history.

Schwartzkopf is one of the most respected U.S. generals of all time. He always did his best to emulate his father, a major general in the U.S. Army. Both he and his father were graduates of West Point. They were men of steadfast striving, constant values, and in pursuit of ideals. Both were men of integrity. (Schwartzkopf continues to be a man of integrity.)

A time of great decision came for the younger Schwartzkopf, when he experienced the defeat of Vietnam. He had served first in 1965 as a captain, and again in 1969 as a lieutenant colonel. In the years following, Schwartzkopf continued his military career. He was forever influenced by the lessons he learned from observing the causes and results of a demoralized army, led by demoralized officers. He then developed his own philosophy of leadership.

Schwartzkopf understood what Eisenhower meant when he said, "It's better to have one person working with you, than to have three persons working for you." He became a brilliant leader and general, without the traditional air of status. He was prepared to lead the transformed fighting force of his own country, coordinate a thirty-three nation coalition, and engineer an inspiring victory in the Persian Gulf War.

Integrity Dictates True Success

"No Excuse!" weaves integrity into the strands of self-responsibility and purpose. It creates a tapestry of life that is beautiful and true.

Integrity is nurtured by living self-responsibly. In turn, your integrity keeps your purpose alive as you strive to become a decisive and action-oriented person. *It is virtually impossible to blame, whine, complain, and simultaneously have great integrity.*

When you lead a self-responsible life of purpose, you grow in wisdom. Look for integrity, in yourself and in the people you choose to work with, work for, and admire. It is mutual respect and integrity that come together to form the foundation for trust in your personal and professional relationships.

Funk & Wagnall's defines integrity as "uprightness of character; soundness; an undivided or unbroken state." *The degree to which you stand firm in your convictions and beliefs, and assume responsibility for what you say and do, determines your level of integrity.* Your integrity ultimately dictates how effective you are as a parent, salesperson, manager, leader, business owner, employee, social worker, spouse, teacher, or anything else. Your integrity dictates the measure of true success that you achieve.

The Key To Effective Leadership

One of the primary reasons for turmoil in any society is lack of personal integrity in political and economic leaders. We need leaders with integrity! It's essential to have self-responsible people in positions of power. They're the kind of leaders needed in government, business, families, and other organizations.

What interferes with good leadership? Ineffective leaders experience the same obstacles effective leaders encounter. Effective leaders learn how to handle obstacles by persisting and being creative. Ineffective leaders need to accept personal responsibility for their actions so they can be more effective. They are often fearful of not satisfying society's empty definitions of success, e.g. large house, fancy car. This sometimes leads them to jeopardize their integrity. They may step on others to accomplish a goal or be dishonest in their dealings. Their fear may cause them to deny responsibility for the consequences of their behavior. They may know what they did was incorrect and want to avoid punishment or maybe even losing their job. Unfortunately, some people think it's easier to forfeit integrity, than to risk not moving up the corporate ladder. This can cause them to live in constant fear of being "found out." Furthermore, the outcomes they create are weakened when they dodge responsibility or act based on their fear. It is likely they won't be pleased with their results.

Parents may be more concerned about being liked by their children, than in fulfilling their responsibility of providing consistent and effective discipline. Without discipline, how can children be expected to develop self-responsible habits and grow into adults with integrity? As a parent, how can you gain the respect of your child if you are not consistent with what you say and do?

The same is true for managers and leaders. Those who take certain actions because they want to please people to be liked are often weak, ineffective, and inconsistent. As a manager or leader, how can you gain the respect of your employees or followers if you are not consistent with what you say and do?

Integrity is key to effective leadership. Trust is a gift given by others to a person who displays integrity. A person of integrity may be thrust into a leadership role as a result of the respect and trust he elicits from others. One of the finest examples of this is the story of Rosa Parks. She demonstrated to the world the power of bravely and simply reflecting one's own basic beliefs. She went "against-the-tide" because she was (and still is) a woman of integrity, committed to principle.

Rosa Parks is a black woman who lived in the then-segregated city of Montgomery, Alabama. It was December of 1959. She believed that a paying passenger had the right to sit on a public bus in any vacant seat. This had been denied to blacks, who were expected to sit in the back. She acted on her belief and sat in the front, whether or not other people agreed with her. She even faced angry threats. She boldly stood up to discrimination by her courageous action. She integrated her belief with her action and caught the attention of an entire nation. Her display of integrity contributed to the nation's increased awareness of racial injustices. As a result, she stimulated the movement toward greater justice and equality of treatment among races. Rosa Parks, now in her eighties, is living in Michigan. She co-founded the Rosa & Raymond Parks Institute for Self Development in Detroit, Michigan. Her latest book is entitled *Quiet Strength*.

Do You Stand Strong For What You Believe In?

How strong do you stand by your beliefs and convictions? When you are expected to act, or make a decision that is in conflict with your values and beliefs, what do you do? Do you waiver back and forth from one decision or behavior pattern to another? Do you stand firm with what you know to be right? If you don't stand for something, you may fall for anything.

Every time a person or group makes a decision that lacks integrity, they experience increased temptation to relinquish responsibility for that decision. It's human nature not to want to take responsibility for decisions or actions we know are morally wrong. These decisions do not reflect our belief system. Therefore, we don't want to "own" them. In these situations, it can be very easy for us to hold someone or something else responsible. If we choose to place blame else-where, and we don't experience the consequences of taking responsi-bility for our actions, we thwart our personal growth in that area.

On the other hand, when you make decisions that correlate with your values and beliefs, you are much more likely to be self-responsi-ble and accept the outcomes. In addition, you are also more likely to correctly anticipate and deal with the results of your actions. Your integrity shows you have the wisdom to develop your values and beliefs and the strength to act on them. As a result, you are likely to have greater peace-of-mind.

My Personal Conviction

I recall an incident in the military where I was asked to sacrifice my integrity to feed the vanity of a higher ranking officer. He shocked me and the patrons of a local establishment by publicly belittling my superior officer. My personal conviction told me to publicly declare his remarks unacceptable. I knew I'd be risking his angry retribution. However, if I chose to say nothing, I knew I would be unworthy of being a leader. My personal convictions prevailed.

There were reprisals, as I knew there would be. I confronted them with all the fortitude I could muster. I responded to the ugly lies. I felt compelled to do these things even though it put my personal ambitions for promotion in jeopardy.

The reports of the superior officers who evaluated my performance, demonstrated how committed I was to excellence and earning advancement and recognition. Here is an example of one of the six reports, all of which were equally complimentary:

> *The most dedicated junior officer I have ever supervised...loyal to subordinate and superior alike....*
> *He is the type of officer a commander wants–he accomplishes every mission in a superior manner.... Never in six years of service have I met a more motivated officer. Respected by subordinates and superiors alike, this officer develops excellent communication with the soldiers– they know he cares about them and the mission.*

I quote this commendation, not to brag, but to show you how important it is to have integrity and establish excellent relationships with the people with whom you associate. To preserve my own integrity, I had no choice but to respond to the officer who, without justification, verbally assaulted the integrity of my superior officer.

My decision to be loyal to my own values negatively impacted a professional relationship with the offending officer. However, the relationship with myself was my key priority. I knew I could not be the officer and person I wanted to be, if I did not heed the call to a higher duty when I heard it. *It is unlikely you will become the person you want to be, if the decisions you make conflict with your values.* Remember, integrity is the driving force and essence of true success.

Success Can Be Learned

The catalyst for true success is learning. Learning leads to knowledge. Knowledge leads to understanding. Understanding leads to wisdom.

"No Excuse!" is an approach for achieving success. Its principles, when you make them a part of your life, will lead the way to honorable behavior and outcomes. The steps of the *THESAURUS Factor* exclude all unscrupulous thoughts and actions. When you are given a choice between taking an action that is against your value system, or declining to do so, "No Excuse!" will give you the understanding to make a wise decision. It'll help you be happy, with no regrets and a clear conscience.

Every successful person experiences times of challenging decision-making. The path of success is paved by one decision after another, and some of them may be tough. Sometimes it may not be easy to make the right decision. As you incorporate the steps of the *THESAURUS Factor* into your everyday life, you'll be able to call on them as a standard for decision-making. I believe you will find the *THESAURUS Factor* a valuable resource for leading a successful life of integrity, happiness, and fulfillment.

Imagine there's a nominee for public office with an incident of questionable judgement in his past. Do you believe he could have made wiser choices if he had used sound decision-making principles based on his value system? There are times when conscientious objection leads men and women to willingly endure sacrifice, while they disagree with a law. This is different than breaking a law because it's convenient and then hoping no one notices. The latter leads to fear and unhappiness.

The road to happiness is mapped out in the *THESAURUS Factor*. It's a guide that helps you protect your integrity as you work effectively toward your goals, so you can fulfill your purpose. As a "No Excuse!" person, you'll have a new opportunity to become a mature, decisive achiever, if you aren't one already. You can be free from the habits of blaming, complaining, and whining. They're losing habits. "No Excuse!" guides you to a life of honesty and integrity, and away from the temptations caused by unscrupulous greed. You'll learn how to develop habits of respect for yourself and others, which can support your efforts to achieve your dreams and goals.

You Are The Commander-In-Chief Of Your Own Life

Generals develop a plan to guide their soldiers in battle. "No Excuse!" teaches you how to be an excellent "commander-in-chief" of your own life. With the basic training of "No Excuse!", you can strategize and set goals as effectively as the greatest generals. You can then carefully choose your role-models, mentors, and associates. Of course accepting responsibility for your decisions is part of a "No Excuse!" life.

"No Excuse!" living encourages you to be the creatively focused engineer of your own life. You can use the *Staircase-of-Success* to examine your actions and powerfully design your own life. There is no need to drift, as some people do, like a ship without a rudder, at the mercy of the life's winds and currents. Your better judgment will win out over the grip of inner passions and needs. With "No Excuse!" self-awareness, you will learn to see what's happening in your life. You'll discover what you're doing to yourself that's not in your own best interest and be encouraged to take action to correct it.

I meet truly happy people every day, and I know their secret. Happiness results from "No Excuse!" living. These people do three things:

- They accept responsibility for their own lives.
- They design a purpose for themselves.
- They establish standards for themselves that they won't violate; they maintain integrity.

Sound simple? I hope so, because it is. Sound easy? I hope not, because is isn't always easy, especially at first. It's like learning to pedal the wheel of the tricycle while steering it at the same time. And like anything else, like any new habit you develop, it gets easier with practice.

How To Make Your Life More Meaningful

"To become what we are, and to become what we are capable of being, is the only end of life."–Robert Louis Stevenson. This simple and powerful statement explains the basic premise of "No Excuse!" *You make your life meaningful by knowing who you are. You make your life worthwhile by fulfilling your potential with integrity. Success is found in that combination.*

The only way to get to know and understand who you really are is to be somewhat introspective. Some people are always focused outward on other people and things. They fail to look inward and realize the power they have to take action in their own lives. Instead they are always fearful and "on guard." They try to protect themselves by finding someone or something else to blame if things go wrong. They spend their lives trying to be right, look good, and cover themselves.

It's impossible for you to fulfill your potential if your life is only a repetition of earlier successes. They are dead ends when they become nostalgic memories that you dwell on. You are safe alright. However, you can end up regretting you didn't move-on. "High-school-heroes" can be found in every community. Some people with potential live on the memories of the glory they achieved in their youth. Unfortunately, they are often afraid of failure. They are often in the "comfort zone" or "familiar zone," commonly called a "rut." They never seem to apply their model of previous success to new endeavors. Re-runs of past successes can be used, instead, to gain confidence to pursue your next adventure. You did it once and you can do it again.

"No Excuse!" helps people break free from faulty thinking patterns which have trapped them much of their lives. Again and again, "No Excuse!" helps people eliminate the habit of blaming others. The energy previously used to avoid self-responsibility can then be transformed into a determined strength. It's almost miraculous to watch as people reach their self-defined goals.

Purpose begins to grow in a self-responsible person freed of the burden of blame. Their accomplishments may be small at first, but they can celebrate each achieved goal. They can continue to move toward fulfillment of their purpose. People of purpose speak a common language; they are happy about their accomplishments. They can better appreciate the good things life has to offer.

"No Excuse!" works like yeast. Your life has bounds that hold and shape who you are, like a bread bowl. You can choose to change many of your bounds and create a bigger bowl. Life also brings in new raw material every day. It gives you experiences to process and develop. These are the ingredients, the stuff of which life is made. Your approach to living is like the yeast that gives growth to the materials brought to the bowl each day.

"No Excuse!" will work for you as long as you wholeheartedly adopt it and persist to make it a daily habit. As you study the lives of successful people, you'll see how they used the "No Excuse!" principles to achieve their goals.

Does Giving Have Anything To Do With Success?

Surely the increased capacity for giving, that comes with success, is its crowning glory. It is wonderful to be able to give freely, whether it is to charity or to assist people in other ways. True success always involves giving. Sure, you can give inherited money. However, this money wasn't the result of your own success, but someone else's. Before you can get to the point where you can give whatever you choose to contribute, you usually need to be a giver of your talents, skills, and caring. After I began implementing "No Excuse!", it became so rewarding I felt compelled to share it to help others enrich their lives. It was the best gift I could give and the best use of my time and talents.

As I looked back on my life, I realized I was happiest giving to others. My greatest joy came by helping friends and associates discover and use their own unique talents to work together to accomplish common goals. That's called teamwork.

At first glance it may appear to be solitary work, rather than teamwork. However, if you look closely, you'll see that the task of empowering others to motivate themselves is an interdependent process. Success for me is knowing that "No Excuse!" is helping others, as well as me, to live a purposeful life of contribution.

Everyone's application of "No Excuse!" will differ somewhat due to personal and situational factors. Your life will provide the container and the ingredients. You will devise the recipe for the success that only you can define for yourself.

"No Excuse!" is effective because you are in charge of your own decisions. You can examine the results of your decisions with new clarity gained from self-responsibility, purpose, and integrity. You can determine whether you meet your own standards of success in all areas of your life.

It's very important to understand that true success is connected to giving without expecting to receive something in return. When you have a "taker" attitude and are solely concerned with what you get, if you are working, you're always only and endlessly just making a living. To design a great life, you need to be more concerned with what you're giving. Your giving allows you to also receive. This is a cause and effect world. You may not receive from the same source to which you gave. It is important to give graciously and receive with genuine appreciation and acceptance.

Is your life a balance of giving and receiving? Do you agree that a life well lived will have both? Can you answer the questions "Did I give today?"; "Did I receive today?";"Honestly and with pleasure?" With "No Excuse!" you can!

"No Excuse!" means paying attention to the people in your life. When you take responsibility for your decisions and actions, it is likely you'll become more open to receiving. People will gladly give you time, money, objects, compliments, friendships, teachings, and counselings. When you no longer need to blame, whine, and complain, or moan and groan, you can really enjoy and appreciate the experience of giving and receiving. As you begin to nourish others with your appreciation of their gifts, you'll notice their ability and willingness to give increases. You're likely to have more strength to stand up to people with negative attitudes. In addition, you'll most likely be better able to find a number of true friends who will support your dreams and goals.

"No Excuse!" is for those who are interested in moving-on. It's for people willing to live with integrity. It takes courage to be honest about whether you have a giver or a taker attitude. It takes strength to humbly accept how important you really are in the lives of others. And nowhere is this fact more likely to be true than in the course of your daily associations with family and friends. Being important to these people implies the necessity of being responsible in your actions toward them.

Building An Army Of Allies

A "No Excuse!" life has a purposeful, self-responsible person at its center. A "No Excuse!" person builds a successful life by reaching out with integrity. A "No Excuse!" person bonds and develops strong, healthy relationships.

The military has a hierarchical structure with a chain of command that needs to be fulfilled. But every great general has known that the chain of command alone is not enough to foster cooperation, loyalty, and productivity. It depends on the bonds between him and his troops. Strong bonds inspire them to do their best. Inspiration is not linear. A small push on the edges of your "limits" can lead you to great victory.

Your relationships with your family and friends, however, do have linear aspects. They are directly affected by the quantity of time we invest in them. Children are ill-served by parents who relinquish their authority. Groups of friends and associates often need leaders too. Family and friends are sò important to "No Excuse!" living that a whole chapter in Part II is devoted to them. Ultimately, the quality of your relationships with them determines your true success in life.

As a society, we are in a time when the definition of family is shifting. Generally speaking, children seem to grow best in families. However, for many of them the traditional family does not exist. In order to compensate, we may need to work more diligently to bring loving care to our relationships.

The same is true of friendships. How many of us have the luxury of daily contact with all of our lifelong friends? Many of us need to nurture some important friendships long-distance. We live in a mobile society. There may be quite a distance between us and them. Therefore, *we have a responsibility to ourselves to make new friends.* We can never have too many friends.

How well do you choose and court (develop a relationship with) people you'd like to have in your life? How well do you treat them once they're a part of it? "No Excuse!" can help you succeed here.

By using "No Excuse!" in your work, you can attract new relationships. You can eliminate the clutter of excuses from your life. You can develop special relationships you'll treasure as you travel on your path of success.

Do You Fear Success?

Many people find that once they learn to stop making excuses for their failures and mistakes, they have a different challenge-- making excuses for their successes! After you've learned to eliminate self-imposed defeatist behaviors, your next step is to allow yourself to enjoy your success. You deserve it!

Success can be uncomfortable, even scary at first, because it also brings increased responsibility. Therefore, increased integrity is required. Some people use excuses to explain why they never accomplish much in life. When they finally achieve some success, the excuse-making habit may still be so strong that they begin making excuses for their achievements. For example, they may say that it was just "luck" when they worked long hours to achieve their goal. When someone makes excuses for their success, they'll feel like a person with losing behavior, even though they exhibit winning behavior.

You'll feel pleased about your success when you eliminate excuses. Give yourself credit for what you've accomplished. Also, give credit to anyone who helped you along the way. Accept compliments graciously from people who appreciate your efforts. Your positive feelings will help you be a more supportive family member, friend, and businessperson. Set your own goals and achieve them with integrity, and both you and others will benefit. Enjoy your success, and invite family and friends to celebrate with you. You'll be free to wholeheartedly enjoy *their* accomplishments too.

You Are Your Own Business

You are your own business; running your life is your business! How you treat yourself affects everything, including your financial picture. Taking excellent care of *you* is important.

You are taking excellent care of the business of life when you surprise a friend with the affirmation "I admire you"; when you affirm a young person's achievements when they aren't expecting attention; when you openly appreciate a golf partner's contribution by saying, "You're on your way to becoming a great golfer"; when you say to someone, "Thank you for being here!" These things will pay off. Your own achievements will be magnified. You'll find yourself surrounded by people who are also committed to live purposeful, self-responsible lives of integrity. *A spirit of generosity goes hand-in-hand with prosperous growth.*

In my mind I return again to the moment when "No Excuse!" was born; the grand opening of my business. The thought that I was in business for myself jolted me into a new awareness. "I'm in business for myself." It seemed to mean that it was all up to me, and in some ways it was.

Being in business for yourself means it's up to you! No one else can set the tone of the life you'll lead. If you believe your life is controlled by other people, you might want to ask yourself, "How come?" and "What can I do about it?" If you want to regain control of your life and you choose not to take action, you are making an excuse; you have lost integrity with yourself.

Start with a clean sheet of paper, and list the names of three people you feel control an area of your life. Beside each name, state at least one undesirable aspect of the power you believe they have. Now, devise a plan. Prepare for a conversation in which you negotiate with that person in order to remedy, or at least modify, the situation that bothers you. Then push all excuses out of the way and go-for-it! *When you use integrity to change or eliminate an undesirable situation, you gain experience in living a more powerful life.* You're starting to "take-charge"!

Having Successful Relationships

"No Excuse!" is a way to develop relationships of a higher order; relationships of mutual respect and support. As relationships grow and change, people sometimes grow apart. Letting go of a grown child, for instance, is the healthy culmination of a career of parenting.

Couples who break-up hopefully have learned something from their relationship. This could be helpful if they choose to build another relationship with someone else. If they don't learn anything from their relationship, they are likely to repeat the same ineffective behaviors with someone new. It's important both partners realize and have gratitude for all the good shared and the lessons learned before entering their next relationship. These romantic courting relationships can serve as a training ground for anyone who seeks to select a mate for a solid marriage.

It takes courage to lead a life of integrity, and to acknowledge the people who have supported you along the way. "No Excuse!" doesn't mean "No Thanks!" "No Excuse!" helps you to be thankful; a person who lights the path to the future with a glow of gratitude for the present and the past.

The first step of the *THESAURUS Factor* is designed to enable you to let go of the pain of the past. This allows you to travel into your future, without the weight of unforgiven ills on your heart, on your back, or on your conscious or subconscious mind. To climb the "No Excuse!" *Staircase,* begin by laying down the burdens of the past.

You've probably *allowed* people to hurt you in the past. I say "allowed" because no one can hurt you without your permission! We need to view an incident in a negative way for it to influence us negatively. It is truly our choice. Almost all of us have let that happen. It is nearly impossible to live in this world without experiencing pain. Some of us are more wounded than others. Outward appearances may lead you to believe that the wounds aren't there when they may be many and deep. You become your own worst enemy when your excuses keep those wounds open. You hurt yourself even more when you use more excuses to infect them. *No one can hurt you without your permission.* You can now look closer at where your wounds and infections are so you can start healing them.

The "Hero-Of-The-Month" Club

Now might be the time for you to start a "Hero-of-the-Month" club for yourself. You can learn from heroes, use them as examples, and fill your mind with their winning ideas and ways. When I ask audiences to name some heroes, I always get a fascinating variety of people of integrity who have influenced our society and how we see ourselves. For example:

- Charles Lindbergh–the gift of daring to bring the people of the world closer together.
- George and Barbara Bush–the gifts of life partners who travel down long and winding roads, committed to each other.
- David Robinson–the gifts of commitment, responsibility, excellence, and helping the future leadership (our children).
- Chuck Yeager–the gifts of guts and determination to explore new realms and break old barriers.
- Martin Luther King, Jr.–the gifts of non-violent protest for social change, and freedom for everyone.
- Amelia Earhart–the gifts of courage and persistence to overcome great obstacles.

No matter what heroes are suggested, I always see by their example that *the first step for attaining "No Excuse!" success is respecting our own desires.* You can respect your desires like these people and other heroes have done. Most people's idea of success includes acquiring something. Your idea of success may be money, cars, homes, or other material things. Hopefully, your success includes personal growth, helping people, championing a cause, and progressively achieving a worthwhile dream or goal. You're probably aware of the basic steps you need to take to get what you want. But remember, "success is a journey, not a destination."

General Ulysses S. Grant knew that he would only achieve complete success when Lee surrendered. He knew many battles, large and small, won and lost, would come before full success was his. This understanding set Grant apart from McClellan. McClellan's reluctance to engage the enemy in preliminary encounters caused Lincoln to replace him with Grant as head of the Union Forces. Grant's success as a general didn't begin with Lee's surrender. It began the moment he sat down and began defining his first encounter with the opposing forces.

Your success as a person in charge of your own life, begins the moment you plan a strategy to meet and overcome the forces that oppose you. If McClellan had realized his inertia was only an excuse, he might not have disgraced himself. Grant, however, used "No Excuse!" principles only in his military career. If he had also used them during his Presidency, he would not have earned disdain for his term in office.

How Can You More Easily Adjust To New Environments?

Grant missed the structure of the military and did not learn to operate from his own principles within the political arena. Some people feel anxious when they leave one environment and enter another. A child leaving home for school for the first time is leaving a place of known boundaries and comforts, for an unknown environment. The boundaries of the new structure will be different. The child will need to develop skills necessary to interact more interdependently as he transitions. These periods require more focus and energy until the new environment becomes more familiar.

The same is true during any time of transition in our lives. We may have experienced success within a certain structure, like school. When we leave that structure, we may find a part of us still wants to return to that comfortable arena. So it's critically important to our future, that we internalize the principles of success. When they are a part of us, they can guide us in any new environment.

"No Excuse!" provides principles we can use as we move from structure-to-structure in our daily lives. The *Staircase* of the *THESAURUS Factor* also guides us to success beyond structures. It can ultimately lead to *the truest success there is–satisfaction with a life you've defined for yourself.* This happens only when you've outgrown both immature definitions and those dictated by someone else or society. It only happens when you have the courage to find out who you really are and who you can be if you are willing to utilize your potential. It happens with sustained "No Excuse!" living.

The Rewards Of "No Excuse!" Living

The rewards of "No Excuse!" living can be immediate and tremendous. They can draw you closer to the goal of the wisdom extolled by philosophers down through the ages: "Know thyself."

Know what you love to do, and what your talents are. Allow yourself room to grow as a person. What do you love about yourself? What do others love about you? What would you love to do with your life? Have enough integrity to be honest with yourself.

People often find themselves working in occupations they don't love, or for which they have little aptitude. They end up toiling away with little reward for their labors, except some regular monetary compensation. Such a life is merely one of existence or survival. It's the same old activities over and over. "No Excuse!" helps you get beyond that to where you can experience greater success.

Your life's work is to grow and become the best you can be. This is not only recommended in your personal life, but in your career as well. "No Excuse!" is practical. It is important to create a balanced, productive life. *When your work turns into drudgery, it means you are ready for a new challenge.* It is recommended you be self-responsible enough to admit it, and maintain your integrity in switching.

If you are unhappy with your work, be honest with yourself. You may want to start looking for other opportunities. This does not mean you look for someone else to blame for the lack of satisfaction you are experiencing. It means you start looking for new ways to be in integrity with your own inner desires and with the people around you. It means sharing an optimism that will create a positive environment for yourself and everyone around you. You are already successful, to some extent, when you've done that much. The rest will come as you continue to grow and become.

Nothing Ventured, Nothing Gained

Ralph Waldo Emerson once said, "It's one of the greatest

compensations in life that no man can help another without thereby helping himself." *One of the most valuable gifts any of us can offer another is our willingness to assist their efforts in being self-responsible.* Helping others is a joy, rather than a burden, when you are sincere.

When self-responsibility is at work, people begin moving out of their "comfort zone" of routine responses. This means taking prudent risks and letting go of irresponsible impulsiveness and cowardly reluctance. It also means living your life with integrity.

Truly successful people take a chance when the time is right. They know they will turn even failure into an advantage by learning from it. In all the decisions you face every day, how well do you weigh the consequences of your choices? How well do you weigh the consequences of your inaction? You can choose to pay the price of success, or you will pay the price of failure by default!

Too many people avoid moving ahead in life because they fear they won't get the results they want, and they will regret taking action. They miss the excitement of a rich and full life experience. If you want to be truly alive, prepare to take risks by living a "No Excuse!" life.

I believe that you've decided to open your mind to "No Excuse!" Remember to keep persisting and maintain your integrity even when you feel challenged. Step right up to the *Staircase* of the *THESAURUS Factor*, confident your efforts will be rewarded. The outcome may be different than what you expect. Nonetheless it will be beneficial. You've had an opportunity to explore the excuses you may have made to keep some or all of your life safely in the "comfort zone." Like most of us who get too complacent, you may be good at making excuses for staying there. Remember Ben Franklin's words, "He who is good at making excuses is seldom good at anything else."

Fleeing The Flea Syndrome

The fact is, there is "No Excuse!" for you not to achieve success in your life. I do mean you. I do mean your life. I wish I could be standing there before you, to take you by the shoulders if necessary, look you in the eye and say, "Yes, you!"

I'd tell you what a wonderful life can lie ahead for you. What joy you'll have when you take responsibility for your own life, if you haven't already done so. You'll be able to convert energy you've been wasting on excuses, that you used in an attempt to guard yourself against criticism and failure. You'll be able to direct this energy into personal growth and the fulfillment of your dreams and goals.

Fleas are trained by keeping them in a covered container. They can jump amazingly long distances; that's how they get to new food supplies. But keep them in a lidded container long enough, and you can remove the lid without them jumping out! As the fleas hit the lid repeatedly, they become conditioned. They believe they can only jump as high as the lid, whether or not it's in place.

"Limits" affect people as well. We often live within the narrow limits we have set for ourselves. Have you been fooled into believing in false limits? It's time to let them go! Are you like a conditioned flea? Or, are you willing to take a chance and jump out of the jar?

Elephants are conditioned too, when as babies they are chained to a stake strong enough to keep them from getting loose. It tries and tries to break free but, of course, it can't. After a while, it becomes conditioned to believe it will never be able to break away. As the elephant reaches adulthood, it can be tied to its stake by only a small rope. It could actually break the rope, or pull the stake out. But it doesn't even try, because it's been conditioned.

Are you conditioned to "break-away" or stay right where you are? The only way you are going to make a difference is by taking a chance. You risk failure but you also risk success!

Most people don't need to see a psychiatrist or go into all kinds of intricate details on how to break "bad" habits and condition themselves to be happy and successful. By reading positive books and listening to positive audio cassette tapes, you can learn a great deal. You can turn idle time into personal growth time by reading. You can turn your car into a "university-on-wheels" by inserting a tape and pressing "play." These are success habits that can help you condition yourself to change your life.

In Part II of this book, we're going to cover the principles of success. You'll discover what it's like to deal with failure, and the impact it has on your life. You're going to learn about the *THESAU-RUS Factor*, and the "No Excuse!" lifestyle that can ignite your potential to help you "jump-out-of-that-jar." You're going to learn principles that can help you "break-the-chain-from-the-stake."

We're going to cover forgiveness, something most people never think about in regard to success. Forgiveness is a fundamental cornerstone of success. This is only one step along the way, and there's a lot more to do. It's going to be an exciting journey, and you're going to have a lot of fun along the line. Hopefully you'll be inspired to achieve greatness in your life by choosing to make a difference in the lives of others, if you haven't already done so.

"No Excuse!" Action Plan For "Integrity"

1. Have integrity in everything you do. Getting what you want is just part of success. Integrity is necessary for you to find true success, no matter what the outcome.

2. Never blame, whine, or complain. It's impossible to have integrity if you do. Be responsible for whatever happens because of decisions you made.

3. Never forfeit your integrity to get ahead. Live consistent with your own values, good morals, and principles. If you make decisions in conflict with your values, it's not likely you'll succeed.

4. Integrity is the key to effective leadership. People will trust you when you operate with integrity. Make a stand and live by it. Give your all to what you believe in, and don't waver.

5. Make your life worthwhile by fulfilling your potential with integrity. Follow through with the activities that are right for you and where you can best serve.

IT COULDN'T BE DONE

Somebody said that it couldn't be done,
But he with a chuckle replied,
That "maybe it couldn't," but he would be one
Who wouldn't say so till he tried.
So he buckled right in with the trace of a grin
On his face. If he worried he hid it.
He started to sing as he tackled the thing
That couldn't be done, and he did it.
Somebody scoffed: "Oh, you'll never do that,
At least no one ever has done it;"
But he took off his coat and he took off his hat,
And the first thing we knew he'd begun it,
With a lift of his chin and a bit of a grin,
Without any doubting or quiddit,
He started to sing as he tackled the thing
That couldn't be done, and he did it.
There are thousands to tell you it cannot be done,
There are thousands to prophesy failure;
There are thousand to point out to you, one by one,
The dangers that wait to assail you,
But just buckle in with a bit of a grin,
Just take off your coat and go to it;
Just start to sing as you tackle the thing
That "cannot be done," and you'll do it.

EDGAR A. GUEST

Part Two

THE

THESAURUS Factor

THE TOUCH OF THE MASTER'S HAND

'Twas battered and scarred, and the auctioneer thought
it scarcely worth his while to waste much time
on the old violin, but held it up with a smile.
"What am I bidden, good folks," he cried, "Who'll start
the bidding for me?" "A dollar, a dollar," then,
two! Only two? "Two dollars, and who'll make it
three? "Three dollars, once; three dollars, twice; going
for three . . ." But no, from the room, far back,
a grey-haired man came forward and picked up the
bow; then, wiping the dust from the old
violin, and tightening the loose strings, he played a
melody pure and sweet as a caroling angel sings.
The music ceased, and the auctioneer, with a voice
that was quiet and low, said: "What am I
bid for the old violin?" And he held it up with the
bow. "A thousand dollars, and who'll make it two?
Two thousand! And who'll make it three?
Three thousand, once; three thousand, twice; and going
and gone," said he. The people cheered, but some
of them cried, "We do not quite understand what
changed its worth?" Swift came the reply: "The touch
of a master's hand." And many a man
with life out of tune, and battered and scarred
with sin, is auctioned cheap to the thoughtless crowd,
much like the old violin. A "mess of potage,"
a glass of wine; a game—and he travels on. He is
"going" once, and "going" twice, he's "going"
and almost "gone." But the Master comes and the
foolish crowd never can quite understand
the worth of a soul and the change that's wrought by
the touch of the Master's hand.

MYRA B. WELCH

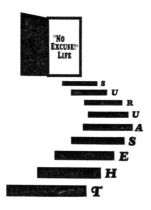

Chapter 4

PRELUDE TO
THE *THESAURUS* F*actor*
Your *Staircase-of-Success*

Folks, Step Right Up!

Picture that our paths have crossed. Imagine we are standing side-by-side at the entrance to a palatial mansion. We are awed by the grandeur before us. We are particularly inspired by the magnificent staircase that seems to stretch endlessly to light-filled upper reaches. We are dazzled by the beautiful, spacious chambers that seem to promise fulfillment of our hearts' desires and abound in all directions. It is a pleasure to welcome you. In our brief time together, you will have an opportunity to learn the secrets of the "kingdom" ruled from this special place.

The *Staircase* may appear awesome to you—insurmountable. But have confidence. Let go of the idea that it needs to be a struggle. Believe you can make it to the top. Understand you will have the opportunity to enjoy each step along the way, and revisit them as often as you wish.

The joy of "No Excuse!" living is not just for those who have reached the top. No! Your success and happiness is right now. Life is sweet for those who live life fully every day.

Take One Step At A Time

The *Staircase-of-Success* is magnificent. In fact, each step is actually a stage: a stage for playing out the best life has to offer; a stage for dancing to your life's music; and a stage that welcomes "another opening, another show." It could be a new show blazing onto the scene like a comet. Or it could be a revival, bringing back a beloved work for a fresh interpretation.

Each step of the *THESAURUS Factor*, your *Staircase-of-Success*, can be adapted to your needs whenever you visit it. And one step is just as important as another. You enter the "mansion" only by way of the *Staircase*.

As you climb the *Staircase* and use the principles, you'll become more self-responsible. You'll experience more peace-of-mind. With this new state-of-mind, you'll come to accept and enjoy periodic solitude or "quiet time," a hallmark of a maturing person's search for fullness of life.

Each step contains opportunities for wisdom, limited only by your openness and willingness to practice what is offered. Once you have reached, acquainted yourself with, and practiced each step, a new freedom to "dance" begins. Your dance is personal and determined by your own wants and needs.

If you need to invest a long time on the first step, great! Give yourself time to understand and use the ideas. Relax as you take a stand on "Totally Forgive," the first step. Don't force yourself to sprint to the next step, "Have Self-Esteem." Wait until you feel satisfied that you have gotten what you need for the moment. At that point it's time for you to move-on.

As you dance along the *Staircase,* determine your own pace. There's a time for marching; that's a dance for a common cause. There's a time for choosing a partner for a waltz under the stars. And then there are times when either slow dancing, dancing alone, or tap-dancing in a chorus line is the thing to do. With "No Excuse!" living, you'll know when those times have come. Listen to your heart.

People who haven't found what inspires *them* may tend to get caught-up in the excitement of other people's dreams. Often they never develop their own. If that happens to you, you can use the skills you've acquired by living a "No Excuse!" life. They can lead you to totally self-responsible behavior. Take a deep breath and search inside for your own "routine" and pace, and you'll discover the desires of your heart. You *can* make your dreams come true.

Is Success Just An Uphill Battle?

Since you're on your own path of success, it doesn't matter whether you're going up or down the *Staircase*. It is important to understand that you can move along the *Staircase* in either direction if you really want to become all you can be. The mastery of each step is a growing process and is interdependent with the others. The *Staircase* is a place for people to learn which step they need to jump to, or carefully step up or down to. Which step you dwell on depends on your needs and what skills you wish to develop.

Your moves along the *Staircase* will be something like those of a xylophone player. He knows the bars so well, his mallet instinctively touches the right ones. His creativity and experience guide him to the perfect tone, the sound that will fill the moment. He may be creating sounds based on the music he hears in his head. Sometimes it's Mozart and sometimes it's a new piece. What's important is that he's in charge. He strikes the bars that will give him the notes he needs to create a fine harmony.

The search for overlapping combinations gives life to music and music to life. Like the musician, you are likely to find your greatest satisfaction along the *Staircase* as you take charge and make your own music. When you have the wit and wisdom to risk leaping about to create new tunes in your life, you can really grow. Since every journey begins with the first step, be kind to yourself if you falter when you hit some sour notes. Gently pick yourself up, dust yourself off, and start all over again! Remember, with practice you'll become more proficient.

The *Staircase* Has A Spirit All Its Own

When the idea of the *THESAURUS Factor* was initially developed, it became clear "climbing" isn't always perceived in a positive way. What is your perception of "climbing"? Negative or positive?

Let's consider the image of a "climber." *Webster's Dictionary* says a climber is "one who goes upward with gradual or continuous progress." Within the context of the "No Excuse!" philosophy, a climber is someone who seeks to develop themselves personally and professionally in all areas of life. The goal is, of course, to live the life you choose.

Why do some people believe it is wrong to strive for a better life? How come some people criticize and shy away from someone trying to achieve something he or she doesn't have or wasn't born with? Quite often, selfishness causes this negative reaction or judgement. Many people feel no one even has the right to dream! How sad.

Some people don't want anyone to have what they don't have themselves. They often feel powerless to change the circumstances they blame for their own unhappiness. They prefer to belittle anyone they believe naively attempts to scale an "unscalable" mountain. They are the people who scoff, complain, whine, moan, and groan. They often have lazy habits and may have a jealous attitude.

Then there are people with selfish attitudes who believe that only those born into "the good life" are worthy of it. They believe only those born with much, deserve prosperity. Snide remarks give these supposedly superior individuals away. Those who snicker and sneer at others usually have either selfish or jealous attitudes.

When climbing the *Staircase* of the *THESAURUS Factor*, it is best to do it with a spirit of generosity and democracy. It is important to believe everyone has the right and responsibility to make the most of themselves. People who are committed to the principles of our founding fathers are most likely the ones who will help keep our country strong and powerful. These visionary men established a society that gives growing room to and nurtures what Thomas Jefferson called a "natural aristocracy," or "meritocracy." In other words, people get rewarded for what they do, as in a free enterprise economy.

When we rise to the occasion and fully contribute our skills and talents, our society prospers. That was the idea in Jefferson's time, and it still offers mankind the best promise for the future.

In the military, success depends on each individual acting responsibly in the best interest of the company. This is similar to the principles of "No Excuse!" Ultimately, a sense of responsibility to be ambitious and generous evolves, oftentimes even with the enemy. This combination turns military triumphs into true victories when the war is over. Peace, harmony, and new mutual understanding can then occur.

Temper ambition with generosity if you want to reap the full benefits of your efforts. Success built on sharing and helping others results in multiplied benefits.

Part of the reason "No Excuse!" living leads you to success, is that it helps you eliminate any anxiety you may have had about other people's good fortune. This anxiety could have robbed you of precious energy, as well as caused friction. Eliminating the anxiety gives you more energy to climb your mountain. You'll have peace-of-mind knowing you did your best. You'll be glad for the company of your fellow climbers. You'll look back only to encourage them to keep up their effort. You'll climb with a lot more assurance than someone who puts others down. Anxious folks are insecure and may use their energy in a negative way by trying to step on the person behind them.

Many people are unsupportive, or neutral at best, toward achievers. They often put down ambitious dreamers who go-for-it. You may have even felt that way yourself at some point. To be more successful, we need to eliminate this prejudice, especially as it applies to ourselves. Recognize the negative attitude you may have toward your own personal desires to be more successful, happy and fulfilled. Sometimes we can sabotage our own efforts because of a negative attitude. We may not even realize it's holding us back!

Take a good look at where you stand on this issue. If you used to look askance at ambitious people, are you ready to accept the fact that you may be one of them? Get ready to dance along the *Staircase-of-Success* by joyfully supporting yourself and others who are adventurous achievers. *Go-for-it!*

DECIDE TO FORGIVE

Decide to forgive, for resentment is negative.
Resentment is poisonous; resentment
diminishes and devours the self. Be the first to forgive,
to smile and to take the first step,
and you will see happiness bloom on the face of your
human brother or sister. Be always the first;
do not wait for others to forgive. For by forgiving, you
become the master of fate, the fashioner
of life, the doer of miracles. To forgive is the highest,
most beautiful form of love. In return you
will receive untold peace and happiness. Here is the
program for achieving a truly forgiving heart:
Sunday: Forgive yourself.
Monday: Forgive your family.
Tuesday: Forgive your friends and associates.
Wednesday: Forgive across economic lines
within your own nation.
Thursday: Forgive across cultural lines
within your own nation.
Friday: Forgive across political lines
within your own nation.
Saturday: Forgive other nations.
Only the brave know how to forgive. A coward never
forgives. It is not in his nature.

ROBERT MULLER

Forgiveness is the fragrance of the violet that clings fast
to the heel that crushed it.

GEORGE ROEMISCH

Chapter 5

TOTALLY FORGIVE
First Step of the THESAURUS Factor

Do You Have Peace In Your Life?

How would you feel about a "potion" so powerful it could free you from the wrongs of the past? How would you feel about using a powerful idea that could help you move-on?

What is it? Forgiveness. What does forgiveness have to do with success? It's amazing. It is associated with your energy. Forgiving frees you from the negative grip of the past. Think of forgiveness as "giving it up," i.e., the resentment and anger. It's simple. If you don't forgive, you're going to waste a lot of time and energy on the past.

Forgiveness provides a fountain of energy. It releases negative energy from the past and unlocks positive energy in the present to help you move into the future. When you forgive, you have more energy to contribute to life. Forgiveness is part of ultimate wisdom. *Forgiveness is love.*

"As you sow, so shall you reap." This biblical phrase is just as important today as it was thousands of years ago. Forgive others and you are more likely to be forgiven.

When a military campaign is over, there's a need for forgiveness; the victor for the vanquished, and vice-versa. The length of any peace depends, largely, on how well each side forgave the other. We've all had occasions where forgiveness was necessary, either on our part or someone else's. *Are you aware that real prosperity is more likely to occur when we are at peace with our past?* When you know the truth, you'll realize there is power in forgiveness. Also, forgiveness may be needed before it is possible to have the necessary cooperation from others that can lead to success.

How Do You Deal With Failure?

Forgiveness can enable you to have abundant, productive mental and physical energy (vitality) in exchange for disappointment, rage, and feelings of failure. If you feel you've been denied, simply forgive yourself for any ill feelings you may have. Also forgive others for what you believe they have done. With forgiveness, you can often eliminate the troublesome feelings usually associated with a loss.

If a person is unforgiving about deprivation and injustice, they may allow it to ruin their lives. Successful people forgive and rise above such challenges to become all they can be. You don't need to let your life be ruled by loss and regret. You can develop the ability to forgive yourself and others when things don't work out the way you want them to.

We've all failed at something; it's just a part of life. Forgive yourself for it and move-on. *Successful people view failure as a learning experience.* In fact, we may literally "fail" our way to success. Failure is an opportunity to grow. It could also be a "wake-up-call" telling us that we need to make a change.

Earl Nightingale once said, "Luck occurs when preparedness meets opportunity." Luck can also be defined as <u>L</u>abor <u>U</u>nder <u>C</u>orrect <u>K</u>nowledge. When you first begin your quest for success, people may say you're "crazy." After you're successful, they may say you're "lucky."

I don't believe in "luck." You can be on the *Staircase-Of-Success*, but if you're sitting still and doing nothing, nothing is likely to happen. The more you do to contribute toward the outcomes you want, the "luckier" you're likely to get. Be prepared for opportunities as they arise and take action on them.

It can be difficult to accept failure, but it's essential if you want to move ahead. As motivational speaker Mike Wickett says, "If you 'lay-an-egg,' stand back, admire it, and move-on!" Love yourself anyway, even if you fail. Failure is just an event, an opportunity to learn something. It can help you be stronger for the next challenge. The best thing to do is face it, deal with it, and move-on.

Plato once said, "The measure of a man is how he bears-up under misfortune." For instance, the average age of a millionaire is fifty-seven. Furthermore, most of them failed five times before they made it! It's incredible. The greater the obstacles overcome, the greater the victory. Many can do well under ideal circumstances. It's when the "going gets tough" that the "tough get going" to become the best they can be.

Old Soldiers Never Die, They Just Forgive Away

Douglas MacArthur was one of history's few five-star generals. He received more medals than anyone of any branch of the American military, including the Medal of Honor, the highest decoration of all.

MacArthur's career was extraordinary, because he was a military genius who took action. He achieved his greatest triumphs because he forgave the opposition and himself. His forgiveness led to peace and the opportunity for prosperity for all.

The prayer MacArthur wrote to his newborn son shows the kind of forgiveness that led to a successful campaign against Japan in World War II. It was his forgiveness that eventually guided that country to a victory of its own.

Build Me A Son

Build me a son, O Lord, who will be strong enough to know when he is weak, and brave enough to face himself when he is afraid; one who will be proud and unbending in honest defeat, and humble and gentle in victory.

Build me a son whose wishes will not take the place of deeds; a son who will know Thee—and that to know himself is the foundation stone of knowledge. Lead him, I pray, not in the path of ease and comfort, but under the stress and spur of difficulties and challenge. Let him learn to stand up in the storm; let him learn compassion for those who fail.

Build me a son whose heart will be clear, whose goal will be high, a son who will master himself before he seeks to master other men, one who will reach into the future, and never forget the past. And after all these things are his, add, I pray, enough of a sense of humor, so that he may always be serious, yet never take himself too seriously. Give him humility, so that he may always remember the simplicity of true greatness, an open mind of true wisdom, and the meekness of true strength. Then I, his father, will dare to whisper, "I have not lived in vain."

THE EMPEROR GENERAL–A BIOGRAPHY OF DOUGLAS MACARTHUR
Norman H. Finkelstein

When the United States entered World War II in 1941, MacArthur was called to direct the Pacific war against Japan. Fighting was bloody and losses on both sides were high. Yet MacArthur could forgive the war for its casualties, for he knew the enormity of what was at stake. He understood that for the Allied Forces to prevail, they would have to take control of the Philippines. And that they did.

To end the war with Japan, the first atomic bomb was dropped on Hiroshima on August 6, 1945. Although seventy-thousand people were killed, Japan still wouldn't surrender. Three days later, a second bomb was dropped on Nagasaki. It killed thirty-thousand people, and finally, Japan was forced to surrender. After the war, forgiveness came from both sides.

President Truman appointed MacArthur to take charge of Japan's transition to a peacetime economy. When he arrived in Japan, MacArthur found the Japanese to be gracious in defeat. They respected him as much as they respected their own emperor! In his speech to the Japanese people, MacArthur spoke, once again, of forgiveness:

> We are gathered here, representatives of the major warring powers, to conclude a solemn agreement whereby peace may be restored.... It is my earnest hope and indeed the hope of all mankind that from this solemn occasion a better world shall emerge out of the blood and carnage of the past—a world founded upon faith and understanding—a world dedicated to the dignity of man and the fulfillment of his most cherished wish—for freedom, tolerance and justice.

Later, in a message to the American people, the general's words showed that, while he was a man of war by training and profession, he was also a man of peace: "Today the guns are silent. A great tragedy has ended.... We must go forward to preserve in peace what we won in war."

Between 1945 and 1951, MacArthur was, in effect, "Emperor General" of Japan. According to orders issued by President Truman, "From the moment of surrender, the authority of the Emperor and Japanese Government to rule the state will be subject to you."

As the Allied occupation got under way, neither the Americans nor the Japanese knew what to expect. The Japanese thought they'd be overrun by soldiers seeking revenge. They were unprepared for Americans who, under the leadership of their esteemed general, learned to put the past behind them. The Americans did not harbor any hatred against the Japanese. Instead, there emerged a feeling of calm and cooperation on both sides. There was much rebuilding to be done, and the effort was to be unified.

Very little happened in Japan without MacArthur's approval. The Japanese were to carry out his orders. His "General Order Number One" for instance, allowed Japanese soldiers to turn in their own weapons. MacArthur knew that if American troops took their rifles and swords by force, the Japanese would feel a shame that might lead to trouble.

American advisors urged MacArthur to order the Emperor Hirohito to appear before him. Many Americans wanted to do away with the position of emperor altogether. Some even wanted Hirohito brought to trial as a war criminal. However, MacArthur did not approve of these ideas. He understood the importance of the emperor to Japanese life. He was the symbol and spirit of the nation. Embarrassing Hirohito would serve only to arouse a Japanese public still humbled by the shock of defeat. He also knew that his own rule over Japan could not succeed without the cooperation of the emperor.

Understanding the nation's need to worship, MacArthur assumed a godlike presence. He ruled, as the emperor had, from a distance. He understood that he was popular among the Japanese because of his cool and grand manner.

During much of his reign, while trying to transform a centuries-old society into a modern democracy, MacArthur focused on the Japanese people. For example, he saw that the Japanese food supplies were short, so he ordered American troops to eat canned rations. He then quickly arranged to import food from the United States.

MacArthur also helped to modernize the Japanese school system and took steps to fairly distribute the country's wealth. He even created a new constitution for Japan, which, when adopted in 1947, forever changed the nation's social and political life.

By accepting the new constitution, Japan displayed both a remarkable willingness to forgive the United States and learn from their defeat. In fact, Japan soon emerged as a strong democratic nation with a love for all things American.

The United States, under the keen guidance of General MacArthur, learned that forgiveness can forge new allies where animosity once ruled.

The First Time His Dad Saw Him Play
There once was a boy who loved football. It was all he thought

about. His mother passed away when he was very young. He was small, thin-boned, and not tall, but he went out for the team anyway. He made the team, but never played. He never missed a practice all through junior and senior high. His father was always there to encourage him and share in the boy's excitement of the game.

The coaches loved him. His teammates loved him because he had such a giving attitude. He was always there for people. He was a continuous inspiration to others because he never gave up, even if all he accomplished was just to make the team.

When he became a young man and went off to college, no one thought he'd make the first string, but he did. He was so excited that he called his father to share his enthusiasm. He even sent his dad season tickets. All through college his dad supported him and never missed a game. He was a loving mentor to his son.

Then, during his senior year, while he was running onto the field to practice, the coach came up to him with a telegram. It said that the young man's father had passed away. Of course, he asked the coach if he could miss the next practice. The coach said, "Sure, and don't worry about the play-offs either."

The Saturday of the big play-off game came. Who came onto the field during the third quarter but this young man. He amazed his teammates that he was even there, let alone dressed to play.

The young man went over to the coach and said, "If there's any game I ever wanted to play, this is it. Coach, let me play." Of course, the coach is thinking, "How can I put my worst player in this game?" But the young man persisted. He kept saying "Coach, please?"

Finally, the team was behind ten points and the coach said, "Go ahead, play." To the amazement of the crowd, the coaches, and the rest of the team, he didn't make a single mistake. He passed, kicked, punted, and caught the ball like a professional. As a matter of fact, within the last minute of the game, he caught an interception and ran it all the way back for a touchdown. The crowd went absolutely crazy.

After he went to the sidelines, the coaches and players gathered around him and said they had never seen him play like that before. The coach asked, "What happened?"

The young man said, "Well coach, my dad and I had a very special relationship. But what you didn't know, coach, is that my father was also blind. This was the first time I knew he could see me play, and I didn't want to let him down!" What a great story.

We All Need A Mentor

When you look at the adversity in your life, you can look at the example of the young man and say, "*No matter what happens there's always someone out there who can inspire me to become all I can be.*" This is mentorship.   Is one of your chief wants in life to have someone who will give you unconditional support and inspire you to become all you can be?   It's true for a lot of people.   Is it true for you?   Do you have a mentor in your life?   We all need someone to help us to empower ourselves to do something we really want to do, yet wouldn't do without some support.   If you are willing to look, and humble enough to recognize your need, I believe you'll find a number of people available who could be your mentor.

Looking to others for inspiration can be uplifting and help us move out of our comfort zone.   It's important to have someone we can follow as an example of how to be and do.   Then, as we continue to personally develop and understand ourselves better, we can become more and more of who we really are.   Everyone needs a mentor.   In fact, some people have a mentor for each area of their life.   And while forgiveness deals with failure, it also relates indirectly to mentorship.   We may need someone who can teach us to forgive. Mentors could include your parents, teachers, or someone else you respect and admire.   An excellent mentor has the knowledge you need and is interested in you and your success.

Why Is It Important That I Forgive Myself?

Forgiveness of self is essential.   We've all failed.   It's how we deal with failure that matters.   We need to forgive ourselves if we want to move-on.   We can cause ourselves a lot of grief by saying things like: "If only I was thinner, smarter, or more educated."   "If only I had done this."   May I suggest that you just accept where you are and let go of your self-destructive thinking?   Otherwise, it's like carrying around excess baggage.   Have you ever been at an airport, carrying your own bags and unable to find a skycap?   Soon your arms may start to ache.   All your energy is directed toward moving those bags, and you're hurting more and more.

If you don't let the past behind, you can't go forward.   You can't get to second base, with one foot on first.

There's a difference between forgiving and forgetting.   You can forgive, but you may never forget.   That's OK, because forgiving makes your memory powerless.   You may always remember who or what you forgave, but the memory won't influence you negatively.

You can remember lots of hurts and pain, but your memories won't affect you after you let them go.

If you don't forgive yourself, it affects your energy. Take the energy you have used by not forgiving yourself, and put it to good use to move-on. Lou Holtz, the Notre Dame coach, once said, "The good Lord put eyes in the front of your head so you can look and move ahead, not focus on the past."

Letting go of the past and taking action are the primary keys to growth and success. Also understand that co-dependency and recovery issues are very important as well. "Co-dependency" means one is dependent on or is controlled by another person who is controlled by compulsive behavior, chronic illness, alcoholism, or drug abuse. "Recovery" is generally used when discussing alcoholism, as well as other addictions.

Recovery could also be used in a more general sense to describe when one is "coming back" from a challenging situation. Among other things this could include mourning the loss of a loved one, recuperating from an illness, coming out of a depression, losing a business through financial challenges, or losing a job.

We can learn to understand why we behave the way we do, what may be holding us back, and how we can change our behavior. Understanding can lead to forgiveness. There are some excellent books, support groups, and organizations available if you want to explore this further.

The key is you need to take that first step. You need to get out of that "comfort zone" to grow, challenge yourself, and change your behavior. When you finally face the fact that the "comfort zone" (sometimes known as a "rut") may actually be more of a "familiar zone." It may no longer be comfortable; you're just familiar with it. It's simply a known quantity.

Forgive yourself for any injustices you may have put on others. They're over and done with. You probably did the best you could with the awareness you had at the time. In fact, you may want to write down all the things you forgive yourself for, crumple-up the paper and throw it away. Once you forgive yourself, you have no reason to blame yourself for anything. You are being self-responsible and are then free to learn and grow.

I'm Hurting. Why Do I Need To Forgive Others?

Forgiveness of others may be more challenging. How many people do you feel you have allowed to influence you in a hurtful way? How many times have you felt that someone did you an injustice? To move-on, you need to forgive them; not for them, but for yourself.

My father's passing away is a good example. It could have been a wonderful excuse. I could have used his death as an excuse when things went awry. I could have said, "If Dad had been here I'd be better off; I'd be more educated; I'd be a better person." The truth is, while he was here, he contributed everything he possibly could to my life. For me to use his absence as an excuse would have bottled-up my energy and prevented me from going forward.

If you use what people did or didn't do in the past as an excuse for not moving-on, you'll never achieve the success you want. If you focus on people you believe hurt you, it's difficult to focus on the future.

Remember, no one can "hurt" (victimize) you unless you let them! You must give them permission. No one has that power over you, unless you think they do. A lot of feeling "hurt" is self-pity. And when you throw a "pity-party," guess who shows up? No one! Saying someone hurt you is not being self-responsible. It's an excuse. As Mike Wickett says, "Blame is like quicksand." You could easily sink deeper and deeper into the quicksand of blame.

When asked who "hurt" them the most, the majority of people say "my parents." The number two response was "siblings," while number three was "children."

Forgiveness of others is essential. We've all felt "hurt." It's just an excuse to say, "If only I had better parents"; "If only I had a better boss"; and, "If only I had this or that when I was young."

This does not mean forgiving others is always easy. It may be a challenge, and it could take time. It is a process. Be patient with yourself. *Forgive for you, not the other person. It helps you heal.* Think about it. If you stay focused on what someone did or didn't do in the past that affected you, you can lose a lot of precious energy that could be directed toward your dreams and goals. You want to look forward and take action, rather than allow yourself to stay "stuck" where you are. You may need to loosen-up; then let go of the control you've allowed someone else to have over you so you can move-on.

A Story Of Two Monks

A little story about two Buddhist monks gives us an excellent example of what forgiving others is all about.

On their way to the monastery one day, they needed to cross a bridgeless shallow river. As they approached its banks, they noticed a young lady standing there. She saw the monks and said, "I cannot go across because I'm afraid." The one monk, who had an easygoing attitude, responded, "No problem." He put the woman on his back and carried her across the river.

When they got to the other side, the woman said "Thanks" and went on her merry way. The other monk, who had an uptight attitude, was upset and angry. He said, "What did you do? We're not even allowed to talk to women, never mind touch them and put them on our backs." He went on and on for over an hour! He kept belittling the other monk, saying, "You are a disgrace to our religion."

The monk who carried the lady was courteous and let the other one badger and go on and on, until finally he was finished. He said, "My brother, I dropped that woman off by the riverbank over an hour ago. How come you are still carrying her around with you?"

Do You Have An Easy-Going, Forgiving, Or UpTight, Unforgiving Attitude?

Are you still carrying around thoughts and feelings that weigh you down? Are you still harboring hatreds and resentments toward others? It all takes energy. What happened cannot be changed, but you can forgive. Forgive for you. It's a very liberating, healing experience. Whether the other person accepts your forgiveness or not makes no difference at all. That's their responsibility. In fact, you may not even choose, or be able, to tell them. How would you feel if that person passed away before you forgave them? Even if they do, you can forgive them in your heart and let it go.

Think of the turmoil you were in before you forgave. Remember the relief you felt when you let go of a life-spoiling burden? It didn't really matter whether you needed to give or receive forgiveness, did it? The feelings were remarkably the same.

What about not forgiving? When we need to give or receive forgiveness and don't, we tend to avoid that person psychologically, emotionally, and physically. We restrict our own freedom. We cut off our options and limit our growth.

Who are we to judge others? As Dale Carnegie wrote in *How To Win Friends and Influence People*, "Never criticize, condemn, or complain." We could add to that, *never compare yourself to anyone else* either. Comparison is just a trap; someone is almost always doing better than you, and someone is almost always doing worse.

Jesus put it well in Luke when he said, "Don't worry about the speck of sawdust in your brother's eye until you take the plank out of your own." Who are we to understand others and decide if their behavior is appropriate? We need to first look inside ourselves and understand what we are about and correct our own behavior. You grow by correcting your own behavior, not by putting others down.

Live by the Golden Rule: "Do unto others as you would have them do unto you." Or you could go one step further and follow the Platinum Rule: "Do unto others as they would like to be done unto." Not everyone prefers the same treatment as you. Love the people that hate you. When you give to others, when you show them you care, it will come back to you! It may not come back from the same person(s). It may not be tomorrow or next week. It may be three, five, or ten years from now. Just let it go. Get out of your "comfort zone" and be confident that you'll get "yours."

Ralph Waldo Emerson once said, "What you are speaks so loudly, I can't hear what you're saying." What we are is who we are. It's important to recognize that we communicate who we are through our attitudes and actions, and they are often imperfect. Therefore, forgiveness of self and others is essential, on a daily basis, if necessary. Have an easygoing attitude; forgive and let go.

Ben Franklin said that "People who do things make mistakes, but they never make the biggest mistake of all, and that is doing nothing." What did we learn from our mistakes? That's what counts. How did we use the experience to better understand ourselves and others? Did we use it to avoid making the same mistake again? Did we forgive ourselves and move-on?

Forgiveness is such a powerful gesture. Here's a story about a remarkable little boy. It'll remind you how empowering it is to have the right tools to face life's challenges.

"It Worked Mom!" - A Story About Forgiveness

A neighboring couple and their three young sons suddenly found themselves a three-generation household. Because of her illness, the husband's mother came to live with them. Grandmother found it difficult to adjust to the rumble tumble of her active grandsons. She was often irritable and critical.

Things seemed to be going OK, until one day the mother found her seven-year-old son sneaking up the stairs. He warily poked his head above the top step before going any further.

The mother realized what was happening. The grandmother commanded a view of the staircase from her bedroom chair, where she spent most of her day. The boy could not come or go without his grandmother seeing him and testily inquiring about what he was "up to."

The little fellow had about all he could take. He was just trying to get to his room without being seen. Then later, in the privacy of the kitchen, he told his mother he didn't like his grandmother.

It was important to the boy's mother that grandmother stay in a designated place, just in case she needed something. It was also important that her son feel safe and free in his own home. She saw the situation. Her son's sense of freedom and privacy was being negatively impacted by an adult with a sour attitude. So he was developing strategies of avoidance.

The mother hoped that some clear communication would help create a better understanding between the two. She suggested the boy stop to visit as he passed by Grandma's room.

"I can't do that, Mom," he said soberly, "I can't look at her."

"What do you mean, you can't look at her?" asked the mother, perplexed.

"I get so mad at what she's saying to me that I can't look at her face," he said.

"Well, this *is* serious," the mother thought. At the same time, she was pleased that her young son was able and willing to put his feelings into words. She wanted very much to help this earnest young man.

"Suppose you try this," she suggested. "Next time Grandma stops you, and you feel angry, look straight into her eyes and say, without speaking the words, 'I forgive you. I forgive you because you are sick, and we all need to take special care of you.'"

"See if saying those words, even if she doesn't hear them, helps make it possible for you to look at her."

Within a day or two the boy reported back, "It worked, Mom!"

The boy's ability to forgive gave him the strength to deal with his anger, which, if unattended, would have interfered with him living his busy life. Being able to forgive gave him options. Avoidance would have kept him stuck.

Later the boy's mother encouraged him to talk to his grandmother and explain that he understood she wasn't feeling well, and he felt upset because he had lost his privacy. Perhaps she could sit by the window in her room. The view was better from there anyway.

He tried this approach and found out from his grandmother that she was feeling lonely. She apologized and agreed to move her chair to the window. He agreed to stop by and visit her more often, even if it was only for a quick "hello" and hug. Everyone won; forgiveness is often necessary to diffuse our negative feelings prior to discussing a sensitive issue.

Forgiving will help you avoid unpleasant encounters that could spell the end to your career, no matter how talented you are. Talent isn't enough. Every successful person anticipates the need to deal with superiors, associates, clients, customers, family, friends, and others whose behavior may sometimes be difficult to handle. They develop excellent strategies for handling these people effectively. However, if the person's behavior is particularly troublesome, and no strategy seems to work, the only thing they may be able to do is forgive them. Frequently, forgiveness is part of the package and opens the way to fruitful relationships and prosperous results.

Say "Goodbye" To Regrets And Recriminations
When we don't forgive someone, we give them power over us. We give them the power to influence us in a hurtful way, even though the event may be long over. Ironically, they may not even be aware that we have been influenced by them. They may have had "good" intentions, but we didn't perceive it that way. Most people are well intended in their actions. Their motive is probably self-directed to avoid pain or gain pleasure. It would seem we were denying *them* something when we refuse to forgive them. However, the reality is that when we are unforgiving, we deny ourselves freedom! We bog ourselves down with negative feelings until we forgive and let those feelings go.

Forgiving ourselves for not acting in our own best interests, or for saying or doing something we regret, is like forgiving another! Say to yourself, "I forgive you (insert your name here) for (insert the event here). I let it go." This is an act of self-love. When you do this, you are recognizing your desire to act differently in the future.

To acknowledge something is to admit it exists. Acknowledging a reality strips it of pretense, strips it of any lingering excuses that might otherwise cloud it. Acknowledging anything gives you a clean slate to work from. You can then recognize the problem for what it is and get to work on the solution. After all, *a problem is just an opportunity for a solution!*

Failure is just an event, not a person! Can you believe that? Can you forgive yourself and others for "failing," and then move-on to success? Reflect on and learn from your past. However, protect your vitality by knowing that *you control your future*.

Why not make an effort to forgive someone right now? Think of someone you feel has harmed you, and forgive them. Envision looking them straight in the eye and saying "I forgive you (<u>insert their name here</u>) for (<u>insert the event here</u>)." You'll experience a sense of relief and feel your face soften, as you give a gift to yourself that only you can give. Do this again and again.

Making a forgiveness list is helpful. Write, "I forgive you (<u>insert their name here</u>) for (<u>insert the event here</u>)." Do this for everyone you need to forgive. One-by-one, give up the hurt and allow in the peace as you resolve to forgive and move-on. You may choose to tell them; you may not. What's in your heart counts more than whether they know you forgave them. Even if you don't tell them, they are likely to feel the difference in your attitude toward them. Remember, forgiveness is a process, and like anything worthwhile, it will take some time. Remember to congratulate yourself each time you successfully forgive someone.

Now, can you forgive yourself? Make a forgiveness list for yourself. Can you "return" to an earlier time and see yourself in a past moment? Was there a time when you did not behave as you wish you had? Perhaps it was when you failed to defend a principle or value. Maybe it was a moment of aggressiveness when you overwhelmed a vulnerable person. Forgive yourself for that failing, and you'll begin to live free of its burden. Forgive yourself for personal behaviors you don't like; maybe it's a habit you'd like to change. *Forgiveness based on honest acknowledgement frees you from regret and recrimination.*

Forgiveness Heals All Wounds

Once you understand the principles of "No Excuse!" living, they seem so obvious, don't they? If forgiveness is practiced, with guaranteed results, why isn't everyone doing it?

How come many people don't know that forgiveness is such a powerful tool? First of all, what we are taught about forgiveness is often misinterpreted. Take, for example, the biblical story commonly known as the "Prodigal Son." Who is the real hero of that story? Why is he frequently overlooked? The father, of course, is the hero. But the drama is stolen first by the son who goes off with his fortune and returns full of regret. It is also stolen by his brother, who hasn't yet experienced the need to ask for forgiveness or learned to grant it.

Forgiveness is a powerful healer. It can resolve difficult, painful, and complex human interactions. Forgiveness is the kind of closure human beings long for.

Do you know what a burden it is to have something undone hanging over your head? Did you ever have something expected of you, that you deliberately "forgot" about, or didn't get around to? Did you get that sinking feeling of failure every time you thought about it?

Whether or not you are consciously thinking about issues that beg forgiveness, they negatively affect you. Get them out into the open. Say to yourself, "So you never did go back to college and finish." "So you walked out of that job when you didn't have another one waiting." "So you made promises you weren't sure you wanted to keep." Look into the eyes of that younger, less experienced, less wise you from the past, and speak kindly.

Where does the power of forgiveness come from? There are two main areas: (1) Ending a wallow in guilt that may really be just an excuse to keep on doing something you are ashamed of, or (2) finally looking at a human error for what it is, a passing event that doesn't need to determine your whole future if you don't let it. Both of these actions require facing the truth and dealing with it, letting go, and moving-on.

When you forgive someone, it's just as freeing. *By forgiving another, you stop seeing yourself as a victim.* You may have allowed yourself to be a victim, but you can stop the endless replay of your victimization (in your mind) by forgiving.

Make Daily Deposits In Both Your Own And Others' Emotional Bank Accounts

Steven R. Covey, author of *The 7 Habits of Highly Effective People*, talks about how we all have an emotional bank account. And like a financial bank account, we make deposits and withdrawals. Sometimes we may withdraw more than we deposit.

Are you depositing daily into the people in your life, or are you just withdrawing from them? Are you building up your emotional bank account or depleting it? When you treat someone with kindness, respect, courtesy, or proper instruction, you add to *your* emotional wealth. You have invested more of what you might need in the future. You have something you can count on. What you gave out will come back through the same or other source(s).

How do you make emotional withdrawals? Do just the opposite: be unkind, disrespectful, and discourteous toward others. When all you do is make emotional withdrawals from others, you are likely to lose their support. Without money you can't pay your bills. When you have no love in your emotional bank account, it's difficult to count on other people to support your dreams and desired outcomes.

Chances are you won't be able to depend on others to help you move-on if all you do is take from them emotionally.

Unforgiveness Is An "Incomplete"

Have you ever left anything undone? When you think about it, unforgiveness is actually an incompletion of some event in your life. Were you ever given a task you didn't finish because of other priorities? You thought something else was more important, or you didn't want to do it, so you just didn't complete it. It was necessary to do, yet you always did something else instead. Did that bother you? Did it seem to control you? You knew you needed to get to it, but you never did. It sapped energy from you, didn't it? Eventually, when you finally completed it, the negative feelings left. What a relief.

Forgiveness works the same way. If you don't forgive, you're letting an incomplete interfere with your progress. Knowing this can help you have the strength and determination to forgive. You're letting it have an influence on you by your own inaction. In a sense, you're giving it permission to influence you.

If you have a document due to someone, and you don't deliver it on time, you may nag yourself about it. You take energy from yourself because you're thinking about it. You may dwell on it. Unforgiveness works the same way.

How do you forgive? Take the "for" away from forgive and you have "give." That's how you forgive. That's how simple it is. In reality though, it can be a real challenge to forgive. *The basic element in forgiveness is giving of yourself; to other people and to yourself.*

"As you sow, so shall you reap." Your world is a mirror of you. How you treat others is how they'll treat you, in most cases. Give kindness and you'll receive kindness. Give love and you'll receive love. You can usually get the response you want from others by treating them as you believe they want to be treated.

Forgive yourself for what you could have accomplished today but didn't. But don't use this as an excuse not to achieve what you want tomorrow. Forgive others for what they did or didn't do to you (or for you), or it'll be difficult to move forward. Don't fall into the trap of using that as an excuse either.

Like anything else, you can become excellent at forgiveness by practicing it; by living it. When you do, you'll start to feel better and have more energy. By letting go of any grudges, resentments, and hatreds, you are freeing-up your precious energy, which you may have wasted before on blaming or complaining. By forgiving, you are becoming more self-responsible because you are doing it for yourself! You are doing it to help *you* to excel and receive the outcomes you want. As a result, you'll be able to help others more, too.

Forgiveness Of The Environment

Once you have learned to forgive yourself and others, you can begin to focus on your environment and your surroundings. Your environment is all the events and circumstances you experience. It is inevitable that there will be environmental factors that can't be controlled by you or anyone else. They will require your forgiveness if you are going to get on with the business of life.

Have you ever been in a traffic jam? It was no different than yesterday's, except you took a different route and thought you had escaped it. Did you get down on yourself for the choice *you* made? Forgive yourself and move-on.

Did your car ever break down? Did you ever swear at it? Did you ever mentally "beat-yourself-up" over it? Forgive the car; don't blame it. It's doing the best it can, considering the attention it has been given! You may need to forgive yourself for not practicing preventative maintenance.

Did you ever notice how people blame the economy or the government for the way things are in their personal lives? It's easy to use what society is doing as an excuse. It's real easy. Then we don't feel the need to take action. We can simply rationalize by saying, "It's all *their* fault."

How about the weather? Did you ever use the weather as an excuse for not doing something? How does the weather affect most things? Not much at all! Yet you hear excuses all the time of how some people let the environment dictate whether they will continue their planned activity. Have you sometimes fallen into that trap?

Will you let the activities and the state of society dictate that you can't be successful? It's easy to blame the economy. It's easy to blame the government. It's easy to blame someone or something else for having a negative impact or influence on where you want to go.

Forgiving your environment. It's essential to do before you can take charge. Do it rather than blaming something external. It's easy to blame something on the outside, even when you know in your heart that it's your internal fortitude that counts. It's "an inside job." Your life is all you really have. How you deal with it is critical. Whether you deny or accept what has been given to you (e.g., situations, challenges, and people) and how you work with it, largely determines your level of success.

When we forgive, we bring new respect to every person and circumstance we encounter. We can start fresh. There's no need to endlessly sort through the debris of the past. It would only hinder our chances to meet and handle future challenges. Where will your new respect come from? It will come from being a powerful forgiver.

The Professor Who Asked For Forgiveness
Many years ago, a professor at the University of Edinburgh was listening to his students as they presented oral readings. One young man rose to begin his recitation, but the professor abruptly stopped him. "You are holding the book in the wrong hand," he criticized. "Take your book in the right hand and be seated."

Responding to the strong rebuke, the young man held up his right arm. He had no right hand! The other students were deathly quiet and began to squirm in their seats. For a moment the professor was dumbfounded. Then he made his way to the student, put his arm around him, and with a tear in his eyes said, "I regret what I said. I never knew. Please, will you forgive me?"

Sometimes, like the professor, it takes humility to ask for forgiveness. It takes knowing that no one is always correct. We need to forgive ourselves and sometimes request the forgiveness of others to move-on. Otherwise we may replay the scenario over and over in our mind and regret our behavior for a long time.

Have You Ever Felt Victimized?
If we are feeling victimized (hurt) by someone or something, it is an indicator that forgiveness is needed. Most of us have felt victimized. We need to realize that, in most cases, no one can be a victim unless they permit it.

Once again, keep this within the context of your use of energy. Where are you directing your thoughts? Where are you directing your feelings? Are they going toward the past or the future?

Certainly, it is important to understand the past. That's part of forgiveness. First, you need to recognize who or what you thought influenced you in a hurtful way, or the nature of the past failures. Then the healing process can begin. In the beginning, part of that healing process is often feeling victimized. This is an important process to work through. As we forgive, we need to take responsibility for ourselves and let go of the idea that we are a victim. Lack of forgiveness adversely affects your behavior and, as a result, your relationships suffer.

What Happens When We Don't Forgive?

Three main types of behavior patterns can develop as a result of lack of forgiveness. You may have seen these patterns of expression in your dealings with people, or even in yourself. The three behavioral types are: "self-pitying," "irresponsibly-justifying," and "abusing."

First you'll want to gain an understanding of each type of behavior to identify it in yourself and others. Then you can consider what the "payoff" is for you or others to behave in these ways. In other words, there are some perceived benefits, or the behavior wouldn't continue. For example, the payoff could be that the behavior causes the person to get more attention than they would have gotten otherwise. To change the behavior, it is important to be ready to let go of the payoff.

"Self-Pitying"

When someone regularly assumes the role of a victim, they are often in a state of self-pity. Have you ever been around someone who constantly feels sorry for himself? Have you ever felt sorry for yourself? Have you ever been around someone who "just-can't-believe" something has happened? They think they can't move-on because of what happened! Have you ever felt that way?

This can be a natural first response to a challenging situation. Most of us have felt helpless at times; full of self-pity. You can see it reflected in behavior. People who are "self-pitying" get "stuck." They don't get beyond this reaction to take charge of their lives and overcome their challenges.

How do you express yourself to other people? Do you often feel sorry for yourself? Or, do you acknowledge the past, make an effort to grow, and move-on from it? It's easy to see this behavior in ourselves.

"Irresponsibly-Justifying"

A person who "irresponsibly-justifies" frequently acts irresponsible and then "justifies" his actions by making excuses. You can see it in their behavior. He's the one who doesn't fill-up the gas tank when it's on "E." He may have a dozen excuses or more. He's the one who leaves the garbage cans in the driveway, rather than picking them up and putting them away with the lids on. Then he complains when they roll into the street and a car runs over them, even though he didn't fulfill his responsibility of putting them away.

People who irresponsibly-justify simply feel justified because they believe people have hurt them or that they have failed. They feel like victims because of what has occurred. They believe they can always justify their actions. They believe they don't need to be as considerate of other people. After all, they perceive others don't have as many problems as *they* do. In reality, many other people may have more or worse situations than they do.

People who irresponsibly-justify believe they don't need to be caring and giving to other people because they've been "hurt." They may be full of resentment and hatred. They believe their actions toward others are justified because of what they believe life has done to them. Have you ever known someone like that? They are hurting because of not forgiving past hurts.

Most of us have felt like people who irresponsibly-justify at times, justifying our actions because we have felt hurt in the past. Most of us have been at a point where we chose to focus on the past so we didn't have to make a decision in the present.

"Abusing"

Then you have people who act in an abusing way. They are in constant denial. They feel victimized and believe they need to have an abusive, mean attitude toward everyone; which is reflected in their thoughts, words, and actions. Most of us have felt like this at times, at least to some degree. These thought patterns also cause us to criticize ourselves. In fact, self-criticism is where it begins.

Can you see how this behavior is not being self-responsible? People with abusive attitudes don't forgive themselves or others. It is not realistic to behave like this and expect to move ahead in life. It just holds you back and keeps you stuck.

How Do You Make Decisions?

Decision-making is a fundamental cornerstone of success. Indecisiveness is devastating to your success. The ability to make decisions is essential to moving-on. Do you accept responsibility for your decisions? Do you "pass-the-buck" if the results aren't what you wanted? Do you say, "Oh no, it's not my fault"? Instead, do as people with winning habits do. Make a decision, and then do what it takes to make it work out.

When you make a decision regarding forgiveness, follow it through with action. When you make a decision to become self-responsible, follow it through. When you make a decision to define your purpose and be successful, follow it through. Make that decision. Take action. Keep making deposits of decisions that help you move ahead into your emotional bank account. Then, as you take action on each decision, feel your self-esteem improving. It's crucial to moving-on.

Why Did I Forgive My Father?

I became a stronger person when my father died. Even though I was worried and frightened by the pitying expressions of sympathy that surrounded me, I vowed I'd "make-it." And I did!

I suffered for many years with the burden of not having forgiven my father for dying. Irrational? Yes, of course. However, the heartache we may experience because of our attitude toward events we have no control over is as real as any other heartache. Our suffering continues, even though we may try to hide it. It's likely to stop once we've accepted the fact that the situation occurred, and we've forgiven all parties involved, including ourselves. We can let go of our sadness and go on to live a joyful life. Lack of acceptance, i.e., continued denial and unforgiveness, kills our joy and peace-of-mind.

The moment came when I could acknowledge the extent of my loss. I finally felt able to look in memory into my dad's eyes. He was the man who was everything I longed to be. He was gone even though I was still eager to spend every possible moment with him.

Finally, I spoke from my heart, "I forgive you. I forgive you for not being here. I forgive you for dying." I did it for me. I did it to let go of the past, enjoy the present, and move-on to the future.

What's Keeping You From Moving-On?

Could it be that you are letting regrets prevent you from finding your way to forgiveness? Could it be the harm done when someone (intentionally or unintentionally) or something interfered with your efforts to make correct decisions? Nonetheless, you felt you had to bear the responsibility for those decisions with dignity.

Have you been caught-up in such a corporate, organizational, or political structure where that has happened? Were you never given the opportunity to take responsibility for and correct your mistakes? Were you never recognized for your triumphs and achievements?

Have you answered "yes" to any of those questions above? Who hasn't had some lost opportunities? Who hasn't felt hurt by people or circumstances? Most of us have. It seems to be a part of the human experience.

So, how come some people get bogged down and begin to drown in oceans of regret, blame, and self-pity? *More depression results from unresolved blame than ever comes from natural causes. The more unresolved regret, blame, and self-pity you hold onto, the more burdened you will feel. Nothing else will hold you back as much as these negative emotions.* Holding on to your "excess baggage" will make it impossible for you to dance along the *Staircase-of-Success* and move-on.

Are You "Stuck"?

Imagine yourself on a five-mile march in heavy combat boots, pulling one foot at a time from the muck and mire of regret, blame, and self-pity. Imagine getting one foot free, only to have to place it back down again, just inches forward, into the oozy "swamp" that seems to go on "forever."

If you have the habit of regret, blame, and self-pity, you'll find that, as more events occur where you feel victimized, you'll feel more and more despondent. It's like a downward spiral. Ultimately, your regret, blame, and self-pity can add up to despair.

There is a way out! The answer to the quagmire of despair is right in front of you. It's simple. It's called forgiveness.

If it's regret that's got you bogged down, forgive yourself. Face up to the injustices you've done to yourself and others. Be courageous enough to list them on paper. You may want to share one or more of these things with a mentor or close friend, provided the relationship is strong, and they have total, unconditional acceptance of you. When possible, share that given a second chance you would do it differently (if that's true for you).

Almost everyone has faced these issues. No one with regrets ever reaches the joy and fullness of life without letting these regrets go and forgiving themselves.

Why Is It Important To Reflect?

Whenever you feel yourself wanting to glance over words in this book and hurry to the next page or section; whenever you find yourself saying, "I know that; that's nothing new; that's not what I wanted to read about," ask yourself, "Why am I so anxious to get through it?" Could it be you feel uncomfortable because the message is "hitting home"? Could it be stinging a bit? When you find a message that strikes a chord with you, close the book, keeping your finger in it to hold your place. Reflect a bit on the message. Give yourself time to reach a new level of understanding and acceptance in this area.

Have you been courageous enough to take responsibility for behavior you regret? Have you admitted to someone that you made a mistake? Have you been able to share all your feelings about the event? Have you forgiven yourself? It is an ultimate act of responsibility to accept what can't be changed and to move-on. *Admitting your regrets doesn't mean they don't exist anymore. It means you will no longer be giving them the power to negatively influence your life or to affect your chances of helping others have a better life.* Go on; do it.

What have you done for yourself lately in this area of growth? Have regrets crept in undetected, their only symptom being that life seems heavy? Are your days beginning to be something to slog through without your really being aware of them? Do you feel burdened, as if the world is on your shoulders? Perhaps it's time to look for the "worm-of-discontent," and send it on its way with forgiveness.

How About Forgetting And Forgiving?

You'll never hear me say, "Forget what needs to be forgiven." Forgetting isn't really helpful when genuine forgiveness is at work. In fact, "forgetting" is frequently a way to avoid forgiving.

To forgive, you need to remember! That's one of the reasons forgiving can be challenging. Memories involving the need for forgiveness often include the misery or regret of the pain of reliving the painful incident. It's often easier to put the memory in the back of your mind, but that's only temporary. It'll fester until it rears its ugly head again. It's our responsibility to remember our incorrect actions if we want to avoid repeating what we regret.

Perhaps you have experienced the freedom that comes from forgiveness. Perhaps the torment has ended, and you have peace-of-mind because you forgave yourself or someone else.

When true forgiveness takes hold, you'll forget about unimportant things. They are discarded like old, worn out clothes. They no longer clutter your life and are easily left behind as you move-on.

Teamwork Makes The Dream Work

This is the key. You rarely hear about forgiveness as a prerequisite of success. Yet it's the first step in moving forward with your life. Why is it important to give to other people? Doesn't society often define success as getting on top as fast as you can? Why consider the feelings of other people? Why take into consideration the teamwork, the team-building aspect of success?

It's simple. You can't become successful alone! Build your success on forgiveness, and you're likely to attract a number of people to assist you. People, in most cases, will feel safer with you and more accepted by you when you have a forgiving nature. This doesn't mean you are acting like a "doormat." You can still be assertive and forgiving at the same time. No matter how assertive you are, people will still need to be forgiven for improper behavior.

The decisions you make about forgiveness are crucial, yet most people simply don't realize it's related to success. When you practice forgiveness, it can make a big difference in your life.

Your dreams can come true. Set your mind and heart to something you love, and you can achieve it. Even if you don't receive the exact outcome you want, you'll be better off for striving. Forgiveness can be a wonderful aspect of achieving your dreams and goals. You can give yourself peace-of-mind with forgiveness. Some people may avoid forgiving because it hurts; it opens up some feelings. Be forgiving anyway. It's essential to your success, happiness, and fulfillment.

What happens when you employ forgiveness in your life? You begin to be more self-responsible. Think about it. When you're not blaming and complaining, you're taking charge. It can be a challenge because you are more vulnerable as you open up to more people. *Vulnerability is an important part of relationships. It helps you reveal the real you and is the essence of true and lasting friendships.* Sometimes, this is an unexpected result of forgiveness.

When you begin to acknowledge areas where you still need to grow, you'll be on the correct path, and something exciting can happen. You'll probably notice that everyone else needs more development in certain areas too, and that it can be fun to work and grow together, helping each other. Just say it's OK. It's OK to make mistakes. You're human. It comes with the territory!

As you employ forgiveness, you'll gain more control over your life. This will help you feel less stressful and more optimistic about the future.

"No Excuse!" Action Plan To "Totally Forgive"

1. Forgive yourself for failing. View failure as a learning experience; it's just an event and not who you are. You can literally "fail-your-way-to-success."

2. Put the past behind you; it's history and cannot be changed. You can't get to second base with one foot on first. Get rid of the excess baggage. Forgiveness is a prerequisite for success.

3. Forgive yourself for any injustices you may have put on others. Write down all the things you need to forgive yourself for, crumple-up the paper, and throw it away. You'll free-up a lot of energy.

4. Forgive others for any injustices you feel they have put on you. Write down their names and what they did or didn't do to or for you, crumple-up the paper, and throw it away. No one can hurt you unless you let them; stop allowing yourself to be victimized.

5. Never criticize, condemn, complain, or compare. Live by the "Golden and Platinum Rules." How you treat others will come back to you.

6. Don't take rejection personally. Say to yourself, "That's just where they are," and you'll mentally remove it as a personal attack. They may be having some serious challenges that day or maybe they're just going in a different direction.

7. Make daily deposits into your emotional bank account. Treat people with respect and be supportive of them. "As you sow, so shall you reap."

8. Let go of mental, physical, and emotional grudges, resentments, and hatreds. You'll free-up a lot of energy. Love the people you "hate."

9. Forgive the environment and the events and circumstances you experience. Take charge of the situation, and you'll no longer feel like a victim.

10. Where you make a mistake, be responsible enough to admit it to the appropriate person and forgive yourself. It'll no longer have the power to negatively influence your life or affect your chances of helping others have a better life.

MY DECLARATION OF SELF-ESTEEM

I am me. In all the world, there is no one else exactly like me. There are people who have some parts like me, but no one adds up exactly like me. Therefore, everything that comes out of me is authentically mine because I alone choose it. I own everything about me—my body, including everything it does; my mind, including all my thoughts and ideas; my eyes, including the images of all they behold; my feelings, whatever they might be—anger, joy, frustration, love, disappointment, excitement; my mouth and all the words that come out of it—polite, sweet or rough, correct or incorrect; my voice, loud or soft; and all my actions, whether they be to others or myself. I own my own fantasies, my dreams, my hopes, my fears. I own all my triumphs and successes, all my failures and mistakes. Because I own all of me, I can become intimately acquainted with me. By so doing, I can love me and be friendly with me in all my parts. I can then make it possible for all of me to work in my best interests. I know there are aspects about myself that puzzle me, and other aspects that I do not know. But as long as I am friendly and loving to myself, I can courageously and hopefully look for the solutions to the puzzles and for ways to find out more about me. However I look and sound, whatever I say and do, and whatever I think and feel at a given moment in time is me. This is authentic and represents where I am at that moment in time. When I review later how I looked and sounded, what I said and did, and how I thought and felt, some parts may turn out to be unfitting. I can discard that which is unfitting and keep that which proved fitting, and invent something new for that which I discarded. I can see, hear, feel, think, say and do. I have the tools to survive, to be close to others, to be productive, to make sense and order out of the world of people and things outside of me. I own me and therefore I can engineer me.

I am me and I am okay.

Chapter 6

HAVE SELF-ESTEEM
Second Step Of The THESAURUS Factor

What Is Self-Esteem?

According to the McGrane Self-Esteem Institute, whose ideas I have integrated into the "No Excuse!" philosophy, "Self-esteem is the respect you *feel* for yourself." It is absolutely essential for success. You cannot respect others either, until you first respect yourself. "You can only give to others what you have, and nothing more!"

"Self-esteem is at the core of all you think, say, do and feel." It affects the seven key areas of your life: Spiritual, Mental, Physical, Family, Social, Financial, and Career. Your self-esteem is always changing, and is always in process; it is intangible and recognizable by your behavior. As a result, you may feel a lot of self-respect one minute, and not much the next.

Self-esteem is not a result of your income, reputation, occupation, race, the clothes you wear, your religion, educational level, ethnic background, possessions, sex, home, car, or zip code. It does not depend on your objectives or your net worth. Psychiatrist and author Carl Jung said, "Simple things are always the most difficult. In actual life, it requires the greatest discipline to be simple, and the *acceptance of self* is the essence of the problems of a whole outlook upon life." Many people base their lives on spiritual beliefs. The religions of the world offer such core beliefs as: "All life is sacred," (Hinduism); "Gaining a complete knowledge of the inner self," (Buddhism); "Love thy neighbor as thyself, " (Judaism/Christianity). Unfortunately, in the past the Western Judao/Christian culture did not encourage us to love ourselves. It was often considered egotistical and unacceptable. Yet we need to first love ourselves before we can love others!

Self-esteem then, is at the core of moving toward spiritual excellence. You can only respect others when you feel respect for yourself. You will learn, grow, have peace-of-mind, be generous, manage, lead, accept differences and responsibility, have Total Unconditional Acceptance (T.U.A.), love, sell, teach, parent, and behave in general, based on your self-esteem. Once again, you can only give away what you possess.

Have you ever believed you had what would bring you happiness? Did you ever feel satisfied, while feeling something was missing? That's called being unfulfilled. Remember, no one has perfect behavior; we are all learning. We all make mistakes, yet we all have talents and skills. We all need other people; no one is an island unto themselves. Self-esteem enables us to communicate, work together, and achieve. People with self-esteem are more likely to be happy.

Value judging is the only thing that will injure or destroy your self-esteem. When you value judge, you compare your value to that of others. About 90% of value judging is done on the subconscious level; you don't even realize you are doing it. However, you *feel* it! Some examples of value judging include: labeling, name calling, sarcasm, controlling, manipulating, put-downs, comparing, criticism, and putting people on a pedestal.

We were all born with intact self-esteem. It's our birthright! As babies, we were open, curious, loving, spontaneous, and accepting. We didn't have the "skill" to nurture and build our self-esteem. Since we were dependent on others for our survival, we learned self-image behavior. We discovered that we were accepted and included by what we did or had. Parents, siblings, relatives, teachers, friends, television, and society all taught us self-image behavior. Society taught us that feelings were *not* as important as knowledge, and acquiring and having material things. Once your self-esteem is replaced by self-image behavior, you never reclaim it until you have somebody who unconditionally supports you, like a mentor, who is genuinely interested in you and can help you reclaim it and make it a skill. You may live your life by self-image behavior if you wish, but be prepared to always be value judging and comparing.

It is true that some people use the word "self-image" when what they really mean is "self-esteem." These people are well-intended. However, like the rest of us, they were probably taught self-image languaging. And as the old cliche goes, "Say what you mean and mean what you say." It's so very important.

How Important Is Self-Esteem?

How can you achieve success if you don't respect yourself? Why would you want to? You'll always doubt what you can achieve if you don't respect yourself. So why do some people lack self-respect?

When you have defined success for yourself, developed a purpose, and begin to forgive, you'll start to *feel* better about who you are. *Success results in bringing out the best in you. Its essence is inside you.* It is an inside experience way before it manifests itself in an outcome which may be visible to others. *Your self-esteem affects all your thoughts and actions.* Without it you are lost; you can never be truly successful. Self-esteem is, in fact, a life and death issue!

How you feel about yourself will help determine the direction you take. How and what you think will largely determine what you become. And as much as we're talking about principles, the secret to success is, in fact, how and what you think and feel. Employ the correct principles, and feel respect for yourself and who and what you are, and you'll be a success.

In his classic, *As A Man Thinketh*, James Allen writes:

> *A man's mind may be likened to a garden. Just as a gardener cultivates his plot, keeping it free from weeds, and growing the flowers and fruits which he requires, so may a man tend the garden of his mind, weeding out all the wrong, useless, and impure thoughts, and cultivating toward perfection the flowers and fruits of correct, useful, and pure thoughts. By pursuing this process, a man sooner or later discovers that he is the master gardener of his soul, the director of his life. He also reveals, within himself, the laws of thought. He understands, with ever-increasing accuracy, how thought-forces and mind-elements operate in the shaping of his character, circumstances, and destiny.*

What Are You Cultivating?

Like a garden, a "No Excuse!" life requires you to grow in many directions. You'll learn how to develop deeper roots. You'll be better able to draw inspiration from other people and events as you strengthen your purpose and resolve.

Your growth will be determined by how eager you are to learn new things and take on new opportunities, challenges, and experiences. You'll likely be better able to deal with whatever comes your way. You will learn how to grow and prosper, even through challenging times. I believe you will find that self-esteem is essential to accomplishing these things.

Would you like to have intact self-esteem, i.e., feel respect for yourself? Does your language and thinking support your self-esteem? The following sections will help you determine that.

How Do You Create An Affirming, Intact Self-Esteem Lifestyle?

What would it be like for you to be free of devaluing yourself? Do you ever wonder what it would take to really enjoy yourself, others, and daily life? People have been asking these questions since the beginning of time. Is getting to the root of these issues important to you?

Many say, "Give me success and I'll figure out how to live with it later." Living a self-esteem lifestyle begins by knowing how you feel and the outcomes you want.

If you always do what you've always done, you'll always get what you've always gotten. Most adults tend to determine their wants intellectually, without consulting their physical or emotional feelings. Just because you were hugged, loved, well-educated, have traveled the world, and have wealth and power, doesn't guarantee you'll feel good about yourself. You need to consciously choose self-esteem. Start by getting in touch with your feelings, both physical and emotional. Then you will begin to recognize the outcomes you really want.

Does Your Language Support Your Self-Esteem?

Words create feelings! Self-esteem is a *feeling*. What language do you use in your self-talk? Examine this, because what you say to yourself will create feelings.

As you go to seminars, read books, listen to audiotapes, and watch videotapes, you may see and hear many words being identified as self-esteem. Let's consider the following words and definitions:

Thinking A mental process utilizing the logical or left side of your brain.

Feeling An emotional state of consciousness utilizing the right side of your brain.

Egotism Self-centeredness. Constant excessive reference to oneself. Conceit. "Unsatisfied hunger for self-esteem." (Schuller)

Self-Concept What you think about your developed and undeveloped areas (skills).

Self-Confidence A belief or trust in yourself. It is a skill developed over time.

Self-Image An imitation or representation of a person. It is what one would like to project to the world. You might even think of "image" as an acronym for "I Measure And Gauge Everyone"! (In other words, image is based on value judging and comparison.)

Self-Esteem The respect you *feel* for yourself. It is a *feeling*.

Be aware of what you say to yourself and how it affects your behavior. Research shows one second of negative thinking takes ten seconds before you can entertain a new thought or feeling.

What is Intact Self-Esteem?

Much like plants, human beings depend on nourishment and endurance. However, unlike plants, we can become aware of who we are, envision what we want to be, and then make it happen.

Who do you think you are? Now there's a question most often asked with an edge. And it's usually asked by someone shocked at another's presumption. Let's play with that idea.

Bill McGrane, (founder of the McGrane Self-Esteem Institute and author of *Brighten Your Day With Self-Esteem*), once said:

"Self-esteem" is the core of a person's physical, mental, and spiritual well-being. You can instantly observe a person's self-esteem by the way they treat you. The entire focus is on a very difficult word for many people: <u>love</u>. First, have love for yourself; then, and only then, can you love anyone else. In other words, you can give only what you have and no more.... Self-Esteem is the respect you feel for yourself.

Babies begin understanding their place in the world by gradually discovering who they are. It is sometimes an alarming discovery and often leads to a loud cry to be held. The baby needs to feel safe, contained, and part of a bigger being.

As time goes on, experience usually teaches the child that it can creep, crawl, walk, run, and tumble. In most cases, it eventually realizes it can independently explore all that lies within reach.

How many times have you held a child who was squirming to get out of your arms? His head and body twisted and turned to keep in sight the delight that had his attention. He envisioned having what he saw and was filled with desire to satisfy that want. Every time a child's desires are understood and respected, not merely fulfilled, a leap in self-esteem occurs.

Self-esteem begins at birth. We are all born with pure potential. As children, we were uninhibited and unafraid until we were taught to be otherwise. All the things we could be or do will never be realized in our lifetime. Therefore, making choices will always be a necessary part of life.

Who Affects Children's Self-Esteem?

When you are born, all you have is *you*! Babies are like a clean sheet of paper. How parents (including other caregivers who assume the parental role) treat their children has a big impact on how the children feel about themselves. Parents have an opportunity to help their children grow up to be adults with intact self-esteem. To do this, it is crucial that parents develop their own self-esteem. Parents cannot teach children self-esteem behavior if they don't practice it themselves. Admittedly, there are other factors affecting children's self-esteem. Teachers, friends, acquaintances, and other societal influences (e.g., TV) all have an impact. However, parents, to a much greater extent, serve as their role models. How parents treat their children affects their self-esteem.

Children take chances based on how they were parented. Parents need to teach their children to recognize and develop their ability to make choices. This will help the child realize his greatest potential, satisfaction, and fulfillment. The ultimate goal is that the children will feel respect for themselves, i.e., have intact self-esteem.

Fear Of Failure and Rejection Hold People Back

Fear of failure is fear of yourself (doing something), while fear of rejection is fear of others (not accepting you). Experiencing some fear is natural, but because of your new understanding, your fear no longer has to be an obstacle to your success. No matter what happens, if you're honest and sincere, you are less likely to fear failure. If you live your life in a way you feel is important, a way that goes along with your values and beliefs, you're not likely to fear rejection either. When your self-esteem is intact, the more likely you are to eliminate those fears.

When your self-esteem is intact, you're likely to take greater risks. When your self-esteem is intact, you're less likely to fear failure and rejection. When you know who you are, respect yourself and know where you are going, you will not be concerned about what others may think or say about you and what you say and do.

A very important part of success is overcoming resistance. An airplane needs to overcome air resistance to fly. A boat needs to overcome the resistance of water and wind to move ahead. People with winning behavior overcome various resistances to succeed.

To be a successful leader, you need to overcome the resistance of yourself and other people. Salespeople cannot be effective unless they learn to overcome resistance to rejection. With intact self-esteem, you are not likely to be affected by rejection. It all boils down to self-respect and belief in yourself.

How you perceive and what you believe about yourself helps structure what you achieve. It all depends on your self-esteem.

The more you know yourself, the more likely you are to allow yourself to become more vulnerable. You will tend to open-up more to other people. You are more comfortable with yourself. Are you sure you want to let people see who you really are? It's OK not to be sure at first. Can you openly and honestly present yourself to others with the attitude, "Here I come, faults and all," while still working to develop your skills? Initially, this idea can cause a great internal conflict until you are peaceful with yourself and who you are. Are you willing to stop "faking-people-out" with an "image" and be the real you instead? It takes courage and you can do it.

Once you reach an understanding about yourself and recognize who you are, it gets easier to open up and let others recognize who you are. The rejection we perceive from others often starts with us and the rejection we give ourselves. We can cause ourselves a lot of pain when we reject ourselves. In other words, once you accept yourself, you open the door for others to accept you more easily.

Fear of failure. Fear of rejection. How many people do you know who are living their lives based on everyone else's expectations? How many "people pleasers" do you know? Are you one of them? Have you ever operated by trying to please other people? Have you ever thought people wouldn't like you, and may even reject you, if you didn't please them? Did you ever stop to think that your perception of what pleases someone may be incorrect? Well, *"people pleasing" doesn't work.* When you do what is truly correct for you, without harming others, it will be correct for them also. They may not realize it at first; they will eventually. Stick with your convictions. You're the only one who truly knows how you feel.

How can you achieve success in your life if you live it based on what others expect from you? Do you find yourself getting angry and wondering "When will it be my turn?" Maintain intact self-esteem, and you'll never have that attitude. With intact self-esteem, if you choose to please someone, it will be because you feel happy doing so, not out of fear of rejection or obligation. The key is, don't let the outside world or society try to manipulate you into doing things that aren't on your agenda. You'll probably feel used and abused if you do. It is your life, and you'll be more respected by yourself and others if you take charge and say "no" to people when necessary.

What Do You Think You're Worth?

Keep things in perspective. You are a valuable and worthwhile person; you were born that way. You most likely wouldn't be where you are already if you didn't have some special qualities, skills, talents, and gifts. Again, ask yourself, "What do I love about myself?" "What makes me the person I am?" It's so important to recognize those things about yourself and to also instill this sense of self-appreciation in your children.

Our children are inundated every day by what society thinks they *should* be, have, wear, and do. If they're not wearing certain sneakers and clothes, are they considered worthless and odd? If they're not listening to a particular type of music, are they thought of as unacceptable? Blind conformity is a sign of unintact self-esteem.

Consider the idea of self-worth. If society considers acquiring money makes you worthy, are you worthless if you're not doing that? *How you feel about who you are and how important you think you are determines how much you let what others say influence you.* When you know you are worthy because you were born that way, your confidence can't be shaken when faced with society's false external value system for determining worthiness. After all, we were all created equally worthy in the eyes of God. He didn't make any junk! We were born to succeed, while society often conditions us to fail.

Self-esteem is vital. You will never achieve true success if you don't feel respect for yourself. Remember that *success and happiness come along the way, not just at the end of the road.* By then the journey is over. Happiness is for today, not just tomorrow! After all, tomorrow may never come. Live each day in the moment, because all you really have is now. Tomorrow is guaranteed to no one. Sir Edmund of Canterbury once said, "Work as though you can live forever. Live as though you were going to die tomorrow."

How Do Criticism and Love in Childhood Affect Fear of Failure?

Two conflicts can occur in children. *The first is the conflict between corrective discipline and criticism.* Children are born with pure potential. Often, however, their parenting (discipline is a major factor) determines how much they fear risk, failure, and rejection.

When children are constantly exposed to criticism, they often develop fear of failure which, as you'll recall, is a fear of self. They develop the fear of trying something new. They fear they won't be able to do it. As a result, they are likely to feel disappointed, possibly angry, and fearful of criticism. When children are criticized all the time, they cannot grow and develop intact self-esteem.

Criticism is a clever symptom of insecurity. How many youngsters could have excelled in sports, arts, music, or academics, if they hadn't felt defeated by a parent's expectations of perfection? How many children have been discouraged by a parent's laughter at their "unrealistic" idea? How many parents have put down their children when they tried to achieve something that was important to them? Was this behavior caused by the parent's general lack of success and vision for both themselves and their children? Or, did the parents try to live vicariously through their children, hoping or expecting them to achieve something at which the parents failed?

"Take care" is an innocent cliché parents and other adults often use. Yet these two words may have done more harm than you might believe. While these words are well-intended, they can set-up an over-cautiousness that leads to fear. When someone is facing an obstacle, challenge, or setback, it might be better to say "take-a-chance." After all, life is an opportunity. Without taking a chance, nothing much happens.

Remember the children's book, *The Little Engine That Could*, by Watty Piper? If you constantly tell that little engine that it can't get over the mountain to deliver the candy and toys to the girls and boys, it probably never will. Parents are usually their children's most influential role models, and therefore they can be their greatest mentors. Children are likely to believe what they hear from their parents more than anyone else. What do you want your children to believe about themselves?

When you yell, criticize a child with anger, or attack their personhood, why would they ever have any need to try something new? Why would they want to take the risk?

Suppose your child came into a room, bumped a lamp and broke it, and you said, "You stupid idiot, you broke the lamp. Go up to your room, I don't want to see your face anymore." That's criticism, which many of us have experienced. Corrective discipline would address the *behavior*, rather than attack the child.

Instead of criticism you may want to consider corrective discipline. Remember that discipline means a disciple of; a way to behave; a way to speak; a way to sing. To criticize means to find fault with the person! Discipline the behavior rather than attack the child.

When using corrective discipline, either with yourself or others, deal with the behavior only and make suggestions to correct for errors and goofs. *A person is not their behavior.* You and others can always correct for errors. No one needs to fail at living.

Corrective discipline might go like this: First, identify your feelings. What is really going on inside of you? How do you feel? Are you playing old "tapes" (things said to you) you heard as a child, or are you able to be objective and deal only with the behavior?

Second, own your feelings by describing them with "I statements." For example: "Jamie, I am very unhappy (sad, angry, uncomfortable) that the lamp was broken." Now say exactly how come you feel this way. "The lamp was from your grandmother and had sentimental value to me. I realize it can be replaced; however, I need to deal with my feelings around this particular lamp. You may be able to identify how I feel because of how you would feel if your bike was run over by a car."

Third, affirm the child and give them the opportunity to describe their feelings. "Jamie, I know you did not mean to break the lamp. How do you feel about what happened?" Allow the child to release the feelings that are going on inside, whether they're appropriate, extreme, or nonchalant. Do your best to practice unconditional love at this moment, with no judgment. Once the child completes describing her feelings, proceed to the last step.

The final step is to go for the solution. What is done is done; it cannot be undone. What are the consequences and responsibility of the behavior? Ask the child, "Jamie, what responsibility do you feel you need to accept for the broken lamp?" Listen for the response, as it will let you know the child's *ability to respond*; that is, you will know immediately how responsible the child is at this particular time.

You may need to say, "Jamie, may I suggest you accept responsibility for your behavior by replacing the lamp? We can go to the store and choose one. You can pay for it with your allowance, your savings, or the money you make doing odd jobs. We can come up with a payment plan once we know the cost of the new lamp. I realize you may not like this outcome; however, it is important you learn to accept responsibility for your behavior. We all make mistakes; and it is up to us, individually, to correct our own errors."

With this response, you are respecting the child and keeping their self-esteem intact. This acknowledges their mistake and separates who they are from their behavior. Corrective discipline may require more thought and time on your part. It takes time to describe feelings, ask questions, and listen to yourself and the child. In the long run, you and your child's self-esteem will be enhanced. You will also be teaching the child "how to" accept responsibility and discover appropriate behavior for all the situations they will encounter in their life

Most people fear failure at some time, regardless of their childhood experiences; it's only human. Therefore, your self-esteem may need repair from criticism. Your self-esteem determines how much you let fear of failure control your thinking and performance. This is true in both your business and personal life.

The second conflict that occurs in children is the one between conditional and unconditional love. Conditional love is given only if something is expected from the beloved. Unconditional love is the pure giving of love, without expecting anything in return.

When children are exposed to conditional love, they frequently develop the fear of rejection. They feel their parents won't love them unless they perform as expected. They don't feel loved just for being themselves. The child feels rejected, and his self-esteem gets injured.

I believe everybody wants to be loved and accepted. Some people will do almost anything to get it. They don't realize that if they need to "do" something to be loved, that's conditional love. To receive it requires the constant effort of performance. They get caught-up in a treadmill of "doing," only to earn fleeting and unfulfilling conditional love. They end up in the vicious cycle of "pleasing" people to get conditional love and approval. When we have intact self-esteem, however, we can handle the rejection of others who may not have our best interests at heart. By handling their rejection confidently and seemingly unaffected, we can acquire the respect of even those who dislike us; we can also find out who our real friends are by how they love us. "Fairweather" friends love us only conditionally. Real friends love us unconditionally. As is true for most people, you may not have many real friends. When you implement "No Excuse!" principles, you are likely to develop more real friendships.

Here's a little story that illustrates unconditional love:

I used to get up around 5:30 every Wednesday morning to perform my duties as a consultant to a local TV station. One morning after I got out of the shower, I found the note "I love you, Dad," written across the steamed-up mirror. Without my knowing it, my daughter, Nicole, came quietly into the bathroom while I was in the shower and left the note.

That's an example of unconditional love; she didn't expect anything in return. She made my day! It was the most important thing that happened all day. No matter how things went on the job, it didn't matter. I had been loved unconditionally that morning, and it was all I needed.

It is necessary for children, troops, and the people we lead or influence to understand the limits of acceptable behavior and to be self-disciplined. Their willingness to live a "No Excuse!" life will depend on the respect they have for themselves and others, which comes from their self-esteem.

Troops who know their commander has a sincere interest in them are more likely to be inspired to achieve victory. Members of an organization who know their leader cares are likely to perform far better than when there is little or no regard shown for them.

Children need to know they are unconditionally loved and respected by their parents, regardless of their achievements or failures. No matter what our age, it makes a difference to be loved unconditionally. It's one of the reasons being a parent who is loved unconditionally by the children can be such a deep human experience.

Young children give us unconditional love. Why would we give *them* anything less? If you have any doubts about the value of developing intact self-esteem (which includes unconditional love for yourself), and working to maintain it, remember that you can't give what you don't have. You need to have self-esteem and unconditional love for yourself first before you can nurture anyone else's self-esteem and give them unconditional love.

Be sure to smile more often—unconditionally. It can help brighten a person's day, as well as your own! Smile without expecting one in return, and you'll probably get a smile back anyway. A smile is universal and lets others know you're friendly.

Unconditional love is not the norm. But when you give it to other people, it is likely they'll feel better, and so will you. Remember, what you give out to others comes back to you, if not from them, then another. In other words, "What-goes-around-comes-around"!

Self-Esteem Is Your Birthright

One of the greatest gifts a parent can give to nurture children is to encourage them to have a wholesome respect for and belief in themselves. Parents can model and teach the skills that lead children to better understand their own uniqueness and capabilities.

Of course, not all parents are even aware of their own talents and potential. All too often, our parents are ill-equipped to be parents.

With all the wonderful things our parents pass on to us, especially the gift of life, they may hand us some less desirable things as well.

Everyone who aspires to be fully mature needs to sort through the lessons learned at home. This is not an indictment of our parents for their imperfect behavior. Be thankful for the valuable lessons they gave us. And other than learning what not to do, we need to lay aside teachings and experiences that have hindered us.

We spoke earlier of the importance of forgiveness. Here's a real opportunity to forgive. Search your memory for instances when you felt injured in your childhood (mentally, emotionally, and physically), not with the thought of "an-eye-for-an-eye" (retaliation), but with the intent to forgive. Accept that you may have to work through some painful anger to get to forgiveness. You can do it, if you keep your eye on the prize. By forgiving, you can reclaim the self-esteem that you had when you were born.

When you follow The Golden Rule: "Do unto others as you would have them do unto you," you'll be better prepared to forgive yourself for damaging another's self-esteem, or injuring them in some other way. In the new awareness of your own restored self-esteem, you're more likely to resist attacking others. You'll reject putting down others as unrewarding and unworthy behavior, which the "old" you may have used in an attempt to "repair" your self-esteem. You have had the opportunity to learn that this technique is ineffective.

Parents have a responsibility to guide their children, and fulfilling it can be risky. Some parents never try; that's called abandonment. Parents can live in the same home as their children and still abandon them in many important ways. Some parents are mentally childish themselves, and know only limited and often spiteful ways to deal with others, including their own children. Some parents have been so unskillfully parented themselves, that they have developed only ineffective patterns which govern their parenting abilities. These patterns can be passed on from generation to generation if no one realizes what harm is being done. With awareness, the pattern can be broken and replaced with skillful behavior.

No matter where poor parenting stems from, the fruits are often all too much the same. Fear of failure and rejection can plague the child's growth in such an environment. *To the extent a child is given love and nurturing, along with corrective discipline, his fears will probably be minimal and most likely won't interfere with his personal growth and development.* The more a child is denied unconditional love and respect, the more his self-esteem may be damaged, and the more his belief in his potential may be negatively influenced.

Who Is That Person In The Mirror?

On average, seventy-five to eighty percent of our self-talk is likely to be negative! Fortunately, this can be changed with practice. When you wake-up in the morning, are you thinking positively about yourself and the day ahead? Do you look in the mirror and say, "I'm excited and happy; this is a great day to be alive"? Do it tomorrow morning and see how you feel. Repeat it several times if necessary.

What you see in others is a mirror of you. You can only see qualities in others that you had, have, or are developing in yourself. Your reflection will undoubtedly be your direction. How you perceive and feel about yourself, in many cases, determines the path you take.

Self-esteem is vital. To even begin succeeding, you need to respect yourself enough to believe (even a little bit) that you can do it and that you deserve success. Henry Ford once said, "If you think you can or you think you can't, you're right."

Tomorrow is promised to no one. Be happy now. Lincoln once said, "A man is about as happy as he makes up his mind to be."

With intact self-esteem, you are more likely to make each day count. This is your life; it's not a dress rehearsal! Your life on this earth is like a movie. It has a beginning and an end. What would you do if you had a year to live? Are you doing it? If not, how come? What's preventing you from living the life you want? Unintact self-esteem?

Our attitude toward the world around us depends on our personal history, our qualities, our beliefs, and how we feel about ourselves. If we have a selfish attitude, we are likely to be suspicious of others. If we have a generous attitude, we are likely to be more trusting. If we are honest with ourselves, we are unlikely to anticipate deceit in others. If we behave fairly, we probably won't expect to be cheated by others. In a sense, looking at the people you've most closely surrounded yourself with is like looking at yourself in a mirror. You'll probably find that as you personally develop, you'll attract more personally developed people into your life. Furthermore, you may no longer be able to relate to some friends who have chosen not to grow with you. This often happens when we choose to move-on and have the self-esteem to know that it's OK!

The Cultivating Of A Leader

The story of General Omar Bradley is a great illustration of the growth of a leader. Following a long and successful battle command, he was Commander of the Joint Chiefs of Staff. The techniques he used to overcome hardships to rise to that position were phenomenal.

Bradley was born into a family of plain Missouri farmers who were "proud, honest, hardworking, and desperately poor." They were people who overcame their difficulties through their inner fortitude. Bradley was particularly close to his father, who was a teacher at a frontier school. Here's what Bradley said of his early years:

> We could not afford a horse and buggy. So my father and I walked to and from school each day carrying our lunch baskets, down dirt roads that were either dusty, muddy or icy, depending on the weather. Father set a hearty pace; seventeen minutes to the mile. This was quite a hike for a young lad, especially on bitter cold days, but having those hours alone each day with my father was spiritually reinforcing to a very great degree.

From his father, Bradley developed a love for books, hunting, and sports. These pursuits promoted development of his mind and body, and gave him an inner strength and fearlessness that would benefit him throughout his life. He was always taught to stretch and achieve his full potential. Once an outcome was realized, he learned to tackle his next challenge.

Bradley's father died on the boy's 15th birthday. But by then he had the self-esteem his father helped nourish. By offering encouragement and support, Bradley's father strengthened his son to develop the basic skills and temperament that would allow him to make the best of himself. He was equipped to rise up from the rickety seat of a one-room Missouri schoolhouse, to the rank of General of the United States Army and beyond. His father left him a priceless legacy, which Bradley put in his own words:

> Thanks to my father, I was determined, no matter how poor we might be, to continue my education all the way through college; to make something of myself; not to squander my time or intellectual gifts; to work hard. He had given me much else as well. A love and appreciation of the outdoors, hunting, and sports; a sense of justice and respect for my fellow man and his property, especially the less fortunate. Integrity. Sobriety. Patriotism. Religiosity. No son could have asked more of his father, nor been more grateful for his example.

Replace "Can't" With "Won't"

Our early childhood experiences teach us to expect certain things from ourselves and the world. Take the Omar Bradley story, for instance. The nature of his childhood experiences helped foster his self-esteem, which greatly impacted his later life.

Sometimes what we were taught as children was incorrect. Later, after we leave home, we are more exposed to the world where negative expectations may predominate. This thinking can cast a gloom on life. Our behavior patterns, if based on our negative thinking, tend to produce the negative results we expected. On the other hand, if we were to expect positive outcomes, our behavior patterns could adjust accordingly to produce positive results. In other words, life is a self-fulfilling prophecy.

You may have entered adulthood with preconceptions that are, in fact, misconceptions. However, you can liberate yourself from these. "How do you do that?" you ask. "How do you sort out misconception from reality?" Reading excellent books about personal and professional growth can help you tremendously. Listening to tapes of people whose thinking is clear and on-target can boost your understanding. Associating with people living in integrity with their purpose and committed to growing and serving can really help.

Every time you want to say "can't," discipline yourself to hold that thought. "Can't" means it is not possible. You give away your power and abandon your responsibility when you say "can't." Instead, say "won't," and see what happens. Suddenly, you're in control. "Can't" is usually just an excuse, a cover-up for unintact self-esteem. "Can't" usually means you're afraid to face someone with the truth that you don't want to do something.

Saying "I can't ski," for instance, may mean many things. Maybe you've never seen snow, never had skis on, or never had anyone show you how. Perhaps you skied a few times and didn't do well. You let yourself feel discouraged and quit before you succeeded.

Saying "I won't ski," (or, "I choose not to ski,") takes self-esteem and an understanding of the issue. You won't vacation where it's cold and snowy, or you won't budget for skiing lessons. You may have explored skiing as recreation and did not find it satisfying enough to invest more time and money into it. Or maybe you found something else you'd rather do.

When you say "won't," (or, "I choose not to,") you're being honest and clear, both with yourself and the person you're talking to. You are showing that you respect yourself and realize the decision is yours. It doesn't matter what that person may think. You weaken yourself by saying "can't" and empower yourself by saying "won't"!

Release the need to please people; it's a "dead-end street"! By saying "yes" to them just to try to get them to like you, you forfeit what you truly want. It may work for the moment, but shortly thereafter you begin regretting or resenting it. Have the courage to say "no." You'll feel a lot better about yourself and give your self-esteem a boost.

Personal growth begins when we start challenging the language we use to describe who we are and what we are capable of doing. It's wiser *choosing* not to do something, instead of accepting ourselves as unable. We feel more in control and our self-esteem is maintained. What does it mean to "ski"? Who can't slide down a hill on two boards? "But that isn't skiing," you say. Even though you may not think it is, someone else may! If you look at it that way, you can indeed ski, to some extent anyway. If you still choose not to, that's OK. It's your decision; you're in control.

What do you think excited audiences when Peter Pan exclaimed, "I'm flying," while zooming around a Broadway stage, suspended by a wire? They exclaimed with Peter because he *was* flying. When you're doing something, you're doing it! Forget the "can't." It's only an excuse! So this was a kind of "flying" made possible by extraordinary means. Most worthwhile things are done with help.

Honesty and integrity are at work when we are brave enough to replace "can't" with "won't" or "I choose not to"! This empowers us to develop the habit of being honest with ourselves and others.

You may be reluctant to let go of the "can't" because it often came from a safe part of childhood. "Won't," on the other hand, may seem "risky." When parents or adults say "you can't do that" to a child, the message often has to do with safety. "You can't cross the street alone," for instance, comes with a heavy-duty warning. It really means you aren't allowed, rather than you're unable. On the other hand, when a child uses "I won't," it often brings a scolding. Therefore, a child may learn to say "I can't," when "I won't" is really what he means. "I can't" seems safer.

According to a recent study, for every positive statement a child hears, he hears fourteen negative ones. They are often statements like: "Don't do that"; "You can't do that"; "You're no good for nothing"; "Sit down and shut-up"; "You'll never amount to anything." By the time the child is eighteen, on average, he's heard something negative over 148,000 times! No wonder his self-esteem gets damaged.

When we begin to believe the "can'ts" that fill our thoughts and language, our self-esteem takes a hit. How you feel about yourself largely determines what you will attempt, let alone achieve. All the great motivators have told us this. If you believe you have a chance to get what you want out of life, you have a reason to work for it. If you still don't believe you have a chance, keep growing and repair your self-esteem. You'll find you'll have more energy, more enthusiasm, and more desire to achieve your goals.

Stop And Smell The Roses

Stop and smell the roses. Say "thank you" to yourself every once in a while. Be appreciative of who you are and what you do. Appreciate the wonderful things; the little joys in life.

Did you ever have a child graduate from preschool? It may seem insignificant, but it's a day most children are very happy with themselves. It's a real self-esteem booster. It may seem inconsequential in the overall scheme of things, but it's very important to the child and often the parents. Enjoy these little successes along with your child.

How about a boy or girl's rise up the ranks in the Boy or Girl Scout organization or their development of musical talent? It may seem so simple, yet it can make such a difference in the child's self-esteem. These things can be an important part of a child's life as he or she becomes an adult. They have created a foundation of success that they can repeat in other areas. Your interest in your child's development here is crucial. It's part of "No Excuse!" living.

Forget about work for a while. Forget about everything that's going on out there. Take a look inside and realize that some of the joys in life you experience are much more important than your daily routine. When we can remember and appreciate these things and take delight in them, we are stopping to *smell the roses*; we're creating more joy in our lives.

We're not talking about anything new here. This is just to refresh and renew you. It isn't anything revolutionary. It's just a way to inspire and help you motivate yourself to experience the fullness of life. It's a way to help you put things into perspective. Tomorrow after you go to work and come home, or whatever it is you do every day, you can say, "Yes. I'm glad to be alive."

Forgiveness is important. Belief in who you are is important. Self-esteem is important. It is also important to instill these things in your spouse, children, other loved ones, and the people around you, even at work and other places.

In the work environment, we may often get the message that these things don't matter. Instead, the emphasis is often on: "You've got to make that quarterly report; you've got to make that bottom-line; you've got to make sure you get this and that done." It will probably get done. But if you destroy yourself in the process of getting there, what do you have? You may develop poor health and a broken family who wouldn't take any more of your neglect and abuse.

If you live your life based on what "everybody else" expects from you, what do you have left? You may find yourself a thin, broken spirited shell, deeply frustrated that you didn't do what *you* wanted to do with your life. This is part of the "mid-life crisis." You may have accomplished a lot with your career but didn't take the time to enjoy anything. How can you be happy unless you enjoy the journey?

When you're constantly responding to the barrage of demands and expectations placed on you, your self-esteem suffers. If you watch the TV news and read the newspapers, it's easy to get the idea that things are not "right," they're not going well, and the whole world's falling apart. You can see how this affects everyone around you, including your family. You can really "bum" yourself out!

How can you better deal with all this negativity around you? How do you enhance your self-esteem? One way is to take time to think and "smell the roses." Take time to engage in a sport, hobby, or recreation. Reward yourself along the way. Remember, "All work and no play makes Jack a dull boy." It's OK, and maybe even essential, to do without these things for a period of time when you are focusing on a business goal, for example. This may be a necessary part of delayed gratification. Then, in the future, you may integrate some sport, hobby, or recreational activities back into your life.

The "Do Right" Philosophy

In his book, *Fighting Spirit*, Coach Lou Holtz of Notre Dame presented a wonderful way to enhance self-esteem. It's called The "Do-Right" Philosophy. It can help you to maintain a sense of integrity within yourself.

First of all, *do the right thing*. What does that mean? It means *be honest and sincere* in everything do you. How could this not make you feel good about who you are? It's when you jeopardize your integrity and are dishonest, that you open the door for excuses to take over. When we are not true to ourselves, when we're not honest, when we don't maintain a sense of integrity within ourselves, it's very easy to relinquish responsibility. It's very easy not to be in control of where we want to take our lives. When you maintain that sense of doing the "right" thing, of being honest and sincere no matter what, you'll feel good about who you are. It's so simple, it's almost insulting. But it's so hopeful that such a simple thing can have such a major influence on your feelings of well-being.

When faced with a choice, are you decisive or indecisive? Rosa Parks (mentioned previously) is a perfect example. She said, "I've had it. I'm not sitting in the back of the bus anymore!" She displayed a sense of self-esteem and value, and acted with integrity.

She said "no more" and stood firm on what she believed in, no matter what the consequences. She made a decision and lived by it.

Are you willing to take responsibility for your decisions, no matter what the consequences?

Have you ever been in a situation personally, or in your career, where you could have jeopardized your integrity? Did you ever compromise your values and morals just to suit the whims of other people, or even to keep your job (or so you thought)? It can be challenging because often you need to make a decision. Do you maintain the status quo, or do you stand-up for what you believe in? Are you going to do the right thing? Are you willing to tolerate that "tug-of-war" in your conscience?

Parenting is much the same way. Many are concerned over whether or not their kids like them, instead of employing correct, effective parenting skills. Think about it. If one day you say this, and the next day you say that, how can you be an effective parent?

Integrity means being decisive, being strong. It means standing up for what you believe in. When you do that, you are congruent with yourself and with your values. You are no longer struggling. You'll have more respect for yourself. No one is here to pass judgment or dictate what values you "should" have. Only you and your heart can determine that, and it's so important.

Secondly, *be committed to excellence.* No matter what you do, do the very best you can. Don't you feel good whenever you go all out for a goal, no matter what the outcome? If you don't pull out all the stops in your pursuit of a goal, you open the door for excuses, which lowers the degree of success you could have achieved.

Be committed to excellence in whatever you do. When you do the very best you can, you'll feel good about who you are. You'll enhance your self-esteem.

Third, *live by "The Golden Rule."* No matter what faith you are or what belief you may have, treat others the way you want to be treated. Most of us want to be treated with respect, kindness, love, and sincerity. When you treat others how you want to be treated, it'll come back to you. How could you not feel good about who you are? Once again, your self-esteem will be enhanced.

If you find that *"The Golden Rule"* isn't working as well as you'd like with a particular person or group, use *"The Platinum Rule."* Maybe their model of desirable behavior doesn't match yours. For example, a friend of mine's secretary has an illness that causes her to feel poorly in the morning. So my friend's cheery "Good Morning" only irritates her since she maintains that mornings aren't good for her. She would prefer "Hi" instead. So this is an instance where treating someone like you would like to be treated may be ineffective. In other words, meet people at their need. If you get caught-up in yourself and forget about other people's needs, it's easy to blame and complain. Do you see how everything interacts? Do you see how even forgiveness enters the picture?

Do you see how being self-responsible determines success and how purpose interacts with this? It's all part of the "puzzle." *As you think and behave, so shall you become.* It's so vital to understand this. How come it works? You'll see the whole picture better as we move along.

There are three primary questions Holtz says that go along with The "Do-Right" Philosophy. **The first question he asks is, "*Can I trust you?*"** Think about that. You may have asked that of your boss. Although you don't come right out and say it, still, in the back of your mind, you may question it. You may feel you have a right to question until he consistently proves he is trustworthy. Or, you may be more trusting, and trust him unless he proves he is untrustworthy.

When you go to buy a car, do you ask yourself if you can trust the salesperson? You see, to one degree or another we are likely to ask that of one another. Clients ask that of consultants. Customers ask that of a business. Parents ask that of children, and children ask that of parents. Managers ask that of salespeople, and salespeople ask that of managers. And the list goes on and on. Approaching people suspiciously is ineffective. However, it is best to be discerning.

This is why maintaining a sense of integrity is so important. What happens when someone breaks that trust? Do you feel the same about that person? Do you feel the same about that business? No way. Then what can you do? You can take a step back on the *Staircase* to "Totally Forgive"! That's why honesty and a sense of integrity are so important. Do people trust you? Always remember that honest, effective leadership paves the way for trust.

The second question is, "*Are you committed to excellence?*" Wouldn't you ask that of an automobile manufacturer? Are they providing a vehicle that lives up to its advertising? Of course, you expect that. The customers and people you serve expect that from you too. In many cases, when excellence is taught at home or school, children expect it from parents, and parents expect it from children.

The "Secret" of Living is Giving

The third and final question Lou Holtz posed was, "*Do you care about me?*" Do you care about me as a person? *People don't care how much you know until they know how much you care.*

Do you wholeheartedly assist, help, and support others? What you give to other people is key. True success comes through giving, which leads to a happy, fulfilled life. If you want to be successful, just help enough other people succeed. Be committed to giving of yourself to others in everything you do. You'll feel good about yourself, and you will succeed.

Do You Care About People?

As an example, let's say you go into a computer store looking to purchase a new computer. Some of us are knowledgeable about computers; some of us are not. Let's say you know very little about computers. Two salespeople are in the store.

The first salesperson comes up to you and says, "Hi, how are you? I've got a 486DX, 100MB hard drive, 8 milliseconds, 20 megahurtz, 5K RAM ...." You stand there scratching your head saying, "I don't know what you're talking about." The salesperson says, "Do you want the computer?"

The second salesperson comes up to you and says, "Before I present you the features of our line, let me ask you a few questions. What specifically are your needs? What kind of things do you do in your office? Are you interested in word processing or desk-top publishing?"

All you said was, "I want to be able to balance my checking account at home, and my kids want to play games. I don't think we need anything real high-tech."

Who would you want to deal with, the one that "knows it all" or the one that cares about your needs? The goal of both salespeople is to sell a computer. I believe you'll want to deal with the one who first cares about you and can meet your needs, even if he doesn't know all the details and consults with someone else to learn more.

Do you care about me? What a difference that makes! If you want to make a sale, show your clients you care. If you want to be a better parent, show your kids you care. If you want to be a better manager, show your employees you care. If you want to have better relationships at work, show your co-workers and boss you care. I believe you will find that if you're going to build a team and loyalties from your people, caring about them can make a major difference in your operation. This is true for families too.

Do the right thing. Be committed to excellence. Treat others as you, or they, want to be treated. And remember the three primary questions people are likely to ask of you: Can I trust you?; Are you committed to excellence?; and, Do you care about me? As simple as it sounds, using The "Do-Right" Philosophy will dramatically enhance your self-esteem.

Let People Know Who You Really Are–Be Yourself

Hugh Prather once said, "Some people are going to like me, some people aren't. So I might as well be me because then I know that the people who like me, like *me*." Why not be yourself? Then you'll really know how others respond to *you*. You can then be confident that they are, in fact, responding to who you are and not an imitation.

No one does everything perfectly, so we can all stand to grow. We were all born with intact self-esteem, but it could have gotten "beat-up" along the way. Read personal growth books, listen to personal development tapes, and attend seminars that help you grow. Put yourself on a continuing education program so people can really know who you are, so people can like the real you.

In the past, you may have hidden your real self from others, and even from yourself. This is called "masking." Before you leave this earth, make sure you let people know who you really are. Let your unique talents, gifts, and skills shine through. Going to a funeral always reminds us that we're only temporary; we're just "penciled-in." Life is too short, so go ahead, be yourself and move-on.

Make the most of yourself, because that's all there can be of you. Let go of the bonds of self-image and let people know the real you. It is gratifying to know your relationships are based on genuineness. It feels wonderful when you know that the people who like you like the *real* you; be yourself and you'll be much happier.

Unless you reach an understanding about yourself, and until you start to recognize who you are, you are unable to really open up to other people and share your real self. When you let other people "in" so they can recognize you for who you are, you are also accepting yourself. If you refuse to do this, you'll get lost in the artificial image you are trying to project. Once you accept yourself unconditionally and let others know you, you've taken a major step toward achieving the outcomes you really want.

Be sure you learn more of what you are all about through your personal development program of books, tapes, and seminars. You are on a mission of self-discovery! After you know more of what you have to give, you can pass it on to others. Your self-discovery continues as you grow into the person you want to be. Share your unique talents, gifts, and skills with the people at home, at work, and with the world. What you have to give is important and can make such a difference. Guess who benefits the most from your growth and sharing? You do! After all, how can you achieve true success and make your dreams come true if you don't use what you were born with and developed along-the-line? Be yourself, yes, and also be willing to grow and become the best *you* you can be.

Self-esteem is one of the fundamental steps along the *Staircase-of-Success*. Forgiveness and self-esteem get you started on your success journey. With a foundation of purpose, self-responsibility, and integrity, the base of your *Staircase* is built on a solid floor.

Believing in who you are, knowing what you're about, and feeling respect for yourself are so important. To be happy and fulfilled, you want to make sure you are living your life based on what *you* expect from yourself. You don't need to let fear control you.

Say "No Excuse!"–Smile And Forgive With Intact Self-Esteem.
Once you have intact self-esteem, wonderful things can begin to happen. I believe you'll want to share it with other people. You're likely to become more self-responsible. And remember, you too can adopt the goal of throwing out excuses. Your attitude can be that there's simply "No Excuse!" anymore. Your goal this week or this month could be to one-by-one, eliminate the excuses from your life. You can "just-do-it!"

When I came home from West Point one time, I decided to throw out my old excuses. Since I was accustomed to saying "No Excuse, Sir!", I used it on my mother. She said "do this" or "why don't you do that?" and I said "No Excuse!" She said, "What?" It was not only productive, but fun!

Say "No Excuse!" to the people you work with and they'll probably be very surprised and think, "You mean you're not going to blame anyone? You're not going to blame anything? You're not going to make an excuse for why you didn't do something?" They may not say those things out loud, but it is likely they will be thinking them.

You'll find it's catching. People will almost inevitably look at you differently. Go in smiling where you didn't smile before. When you go into work having intact self-esteem, it can spread to others who are interested in making a change in their lives. When you go in to work looking for something in life other than what everyone else expects, you have a better chance of finding that there's a person of worth inside you. Once you do, you'll probably want to share that with other people. How do you do that? It is reflected in your attitude, which is the third step on the *Staircase*.

When you forgive and let go of the past, you have no reason to harbor ill feelings for other people. When you begin to live an intact self-esteem lifestyle, you can let go of self-doubt.

How Good Are You At Giving And Receiving Compliments?
How do you feel and respond when someone pays you a compliment? Do you say "Thank you"? Or do you say, "This old thing. I've had it for years," or "I really need to wash my hair. I can't believe you like it." How you respond to another's gratitude and sincerity is an indication of whether your self-esteem is intact. Do you feel respect for yourself and believe you are worthy enough to receive that person's generosity? Do you realize that it is a gift they are giving you? When you negate their gift, you are doubting their judgment and rejecting their compliment. Just say "Thank you!"

Have you ever had anyone, particularly a friend, offer to buy you lunch, but you refused to let them? Do you realize how that might feel to them? Aren't you rejecting their offer? The kindest thing to do is to just say "Thank you!" Be a gracious receiver. Perhaps at a later date you can offer to buy them lunch, if you want to. Then you'll realize how good it feels when they say "Thank you" to you.

You see, what's inside you is the only thing that can come out. You can only give what you have inside. If you don't have a generous attitude, you may have trouble accepting generosity. Are you open to receiving? Is your self-esteem intact? Be positive. Smile often. Not only can you brighten someone else's day, but yours as well.

When you get to work tomorrow, smile at someone who never smiles. They may not smile back; it really doesn't matter. The point is, *you're* going to feel better. When you smile, you're giving a gift to the other person. You are giving them a compliment. Your smile says, "I'm happy to see you." Remember, success comes by giving, and whatever you give away will come back to you. When you operate with self-esteem, you'll feel better about yourself and be better able to give. You'll discover that giving is fun and rewarding.

Do you feel good when you give to your church or a favorite charity? How do you feel when you help an elderly person cross the street? Do you feel good when you help someone less fortunate than you? I believe you do. Giving is a sign of a successful person. Giving is a sign of intact self-esteem.

"No Excuse!" Action Plan To "Have Self-Esteem"

1. Love and feel respect for yourself, and you'll be able to love and respect others. You can only give away what you have.

2. Never value judge; it's the only thing that will injure or destroy your self-esteem. Value judging is labeling and comparing, and that will give you nothing but pain.

3. Find a mentor who can help you replace self-image behavior with self-esteem behavior. This is essential for you to truly succeed.

4. Get in touch with your feelings, both physical and emotional, and you'll begin to recognize what you really want. Major decisions are most often made based on emotions, backed-up by logic.

5. Use self-esteem language when you talk to others and also in your self-talk. Words create feelings which affect your behavior.

6. Make decisions, then make them work out. It's impossible to do everything, so making choices is always necessary.

7. Repair your self-esteem, and your fear of failure and rejection will decrease. It boils down to having self-respect and belief in yourself. Then you can help others get it, too.

8. Do the things that are in your heart, not to please people, but to follow your dreams. Don't let other people manipulate you into doing things that aren't on your agenda and not in your best interest.

9. Work as though you could live forever; live as though you were going to die tomorrow.

10. Love unconditionally and smile more often. You'll brighten someone else's day, as well as your own.

11.   Replace "can't" with "won't" (or "I choose not to"). "Can't" is usually an excuse. It's often irresponsible, and it usually means you are afraid to face someone with the truth. Saying "won't" means you're taking charge of the situation.

12.   Stop and smell the roses. Appreciate who and what you are, as well as life's little joys. Enjoy the trip.

13.   Be yourself. Let people know who you really are. Don't try to be like anyone else. Then you know that the people who like you, like you for who you are and not just what you do.

14.   Accept compliments simply by saying "Thank you!" Appreciate the gift you were given.

15.   Give unconditionally, without expecting anything in return. You'll feel good about yourself.

ATTITUDE

The longer I live, the more I realize the impact of attitude on life. Attitude, to me, is more important than facts. It is more important than the past, than education, than money, than circumstances, than failures, than successes, than what other people think or say or do. It is more important than appearance, giftedness or skill. It will make or break a company...a church... a home. The remarkable thing is we have a choice every day regarding the attitude we will embrace for that day. We cannot change our past...we cannot change the fact that people will act in a certain way. We cannot change the inevitable. The only thing we can do is play on the one string we have, and that is our attitude....I am convinced that life is 10% what happens to me and 90% how I react to it.

*And so it is with you...
we are in charge of our ATTITUDES!*

CHARLES SWINDOLL

Chapter 7

ELEVATE YOUR ATTITUDE AND ENTHUSIASM
Third Step Of The Thesaurus Factor

An Elevated Attitude—Your Esprit de Corps

William James once said, "It is one's attitude at the beginning of a difficult undertaking which, more than anything else, will determine its successful outcome." In fact, you can alter your life and affect the lives of those around you simply by changing your attitude. So may I suggest that you prepare yourself to develop and maintain an elevated attitude and enthusiasm.

The dictionary defines *attitude* as "a state of mind expressing a certain opinion. A position of the body that indicates a certain expression or opinion. Posture. A feeling or emotion toward a fact or state." It defines *enthusiasm* as "strong excitement of feeling. Something inspiring, zeal, terror, warmth or eagerness."

Elevate Your Attitude And Enthusiasm is an "express" step on the *Staircase*. Think about it. How you express yourself helps to determine the ideas and feelings people have about you. It also influences how fast you move toward your desired outcomes. Learn how to express, rather than impress!

When you learn to like and respect yourself more, and appreciate the possibilities that exist for you, guess what happens? A natural tendency to "shine" kicks-in; you're on your way to becoming a leader. An elevated attitude and enthusiasm are marks of a leader, and *esprit de corps* (enthusiastic comradeship) is the mark of a group led by that person.

Of course, to "have an attitude" (a "tude," i.e., arrogance or a nasty attitude) is another thing altogether. Having a "tude" is to cut off communication. Ultimately, it's the mark of a loner. A true leader skillfully maintains morale in the group that has confidence in his ability to lead them.

An elevated attitude begins when you understand what you want, and start to resolve the conflicts in your life. In our hectic society, many people are often fragmented and unfocused in their thoughts and behaviors. They may be in the survival mode, not looking at the bigger picture of what they really want. An elevated attitude helps us to have the desire and energy to remain focused on what we want to accomplish. As we continue to focus, take action, and start to get the results we want, we become a role model to others. Our elevated attitude and enthusiasm can inspire others to also take action in their lives. In other words, it can be contagious.

An Attitude Befitting A King

Throughout history, it has been well documented that military leaders have maintained an elevated attitude. For generals, and real and fictional kings alike, a positive and enthusiastic outlook seems to be their most effective means of rallying troops to the cause. In Shakespeare's famous play "Henry V," penned almost 400 years ago, elevated attitude and enthusiasm take center stage.

King Henry was at his best when he fulfilled his patriotic functions in the crusade against France. Once he became committed to the virtues of his cause, he displayed great enthusiasm. His most difficult to understand trait was his jaunty disregard for the enemy.

By conveying his enthusiasm to the bedraggled troops, he became the ideal man of action and the almost perfect leader. He called his men "very valiant creatures" who, supplied with beef and iron and steel, "eat the wolves and fight like devils." Henry stirred his men to action because he made it his business to elevate his attitude and be enthusiastic.

Where Does Elevated Attitude And Enthusiasm Begin?

When you are self-responsible, define your life's purpose, and stop making excuses, i.e., don't blame anybody or anything, your life will be different. As you forgive, and direct the energy previously wasted on resentment and anger to where you know it can make a difference, you'll feel better about yourself. You're likely to want to share this "revelation" with others. And that's where your attitude and enthusiasm come in, as you share these ideas with others.

Earl Nightingale once said, "Attitude is the magic word." And it's so true. It can provide "magical" results both at work and at home. *It's your attitude and not your aptitude that determines your altitude in life.* It tells you and others where you are. For example, it communicates whether you have a forward thinking mentality and are living a purposeful, passionate life. Or do you just have a "poor soul" mentality, existing in "gray mediocrity"? Your attitude helps determine how other people respond to you.

Are You Smiling?

When you wake up in the morning, are you happy? Do you say, "Good God, it's morning!" or "Good morning, God"? Do you look at your spouse next to you in bed and say, "I love you"? Does he or she smile about that?

Is your glass half-empty or half-full? Your attitude is one of the first indicators that tells others what kind of person you are. As Dr. Robert Schuller says, "Happy is the person who is motivated to be a beautiful human being."

How come some people don't smile? Do they think it's silly? Are they afraid to let people know they like them or at least that they're a friendly person? Are they always focusing on the negative, and therefore frown? Smile! When you do, others will usually smile back.

Some morning on the way to work, see how many people look happy as they wait for the traffic light to change. You probably won't find one! In fact, you might notice some pretty grumpy-looking faces. We're not suggesting drivers should be jumping up and down and waving to everyone! All we're saying is that a cheerful expression would help brighten their day and that of others. This can be accomplished by relaxing your facial muscles and thinking pleasant thoughts. Let go of your frown! A lot of people don't realize they look angry, and because of that, people may be afraid to approach them. Wear a relaxed and happy countenance. It attracts people.

Almost everyone gets discouraged. Your attitude can help you overcome it. Your attitude largely determines the first impression you give other people. Your smile can make a difference in other people's lives. When you get a person with a negative attitude to smile, their attitude becomes a little more positive. It's amazing to see what happens to our attitude when we choose to smile instead of frown. Our attitude can spread like wildfire.

If, rather than being pleasant, you project a negative attitude toward the people you're speaking to, it is unlikely they will want to be around you, unless they are negative too. You may literally repel them to the point where they only associate with you when they feel they "have to."

The word *communication* comes from the Latin word "communical," which means *to share*. A smile shares joy. A smile says, "I'm happy to see you." It is a form of communication. The intent of this book is to share techniques that can make a difference in your ability to overcome obstacles and reach new levels of personal growth, success, happiness, and fulfillment. I believe applying them in your life, and sharing them with others, will help you take giant leaps forward.

Be positive with other people. Be positive with yourself. Much of your self-talk may be negative. It is important to change that; talk positively to yourself if you expect to be more successful. If we aren't careful, we can fall into the trap of negativity and discouragement because of various challenges. Circumstances can affect our attitude only if we let them. Face your challenges with a smile. Most of them are temporary. If you adopt the attitude of "this too shall pass," it is often helpful.

How Does Perception Affect Your Attitude?

The key to your attitude is your perception. How do you perceive the situation? Will it matter five years or even five minutes from now? How important is it, really? Are the people's feelings more important in the long run than the situation itself? How do you perceive life? Is it your perception that life is meant to be perfect with no challenges? If so, you are setting yourself up for many disappointments.

Do you remember the last time you went on vacation? What did you focus on before you left? The cost? The kids being with you because no babysitter was available? The drive to the airport? Dealing with airport parking, tickets, bags and everything else? You may have put yourself in such a "huff" that, before you even got on the plane, the vacation seemed ruined!

How do you look at things? Do you focus on the work of getting there or the pleasure awaiting you, like walking on the beach? If you feel what you have to do before you get on the plane is a big hassle, you'll discourage yourself. But if you focus on relaxing on the beach, or whatever else you enjoy, it will be easier for you to handle all the challenges with a positive attitude. It will seem worth it. Focus on the desired outcome rather than the details. The details will all get done a lot easier when you focus on what you want.

Do You Tend To Have A Positive Or Negative Attitude?

Do you look at the positive aspects of work? Do you have positive feelings about your home and family? Do you focus on the negative or positive aspects of your life? The self-responsibility way is to admit that *you* put yourself where you are, so you might as well make the best of it. Of course, you also have the power to change certain aspects of your situation: get another job; move to a different location; start your own business; or whatever else you may decide to do. You are not stuck! That alone is a positive aspect; you have the power to choose.

Attitude Versus Aptitude—Which Is More Important?

What's your attitude doing? Is it helping you or hindering you? About ninety-percent of the results you get from life stem from your attitude, while about ten percent come from your aptitude. For example, let's say you are in a position to hire someone. If that person goes through the interview with his head down, whining and complaining about benefits, you're not going to hire him no matter what his aptitude is. On the other hand, when a person is enthusiastic and positive about who they are and what they can do for you, you'll be more likely to want to hire them. Then you can train them. That's the easy part when they have a positive attitude.

How Do You Measure Attitude?

You can measure your attitude by the way other people react to you. When you're positive, people are more likely to respond positively to you. If you're negative, and a real "headache" to be around, forget it. Other people are likely to react the same way and avoid you whenever possible; most people don't want to be around negativity. They have enough of their own challenges. They need to be uplifted rather than "negged-out." Of course, you may attract other negative people to join you in the "muck-and-mire" of your attitude. They will only contribute to your negativity and lack of success. It's like a downward spiral.

The more you know yourself, the better you can understand and work on your own unskillful behavior. The more you accept yourself and other people, the more positive you'll be. When you look at life as an opportunity rather than a burden, a struggle, or a headache, you'll have a more positive attitude and greater enthusiasm. This takes time and effort, but it's worth it.

How Is Your Health?

There are plenty of books and tapes available to help you be as healthy as possible for you. You may have some health challenges to work around. Your health may affect your attitude and enthusiasm. If you are "dragging yourself" through the day, you will have less energy and enthusiasm for creating a successful life. There may be some simple things you can do to feel and look better. Here are some questions to consider:

Do you eat balanced meals? Do you take vitamins? Do you drink 6-8 glasses of water a day? Do you sleep 6-8 hours a night, or whatever feels best to you? If you have a late night, do you take a 30-40 minute nap to refresh yourself? Do you do toning and aerobic exercise regularly, according to your physician's recommendations? Do you get regular check-ups? Do you breathe properly? Do you maintain your correct weight? Do you get enough fresh air, perhaps opening your window a little at night as you sleep? Do you visit the dentist every six months? Do you pace yourself? Do you pay attention to your thoughts and feelings and observe their effects on your body? Do you smoke? Do you drink too much alcohol? Do you take illegal drugs? Do you get your eyes examined at least every two years? Do you relax regularly? Do you take regular vacations? The more questions you said "no" to, the more attention you need to pay to your health.

You might say you have heard these things a million times before. You may be surprised at how many people take better care of their homes, yards, cars, pets, and clothes than their own health. It is vitally important to take care of yourself. It is not selfish. It is essential! The healthier you are, the easier it will be to fulfill your purpose and live the life you want. Be enthusiastic about your health! Without it, life's not much fun.

The Man Who Sold Hot Dogs

Once there was a man who sold hot dogs at his stand on the sidewalk of a major city. He was partially deaf so he didn't listen to the radio very much. His eyesight was so poor he didn't watch TV or read the newspaper. However, he sure did sell hot dogs! He enthusiastically encouraged people to buy his hot dogs. He had a cheerful sign advertising how delicious they were. He even bought a big stove to take care of all his customers.

Then something happened. His son came home from college and said: "Dad, haven't you been listening to the radio? There's a big recession coming on. Haven't you been reading the newspapers or watching TV? The political situation is in complete turmoil. The world's a mess."

That made his father think, "Well, my son's been to college, he would know." So the father cut down on his hotdog roll and meat orders. He reduced the number of his advertising signs. He no longer stood by the side of the road to sell those wonderful hot dogs. Sales fell fast, almost overnight!

The father looked to his son and said, "You were right, son. We're certainly in the middle of a great recession. There just isn't any business."

What changed to make the man's hotdog sales fall? His attitude! Before his son threw a lot of negative ideas his way, his sales were fine. His new doubtful attitude caused him to believe he would experience reduced sales, and he then took action that caused his sales to go down.

Is There Opportunity In Failure?

How you perceive situations, and how you let society and the outside world influence you, affects your attitude and enthusiasm. Do you perceive a recession as a negative or an opportunity to shine, be innovative, and use different approaches? Every potential failure also has potential opportunity. Have you ever noticed that? You might think you experienced the worst failure of your life. Then, by golly, it turned out to be your greatest lesson, which helped to propel you to even greater success.

Woodrow Wilson once said: "I would rather fail at a cause that I know would ultimately succeed, than succeed at a cause that would ultimately fail." In other words, it's better to attempt something great and fail than attempt an unworthy project and succeed. The great projects will never die, even if you failed in your contribution. On the other hand, unworthy projects will eventually fail, even if you've succeeded in your contribution.

What Difference Does Attitude Make At Work?

Attitudes have a tremendous influence at work. What happens when the boss comes in with his head down, angry and slamming his office door? His attitude can be assessed by observing his body language and emotional state. Would you be as motivated to be productive and efficient, manage your time well, and communicate with the people around you if your boss is negative? Unless you have an elevated attitude and enthusiasm, you are likely to be de-motivated. It is your choice whether or not you let someone else's attitude affect or determine your own. If the people in the hierarchy don't care, why would you? Would your attitude sustain you?

When the people in the hierarchy smile, the atmosphere is different. Enthusiasm can have a powerfully positive effect on people. A smile seems to make everything more worthwhile. It's amazing. It's fascinating to see what effect your facial expressions can have on yourself and others. Experiment with smiling, frowning, and neutral expressions, and see how others react. You may be surprised. You may find that people will smile back when you smile first. When you frown or exhibit a neutral expression, people may not acknowledge you. They may even avoid you.

What About Your Attitude At Home And Other Places?

Strive to elevate your attitude and be enthusiastic, both at work and at home. As we progress along the *Staircase,* you'll see how vital, how important home is. "No Excuse!" isn't just for work. These steps and this entire program are for everyday life. Everyone carries their attitude and enthusiasm (or lack of it) with them wherever they go, whether it's at home, work, church, stores, school, or recreation.

The same success principles that apply at work also apply at home and everywhere else you go. If you're honest and have integrity at work, what would cause you to be any different at home? If you forgive at work, wouldn't you forgive at home? If you believe in yourself and want to instill belief in other people at work, would you be equally inclined to do that for your family at home? Some people treat virtual strangers with more respect and caring than their own families. This can be devastating to their family relationships and lead to a lot of avoidable grief. Some people take their families for granted. Be wholehearted in your enthusiasm and attitude, and uplift everyone you can wherever you are.

You see, there is no difference. Success is for work, family, and other parts of your life. Your attitude and enthusiasm are a major part of your first impression. They're also vital parts of the first *expression* you give to other people. When you elevate your attitude and enthusiasm, they'll produce "magic" for you.

The Best Pitcher In The World

Children can teach adults about attitude and enthusiasm. One day, a gentleman was walking past a playground when he noticed a young boy with a baseball and bat. As the man got closer, he overheard the boy saying, "I'm going to be the best hitter in the whole world." The boy had been throwing the ball into the air, trying to hit it. He threw the ball up, swung the bat, and missed. He did it again.

The boy continued; he wouldn't give up. He picked up that bat, threw the ball up in the air and said again, "I'm going to be the best hitter in the whole wide world." He swung the bat and missed. It was interesting to see the man's fascinated observation as the boy persisted. For the third time, the young boy said, "I'm going to be the best hitter in the whole world." He threw the ball up in the air, swung, and missed.

At that point, the boy noticed the man looking at him. The boy then turned around and said to the man, "Hey mister, did you see that? Three balls up in the air, three strikes, no hits; I'm going to be the best *pitcher* in the whole wide world!"

It all depends how you look at things. As the young boy did, we can all learn to look at things differently, to have a more positive attitude and greater enthusiasm. There's always a positive in every negative situation. The man *perceived* the boy was failing at his effort. The boy chose to view the situation in a positive light. Your attitude and enthusiasm can help you find it. Remember, there is usually someone who has a worse situation than you. You might be doubtful and ask, "Where is that person that has it worse than I do?" Remember that *life has too much potential for joy to waste time on everything that seems to be wrong with it.* There's so much to be gained by having a positive attitude and being enthusiastic with other people.

The Power of Positive Thinking

It takes a combination of courage and hope to elevate your attitude and enthusiasm. It's called "*chutzpa*"!

Eleanor Roosevelt, a woman of elevated attitude and enthusiasm, once said, "No one can make you feel inferior without your consent."

ON BEING YOUR OWN CHEERLEADER

*The real secret of success is enthusiasm. Yes, more
than enthusiasm, I would say excitement.
I like to see people get excited. When they get excited,
they make a success of their lives. You can
do anything if you have enthusiasm. Enthusiasm is the
sparkle in your eye, it is the swing in your gait,
the grip of your hand, the irresistible surge of your will
and your energy to execute your ideas.
Enthusiasts are fighters. They have fortitude, they have
staying qualities. Enthusiasm is at the bottom of all
progress. With it there is accomplishment.
Without it there are only alibis.*

WALTER CHRYSLER

*ENTHUSIASM is more important
than INTELLIGENCE.*

ALBERT EINSTEIN

She recognized the threat we are to ourselves when we succumb to someone else's low opinion of us. Eleanor knew the courage it takes to insist on our own worth and to take action to fulfill our potential.

Think of George Washington at Valley Forge as he walked alone on cold winter nights, between the tents of his sleeping soldiers. He believed the new nation had a right and responsibility to exist. It was truly Washington's elevated attitude and enthusiasm that helped keep the spark of hope alive in his men. It helped them endure the bitter winter and persevere without quitting.

In the military, the true test of a commander is his troops' morale. According to the dictionary, *morale* is "the state of the spirit of a person or group as exhibited by confidence, cheerfulness, discipline, and willingness to perform assigned tasks." Performance improves when the morale of the troops is high. When morale is low, energy is spent on negative thinking, which weakens the will to win. This also holds true in civilian life.

Attitude And Enthusiasm Affects Our Success

Whenever possible, associate with people with positive attitudes and enthusiasm. This will help you to maintain a great attitude and stay enthusiastic.

Did you know that attitude and enthusiasm follow the laws of physics? One of Newton's Laws states that an object at rest tends to remain at rest unless acted upon by another force. Also, an object in motion tends to remain in motion unless acted upon by another force. This is true for people's attitudes, which will stay negative unless influenced by a positive attitude. Attitude and enthusiasm can be the force needed to get beyond negativity to the outcomes we want.

What About Dealing With People With Negative Attitudes?

Although you may not want to hang around people with negative attitudes, they *do* need your encouragement. How can you success-fully deal with them? The key is to change your perception of them and their behavior. Their intentions may be good; look for the joy, the positive, and the benefits. Realize they may be hurting inside. Most people are, to one degree or another. They may just need some attention; someone who cares about them. Look at things in a different light, and you can feel kinder toward them. *How you perceive what you believe will help structure what you achieve.*

Here's an example of changing perceptions. You may see a "Beware of Dog" sign on someone's fence. Your perception may be that a dog probably lives there. Imagine taking that sign and putting it on your boss's office door. (Fun to imagine, isn't it?) Now you probably have a different perception of what that means. You may think there's a dog in there, but more likely something else. Your perception depends on how you interpret the information you receive.

For example, suppose you change the frame around a picture. The picture may appear different to you. The new frame may enhance the picture. It may cause the picture to look larger or smaller. When you put a different "frame" around a certain situation, you'll find it tends to change your belief about it. You're looking at the situation a little differently. For example, you can view a person's unskillful behavior with either an angry attitude or a caring attitude, giving them the benefit of the doubt. When you "re-frame," imagine no harm was intended by the people you may have thought intended to harm you. Their intentions may have been fine, even though their behavior was unskillful.

A Sense Of Meaning Elevates Your Attitude And Enthusiasm

A great book that demonstrates the importance of attitude is *Man's Search For Meaning* by Viktor Frankl. If you've never read it, you might want to, especially if you're ever feeling down and out. He talks about the horror of the Nazi concentration camps, what he went through, and how he survived.

Frankl basically said that *life is 10 percent what you're given and 90% how you react to it.* He said he never lost his sense of self. He shared that they could physically abuse him, torture him, and take all the basic necessities away from him, but they could not destroy what he was about. No matter what they did to him, he maintained his attitude.

Frankl said people who survived the camps (about 5%) had a reason to live. Frankl wanted to see his wife again and get his first book published. He had a reason to live; he had a purpose. Those who gave up hope and lost the reason to live didn't make it.

Life's the same way for us too. Those who have developed a purpose, a mission beyond just "getting by" (survival), are more likely to become successful, happy, and fulfilled.

Frankl's book is deeply inspiring. It can be a powerful experience to read about someone overcoming hardships. Oftentimes, you can imagine yourself in their place. You can often relate their difficulties to your own challenges. Then you can bring yourself to a new level of understanding, realizing that you too have a chance to make a difference in this world. I believe you know in your heart that you have an opportunity to take what life has to offer and use your skills and talents to benefit other people.   What a wonderful sense of significance you can have.

Man's Search For Meaning; what a great title!   What is the meaning of life?   If you still don't know the answer, rest assured, you are not alone.   Many of us are still searching.   You'll know the answer when you find it.   For me, life is an opportunity to grow, while helping others grow, through teaching "No Excuse!"

Many believe the meaning of life is "to love."   This can be achieved through caring about others and doing what you love to do; sharing your talents and skills with others.   William James once said, "The most important thing in life is to live your life for something more important than your life."   *How you think structures what you become and whether you use your talents and skills.   Thinking is the essence of success.   Your attitude and enthusiasm are core parts of your thinking; they affect your success, happiness, and fulfillment every day.*

Fulfillment

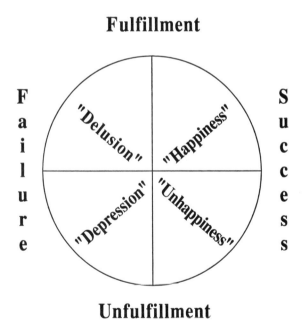

Unfulfillment

The Success-Happiness-Fulfillment Relationship

Based on the teachings of Dr. Viktor Frankl, I have developed a pie-diagram to show how success, happiness, and fulfillment relate.

When we are successful and fulfilled, we are happy. When you define and work toward what being successful really means to you (deep, down inside), without any outside influence or trying to please someone else, you feel fulfilled as you go along. The result of going toward your vision is called happiness; it is a by-product.

When we are "successful" yet unfilled, we are unhappy. For example, say you achieve great success in your career, but you did it for the wrong reasons. Perhaps you defined success based on someone else's expectations, like maybe what your parents wanted you to become. You didn't do what you really wanted to do because you thought you wouldn't be accepted if you did. After you "woke-up," perhaps after going through a mid-life crisis, you "suddenly" understood why you were not happy, even though you had achieved. This leads to unhappiness, and possibly other undesirable behaviors, in an effort to compensate for your lack of happiness.

When we are unsuccessful and unfulfilled, we tend to get depressed. Nothing we do seems to work or give us any satisfaction. Perhaps you never defined success for yourself in the first place, and you have no idea what you want out of life. If you have no purpose, there's nothing you are going toward. You have, in effect, failed by definition and default. If you don't know what you want to accomplish, it's impossible for you to become fulfilled. If this keeps up, long term depression can turn into despair.

Finally, we have "delusion." When we feel fulfilled by what we do, without having or recognizing our true purpose, we are only deluding ourselves. An example of this could be a situation where you love your job, but you don't earn enough money to properly provide for your family. You are fulfilled by your work, but certainly not successful. You've failed your family. This individual is basically acting selfishly, and all kinds of problems could develop.

Are You An Optimist Or A Pessimist?

Have you ever heard the story of the little twin brothers, Harry and Larry? Harry was a pessimist and Larry was an optimist. The little pessimist was always complaining and very negative. The little optimist viewed everything through "rose-colored glasses." It was their birthday, and their father decided to test their attitudes. He bought every kind of toy imaginable for the pessimist: a new bike, a basketball, a rifle, and dozens of things that could give any little boy pleasure. For the optimist, a pile of horse manure was his only gift.

As soon as Harry, the pessimist, saw all of his beautiful gifts, he began to complain, "If I ride this bike on the street, I might wreck it and hurt myself. I know if I take this basketball outside, someone will probably steal it. This rifle is dangerous. I'll probably end up shooting somebody's window out." Harry went on-and-on with his deep negativity. He turned his birthday into gloom and doom. The little pessimist saw life in a negative light and found fault.

Then it was the little optimist's turn. When Larry saw the pile of horse manure with his name on it, he got excited. He began to run through the house looking in all the rooms, in the garage, and in the backyard. When his father caught him by the arm and asked, "Son, what are you looking for?" Larry replied, "Dad, with all the horse manure you gave me, I just know there's gotta be a pony around here somewhere!" The little optimist was an example of a person with an elevated attitude and enthusiasm. Optimists look for the good in people and situations.

What's "Realistic"?
Some people think they are recognizing reality when they think negatively. But when your idea of reality allows *only* for the negatives, your sense of reality is seriously flawed. Furthermore, positive outcomes are possible from negative situations when you look at them as opportunities. There's a silver lining behind every cloud, and you can't have a rainbow without rain. In other words, *realistic for you is whatever you believe.*

As an example, in the business world, patterns of *hiring* and *firing* have evolved. (Lay-off is sometimes a gentler term for firing.) The reduction of staff may be called "re-structuring," "down-sizing," "right-sizing," or eliminating departments. Such events, coupled with an employee's desire to make changes, means the average working person could experience three to four *career changes* or more over their lifetime. Be prepared to negotiate these "rapids-of-change."

"Firing" isn't as negative as it first appears. Can you picture yourself "fired-up" for all the good things that can come when you are free to make new choices? Whether the decision to move-on has been yours or not, it can turn out to be the best thing that ever happened to you. It can give you time to learn more about who you are and what you want. The people who make well-thought-out decisions about what comes next in their lives can reap great benefits from adversity. They may find the career, whether it's a job or a business, of their dreams. These people have an elevated attitude and enthusiasm. They face challenges with a sense of adventure. In other words, what they believe becomes realistic for them. They recognize and use adversity as an opportunity to move-on.

Can You Find The Sunny Spot On A Rainy Day?

Think of all the things people choose to be "down" about. Think of the weather. How many times do you hear people say, "I can't take this weather anymore." It doesn't matter whether it's sunshine or rain. Whatever the weather, if the same pattern goes on for awhile, you'll probably hear someone complain. When you hear those words, ask yourself, "Do I have a problem with my attitude? Am I allowing rainy weekends to negatively influence my attitude? What can I do about it? Ah ha! Maybe I'll spread that fertilizer on the lawn so the good earth can soak it up and really make my lawn green."

Ask yourself, "What one outrageously fun thing could I do to help me cope with another rainy weekend?" Why not reserve a suite with a hot tub and invite some friends to grab their swimsuits and drop by? They may be feeling the same way about the weather as you do. You'll provide the spark people depend on from their leaders. You could make the jacuzzi a "think tank" to brainstorm a business challenge. Or maybe you could develop a plan to support a worthy cause. Maybe you could just relax and share funny stories and jokes.

The point is, unconventional settings can stimulate creative thinking. When you elevate your attitude and enthusiasm, people around you are more likely to do the same, and creative thinking can flourish. You can help other people turn their negativity about the weather into a creative positive.

A word of warning. Elevating your attitude and enthusiasm does not mean endless "rah-rahing." You want to be genuine, and show a lot of respect for where other people are in their lives. Give people space to experience their challenges, acknowledge their situation, and gently uplift them with your encouragement.

Just as there is day and night, there are fruitful and fallow times in life, especially in the creative area. A time of tremendous growth is often followed by a period of introspection that can almost appear as dormancy. Recognize these situations as a time to regroup; a time to refresh and renew; a time to consider new objectives; or a time to prepare and strategize for your next challenge. During these times, when the fires of expectation are low, repairs can be made to the furnace. An elevated attitude and enthusiasm really shine through. They protect and shelter your hopes and dreams. As a leader, you help protect and shelter the faith and trust of those around you.

How "Attachment" Affects Your Attitude And Enthusiasm

When you are "attached" to a person, thing, idea, outcome or event, you are "holding-on" to your belief of how things "should" be. You may be unaware of other options or concerned about the unknown.   Being attached is unhealthy, and it shows you are inflexible, fearful, and anxious. It's like you're "hanging-on-for-dear-life," so to speak, and if things don't go your way, it'll be a tragedy! In other words, you don't have the faith to believe things will turn out in your best interest. This is a sign of insecurity and lack of confidence.

Attachments often occur in relationships. For example, say you finally find the person you want to marry. You may hang on to them desperately, hoping they won't leave. You may believe your overly attentive behavior is love. However, you may be "smothering" the person and depriving them of some much needed private time and the opportunity to stretch and be who they are. Attachment may seem endearing at first, but it can quickly become "old" and stifle the relationship. Attachment can lead to manipulation and other tactics that could drive the person away. This is the exact opposite of the desired outcome of a healthy, balanced relationship!

You can't force a successful relationship by being attached to it. Part of your responsibility is to "let go" of attachments by letting that person decide if they want to participate in the relationship, and to what degree. If they choose to participate, great! If they don't want it and you try to force it, you'll probably drive them away. Grow through the experience. Their not wanting a relationship may be the best thing that could happen. This may not seem true until later.

If you think being attached to someone makes you happy, you'll probably be in for a rude awakening. Nobody can make you happy; it's a personal choice. You can't get all of your emotional needs met by someone else either. Imagine being around a person with an unhappy, negative, taking attitude, who is trying to get all his emotional needs met by you! What an energy drain. Happiness is an attitude that you can carry around with you wherever you go. It comes from inside.

One way to let go of an attachment to an outcome is to ask yourself, "What is the worst thing that could possibly happen?" Then just accept it! Once you've done that, you'll be grateful for practically any result you get, as long as it's not the worst case scenario.

Another example of being attached might be when you apply for a promotion in your company. You may think that "without a doubt," the new job is the one for you. Being attached can be like a mental "latching-on." You may appear desperate and anxious. What do you do? Of course you want the job; it pays more. You'd have a bigger office and other perks. Who wouldn't want that? To "protect" yourself, you could adopt the attitude that "I *prefer* to be promoted to that job; however, I am not *attached* to it. I am flexible. I'm confident that if I don't get the promotion, another opportunity as good or better will come along." By not being attached, you're also less likely to feel disappointed if you don't get the job.

To maintain an elevated attitude and enthusiasm, it is crucial to learn to *let go of attachments and state preferences instead.* You can apply this approach to any area of your life where you may be "holding-on." Your new flexibility will help you adjust to the ebb and flow of life, which often has elements that are outside your control. You can then maintain an elevated attitude and enthusiasm throughout much of life's challenges. You could look at it like this: *What happens to you, happens for you!*

What Is The True Mark Of A Leader?

I have always been inspired by excellent leaders, beginning with my parents. They both had strong personalities, and set and worked for personal, family, business, and community goals. There were also adults in my extended family, teachers, and friends with similar qualities.

I enjoyed something of a leadership role early-on with my military peers. I first realized I had an ability to influence and help others to be motivated, in the summer between my sophomore and junior years at West Point. Every cadet has several options from which to choose a summer training session. I chose Cadet Troop Leadership Training and was sent to Schweinfurt, Germany to serve as a tank platoon leader for "C" Company, 2nd Armor Battalion, 64th Regiment. Still a cadet, I would experience the responsibilities of a 2nd Lieutenant. Pretty heady stuff, I thought.

I was ready to use some of the skills I was learning at West Point, so I jumped right in. I sincerely cared for the troops under my command and they knew it. My self-confidence was bolstered by their positive response to my leadership. My ability to lead boiled down to communicating positive expectations that we could accomplish whatever goal we set. I consciously conveyed my belief in them and saw them grow. The power of elevated attitude and enthusiasm worked.

At the end of that summer, the troops and I parted company, and I went back for my last two years at the Academy. I was elated that I was capable of being what I had set out to be: a leader who could inspire others to rise to challenges. The officers and soldiers with whom I spent the summer, openly expressed their admiration of my abilities and the path I had chosen. This experience is, to this day, a powerful reminder of the link between leadership, attitude, and enthusiasm. I believe excellent leadership is only possible with an elevated attitude and enthusiasm.

As a young soldier, I was happy about being given the opportunity to grow as a leader. For all that I remember with a golden glow, I also remember certain negatives. I wouldn't compare them to the difficulties of Valley Forge, but they were tests of my ability to elevate my attitude and enthusiasm and stay positively motivated. Not everyone around me had the same attitude. Most people are negative at times, but some are habitually negative. I'd rather be surrounded by habitually positive people. Encouraging people around you to change their attitudes can be challenging, but it is the mark of a leader. To the degree I was able to do that, I became a better leader that summer.

Get Rejuvenated By Elevating Your Attitude and Enthusiasm!

Attitude and enthusiasm are like static electricity. They can rub off and cling to someone else. Attitude is your first indicator for success, while enthusiasm helps you sustain it.

If you are a salesperson, do you have a positive or negative attitude when you call on someone? If it's negative, it's highly unlikely you're going to close the deal. When you get home, is your attitude positive or negative? If it's negative, you're less likely to get much done. Also, you'll feel miserable while doing your work.

If you ever feel your attitude and enthusiasm slipping, it's time to go back to this step for a refreshment of your positive energies. Dr. Norman Vincent Peale wrote a great book called, *Enthusiasm Makes The Difference.* Your elevated attitude and enthusiasm can produce seemingly magical results at home, work, play, or wherever you go. They do make a difference.

Get some of this special magic going in your life. Elevate your attitude and enthusiasm and you'll open up to the exceptional things that go on around you every day. Open your eyes to the remarkable opportunities that are out there for people with elevated attitudes and enthusiasm.

Elevate your attitude and enthusiasm and you'll be well on your way to becoming happier and more successful; you'll be better able to make a difference.

"No Excuse!"Action Plan To"Elevate Your Attitude and Enthusiasm"

1.   Learn how to express, rather than impress! How you express yourself largely determines the ideas and feelings people have about you.

2.   Smile more often and be enthusiastic. When you do, others will usually smile back. You'll brighten their day, as well as your own. It's contagious.

3.   Maintain a positive mental attitude, no matter what, and people will want to be around you. It's your attitude and not your aptitude that determines your altitude in life. Whether you find your work a bore or a pleasure depends largely on your attitude and often not on the task itself.

4.   Talk positive to yourself. Circumstances can affect your attitude only if you let them. Life is 10% what you're given and 90% how you react to it. It's a choice.

5.   Be a good finder. Behind every adversity is the seed of an equal or greater benefit. Look at life as an opportunity rather than a struggle; you'll have a more positive attitude and greater enthusiasm.

6.   Insist on your worth and take action to fulfill your potential. No one can make you feel inferior without your consent.

7.   Change your perception of people with negative attitudes; their intentions may be good. Look for the joy, the positives, and the benefits. Realize they may be hurting, and you can feel kindly toward them. How you perceive what you believe will help structure what you achieve. Encourage the people around you; it's the mark of a leader.

8.   Get "fired-up" over change. Remember, you'll always get what you've always got, if you continue to do what you've always done. The only constant in life is change. Embrace it and get excited about it. In order to change your life, you need to make some changes in your life.

9.   Give people space to experience their challenges; acknowledge their situation, and gently uplift them with your encouragement. Elevating your attitude and enthusiasm does not mean endless "rah-rahing." Be genuine, and respect where other people are in their lives, and meet them at their need.

10.   Don't be attached to anything. It's a sign of anxiousness, inflexibility and fear, and will drive people away. Be a little "hard-to-get." State preferences instead.

CONTROL YOURSELF AND YOU'LL CONTROL YOUR LIFE

*Many people have the ambition to succeed; they may
even have a special aptitude for the job. And yet
they do not move ahead. Why? Perhaps they
think that since they can master the job,
there is no need to master themselves.*
JOHN STEVESON

*He that hath no rule over his own spirit is like a city
that is broken down, and without walls.*
THE *BIBLE*, PROVERBS

No man is free who is not master of himself.
EPICTETUS

*It isn't until you come to a spiritual understanding of
who you are—not necessarily a religious
feeling, but deep down, the spirit within—that you
can begin to take control.*
OPRAH WINFREY

Most powerful is he who has himself in his own power.
SENECA

*Self-control is the quality that distinguished
the fittest to survive.*
GEORGE BERNARD SHAW

*What we do upon some great occasion will probably
depend on what we already are; and what we are will
be the result of previous years of self-discipline.*
H.P. LIDDON

*There is little that can withstand a man
who can conquer himself.*
LOUIS XIV

*He that would be superior to external influences must
first become superior to his own passions.*
SAMUEL JOHNSON

*He that is slow to anger is better than the mighty;
and he that ruleth his spirit is better than
he that taketh a city.*
THE *BIBLE*, PROVERBS

Chapter 8

SUSTAIN SELF-CONTROL
Fourth Step Of The THESAURUS Factor

Take Charge Of The Battle Within

Self-responsibility is the essence of self-control. The key word here is SELF. *Being in control of anything most often depends on how well you are able to control yourself. Webster's Dictionary* defines self-control as "restraint exercised over one's own impulses, emotions, or desires."

What happens when someone loses control? It changes the atmosphere immediately. In dangerous situations, it spells disaster for anyone who lacks self-control, especially a leader. Even situations that don't start out as dangerous can become so.

Self-control is the testing ground for how effective you are in employing the other principles of the *THESAURUS Factor*. Your self-esteem and how well you know yourself largely determines your degree of professionalism in your career and maturity, as well as how you deal with others in general. These attributes are related to your self-control. If you have a negative attitude, you will probably not have nearly the degree of professionalism and self-control in thought, word, and deed, as you would if you had a positive attitude.

If you're dwelling on the past, blaming and complaining, whining and moaning, it's difficult to maintain self-control. Your professionalism and determination to take charge of your destiny slips away. It's a choice, not a chance!

Self-control is a gauge of where you are at all times. How you handle yourself, day-in and day-out, is a measure of your self-control. Self-discipline, a part of self-control, is your first "test" for all the steps along the *Staircase*. *Webster's Dictionary* defines self-discipline as "... controlling oneself or one's desires, actions, habits, etc."

If you perceive yourself as weak, and you lack self-control and self-discipline, you are also likely to let circumstances influence you negatively. If you think you are weak, you may lose control when you're bombarded by things that test your professionalism, maturity, self-control, and knowledge of who you are.

When you perceive yourself as strong, have control of yourself and exercise discipline, you can "rise-to-the-occasion." Circumstances just won't matter. Did anyone ever say to you, "Well, under the circumstances..."? That's really just an excuse! Did you ever say that to someone? Weren't you just blaming the environment; using it as an excuse?

There have been brilliant military officers who have damaged their careers and lost the respect of their peers, superiors, and subordinates. They didn't maintain self-control at a social event or while on duty. This may have occurred because they were frustrated by someone else's failure to meet their expectations, or they may have been under the influence of alcohol. Regardless of how exceptionally they may have performed at their job, it no longer mattered to those observing their behavior when they "lost-it." *Self-control becomes jeopardized when you let your emotions control your behavior.* Loss of self-control can damage your career and put everything you've worked for at risk.

When a crisis occurs at work, how do you react? Do you get emotional or angry and lose your "cool"? Do you go absolutely bonkers and look for someone to blame? Or do you look to see why the crisis occurred in the first place? Do you maintain a sense of professionalism, contain your emotions, and then respond to the crisis? Take care of the situation, solve the crisis if you can, and move-on. After that, you can concern yourself with who's responsible or why the crisis occurred to begin with. In other words, wait until the dust settles! By the way, this is also true for handling crises at home.

For life to be well-lived, we need to exercise self-control. Yet there are so many talented, attractive, and accomplished people who get near the top (the highest position of rank or achievement) without developing self-control. That's just it. They only get *near* the top. Because they lack self-control, they often blow their chances for true success. Their out-of-control emotional reactions get them into trouble. If they make it to the top and they lose self-control, they will lose the respect of their peers and the people they oversee. They may also lose their position.

Self-control is very much a measure of where you are within yourself. How much do you believe in you? How much are you in touch with how you feel about yourself? If you don't have an excellent relationship with yourself, how can you have one with anyone else? How's your self-esteem? The respect you feel for yourself largely determines how much you maintain your sense of self-control; it is synonymous with your happiness.

Sustaining Self-Control Is Easy When We Eliminate Anger

Can someone or some event make you angry, cause you to lose control, or otherwise control your emotions? It is a common belief that there's no doubt about it; people and events can make us angry. But wait a minute. Let's stop and think about it. Is that really true? You may hear people say that "all the time," but is it really true? Of course not! That would be real scary if someone or something had that kind of power over you, now wouldn't it?

Consider this example: What do you get when you cut open a lemon and squeeze it? Lemon juice, of course. So, what do you get when you "cut open" and "squeeze" an angry person? What comes out of them? Anger, of course. If there's no anger inside of them, no anger can be squeezed out!

People or events can't make us angry; all they can do is trigger the anger that's already inside. When we're self-responsible, we own all of our emotions. Nobody can "do it" to us. Self-responsible people don't put the burden of their happiness on someone else. They know it's a matter of their choice.

Anger can be an excuse to blame, rather than accepting responsibility. It may be the stance of a victim, with its root being unforgiveness. It often stems from harboring hatred, resentment, and disappointment, which comes from an unwillingness to let go of the past.

Anger is also used to dominate, control, or manipulate. When people are honestly and openly communicating their needs, wants, and values to determine a mutually beneficial course of action, anger is less likely to be triggered.

If you get angry easily, you probably have some unresolved issues. You need to identify them, let go of them, and move-on. Go back and re-read the first step, Totally Forgive. Forgiveness is the greatest way to eliminate anger and make sustaining self-control easy. When you have no anger inside you, no one can "rattle-your-cage." You'll maintain your "cool" and sustain self-control.

Note that a conscious "show-of-anger," used in a deliberately proactive way to make a point or get someone's attention, is different. With some people, for example, it's sometimes necessary to raise your voice to get through to them. Here, you are well aware of what's going on. You're not just reacting. Nobody triggered your anger. You're just taking charge of the situation.

The "Slap-Happy," Unhappy General

This story about General George S. Patton is a good example of how his self-control weakened, jeopardizing his career, and undermining the respect of others.

Surely, Patton had achieved legendary status as a military genius. But what happened during the two famous "slapping incidents," when he lost his self-control, also went down in history. Unfortunately, they tainted the reputation he strived so diligently to earn.

The first incident took place on a hot August afternoon in Italy in 1943. Patton arrived at the 93rd Evacuation Hospital in Sicily to visit the wounded. This was his usual practice. In the tent were about ten to fifteen soldiers who had suffered casualties. The first five or six he talked to had experienced battle wounds. He asked each man about their condition, commended them for their excellent fighting, and wished them a speedy recovery.

Patton then approached one patient who said he was sick with a high fever. The General dismissed him without comment. The next patient was sitting huddled and shivering. When asked what his trouble was, the man replied, "It's my nerves," and began to sob. The soldier was suffering from the combat fatigue called "shell shock."

The General screamed at him, "What did you say?" The soldier replied, "It's my nerves. I can't stand the shelling any more." He was still sobbing.

The General yelled at him, "Your nerves, hell, you're just a Goddamned coward, you yellow son-of-a-bitch." He then slapped the soldier and said, "Shut up that Goddamned crying. I won't have these brave men here who have been shot seeing a yellow bastard sitting here crying." He struck the man again, knocking his helmet liner off and into the next tent. He then turned to the Receiving Officer and yelled, "Don't you admit this yellow bastard, there's nothing the matter with him. I won't have the hospital cluttered up with these sons-of-bitches who haven't got the guts to fight."

He turned to the soldier again, who was managing to "sit-at-attention," though shaking all over, and said, "You're going back to the front lines and you may get shot and killed, but you're going to fight. If you don't, I'll stand you up against the wall and have a firing squad kill you on purpose." "In fact," he said, reaching for his pistol, "I ought to shoot you myself, you Goddamned whimpering coward." As he went out of the ward he was still yelling back at the Receiving Officer to "send that yellow son-of-a-bitch back to the front lines."

The second slapping incident happened much the same way. When a solder complained of shell shock, Patton struck the man across the face with his gloves, yelling, "I won't have these brave boys seeing such a bastard babied."

Patton's suppressed hysteria was prompted by tremendous stress. It was never easy for him to see the wounded, yet visiting hospitals was his duty. He forced himself to carry out that burden. He had to keep a tight grip on himself to avoid breaking into tears over men who had sacrificed their lives for their country, as well as for him.

Other pressures hammered at him. He resented the need to submit to British command. He was upset because the enemy, in possession of favorable defense terrain, was dictating the course of the battle. He was angry because Allied aircraft had bombed American troops by mistake on several occasions. Those were just a few of the battle thorns lodged in the General's side.

Above all, Patton was tired due to what he called "intense mental and physical activity." Driving himself savagely in the heat of summer, despite his age, he was close to exhaustion. This is something many of us need to be careful about. Sometimes, rather than assuming all the responsibility of a project or activity ourselves, we may need to delegate the responsibility and "share the load." Furthermore, the battle within himself wore him down, loosening his grip on himself.

As a result of his loss of self-control, Patton suffered an even more devastating outcome. He lost the confidence of his commander, General Dwight Eisenhower. Though he was spared a general court-martial, Patton was denied the choice combat assignments as well as further promotions. Eventually, when the story of the slapping incidents leaked to the public, he lost much of the respect of the American people.

The purpose of this chapter, then, is to help you learn to take command of yourself. When the going gets tough, you'll be able to prevent a "slapping incident" of your own.

Are You A Doer Or A Watcher?

Doers have a vision. Watchers just observe. Doers have a dream and act on it. Watchers toss and turn. To be successful, you need a vision. The *Bible* says, "Where there is no vision, the people perish." All successful people know where they're going, and they take action. When they are faced with a challenge, they are more likely to be clear and focused in their response and exert self-control.

When you have a challenge, look beyond it to what you want for yourself, your business or job, and your family. It's generally a mistake to just react to things. Your self-control is a measure of how well you *respond* to challenges; it has to do with responsibility.

Self-Control At Home

Of all the places in our daily life, where do you think self-control is most important? At home! But is that where it's practiced most? We may be "nice" to people all day long. We may put on a facade at work, even if we don't care for someone or something, just to keep the job or the employee. You might meet someone who behaves obnoxiously, but because you're at work you do your best to maintain a sense of professionalism and self-control.

We may be patient with co-workers or staff all day long, but what may happen when we get home? We may pull into the driveway, open the car door, and our self-control may fly "right-out-the-window." You get home and the last thing you may want to be is nice. You've been nice all day. You may feel you don't have any more self-control left. All you may want to do is go open that refrigerator, grab something to drink, sit down in front of the TV, and "zone" for awhile. The slightest interruption to this may "set-you-off," no matter who does it. Boom! It may have been just that easy to lose control.

It's difficult to justify losing control with your family. Self-control affects every part of family life. Maintaining integrity, sincerity, and maturity is essential so you can correctly communicate your feelings at home. It's hard to justify not doing that at home, while you may be doing it for a complete stranger at work. How come? Is money more important to you than your family? Only you can decide that.

If arguments and anger erupt every time a challenging situation occurs at home, it becomes more difficult to continue the relationship(s). It's far better to prevent the anger, otherwise, family relationships may be jeopardized. Who wants to be abused or accused? What would cause you to want to deal with that? Just avoid the anger. Resolve the situation with kindness and move-on. If you have an occasional flare-up, apologize and work it out without additional anger.

Self-Control At Work

Self-control in thought, word, and deed is so important. When you have a task at hand, do you have the discipline and desire to get it done? Can you maintain that sense of professionalism and control? Are you decisive? Self-control is essential because it affects every aspect of the operation of an organization. How do you think self-control affects your organization?

If your boss reacts with anger every time you present a situation to him, do you want to continue the relationship? Do you feel inclined to be as helpful to that person as you had in the past? If you are the boss, and it is you who is reacting angrily, how do you think you are affecting your relationships by your lack of self-control? Self-control deals with communication, either self-talk or with others, whether it's at home or work. Think about it.

The same thing can happen throughout the organization. If you don't communicate effectively with people by listening to them and letting them share their ideas and concerns, you're going to have unwanted situations. You can discover most of the problems in an organization by listening, asking questions, and listening again.

People who lack self-control don't listen, or at best, listen ineffectively. They may be more interested in what's on their mind rather than what the other person is saying. If anger erupts at work, use self-control to avoid "fueling-the-fire" and igniting the potential for emotional hurt and negative feelings. Listen to what people are saying. We need to be excellent listeners to be excellent leaders who can diffuse "hot" situations.

If we intervene, it is best to do so using a calm, soft tone of voice. We want to allow others to "get-it-all-off-their-chest" as we ask if there is anything else bothering them. As we continue to maintain self-control, we keep asking if there's anything more they'd like to say.

After they have "cleaned-their-slate," we can go in and share what we believe is helpful to resolve the situation.

If the leadership isn't consistent in making correct self-controlled decisions in business (and at home), there is likely to be a breakdown. No organization (or family) does well when its members are frequently emotional, angry, and focused on the negative. If there's little or no self-control, you're not going to move ahead effectively.

Three Ways To Maintain Self-Control

How do you maintain self-control? At times it can be challenging. When you deal with the same people every day, it's going to be tested. You could become a little "short-fused" if you aren't skillful. **Here are three steps to help you maintain a measure of self-control in everything you do:**

1. Listen before you think. The most effective salespeople, for instance, are those who listen the most. How can you sell a product or service to someone if you don't take the time to listen to their needs? If you are an employer and you don't listen to your employees before you make a decision, you may not know the whole story. You are reducing your chances of making an informed decision or developing the correct solution. You may need to ask questions to get more information. Listen to their answers carefully.

If you immediately let your emotions override practicality, how can you create an appropriate solution to a problem? If you "short-circuit" (interrupt) everyone along the way, you're likely to create *more* problems. Listen *before* you think. It is important to listen well and gather the information before your emotions and your self-indulgences can interrupt. Then you'll have a chance to think and decide how you're going to solve that problem. *Listen.*

2. Think before you assess. Collect the data, then assess the situation. If it's a very emotional situation, try to separate emotion from fact. *Think.*

3. Assess before you act. After you collect the data, it's time to make an assessment. After that, implement whatever policy or action you're going to take. *Assess.*

Certainly, there's nothing revolutionary here. We all need to remember these steps, as simple as they may seem. It's just that we may get so caught-up in everything that's going on day-to-day, we may need to remind ourselves.

When you come to the end of the day and go home and reflect on it, do you generally feel satisfied that you accomplished what you wanted? Were you focused and self-controlled? Do you feel each day you are making progress toward fulfilling your purpose? Are you working on fulfilling your definition of success and heading toward your dreams? How do you feel about yourself in these areas?

Do You Feel All Stressed-Out?

Did you ever watch a hamster running in a circular wheel? Is he going anywhere? He's running and working up a sweat. His eyes are "bugging-out," but he's going nowhere. Have you ever felt like that? If you have, you are not alone.

Where are people going during rush hour every day? They may be working hard, but where are they going? Are they heading toward their vision, or are they in a rut? Are they feeling all-stressed-out, just waiting for the weekend? What's the difference between a rut and a grave? You could almost think of a rut as a grave with no ends! Surveys show that at least 70% of the people hate their work or some aspect of it. No wonder many people aren't happy. Work is usually such a large part of life. If there's no fulfillment for you in your work, it can lead to problems. It can also affect your self-control.

It's important to use your time wisely, investing it in things that are going to be productive for you. Self-control helps you stay on track to get the outcomes you want. It helps you maintain focus and a sense of direction. When you know where you're going and you work on it every day, you can avoid feeling all-stressed-out. Stress often results from lack of direction and self-control in life. Purpose gives your life meaning and makes it easier to maintain self-control.

Is Your Clock Too Fast?

A talented basketball player found success in his game when he learned to slow down. Before that, all his natural talent, plus years of excellent coaching, practicing, and playing, had not enabled him to reach his potential. He knew it was because, as he put it, his "clock-was-too-fast." Some people call it "hurry sickness."

He had developed the self-control which enabled him to focus his energies on the skills he needed to be a formidable player. He had the self-responsibility to maintain the physical conditioning that allowed him to come to every basketball game in peak condition. He was missing the ability to be on the court playing *his* game, to be proactive, to never let the game play him.

It all came together for this young man when he learned to let his clock tick "slower." He learned to keep working the ball and scanning the court. He just looked for the right opportunity for that "perfect" pass to the free agent poised for a shot. He became an excellent point guard and led his team to championships by keeping his clock steady.

This timing factor is also true for other areas of your life. Some people confuse self-control with denial. *Equate self-control with your willingness to patiently await results.* Getting what you want is much sweeter when you know you had the wisdom, faith, and patience to wait (while diligently working) for the jackpot. This is far better than later realizing you "cashed-your-chips-in" too soon for a minimal and often self-defeating payoff. William J. McGrane, CPAE, in his book *Brighten Your Day With Self-Esteem*, said that research shows it takes an average of 15 years to be an "overnight success."

Self-Controlling A Crisis

The amount of self-control used in a real crisis, or a crisis created by someone out-of-control, often determines the chances for a desirable outcome. A person in control lays anger and frustration aside while the situation is studied. He evaluates the possible consequences of any remedial action. Finding the cause(s) can then help define the remedy. Measures may then be taken, if possible, to avoid a future occurrence.

Personalities become incidental when the search for meaningful response is led by a person with self-control. In fact, as in Patton's case, it is often a sign of "burn-out" to have a normally capable leader lose self-control in a moment of crisis. Such behavior inevitably worsens any situation because the morale of the group being led is negatively impacted by this sign of weakness.

Like that basketball player, a leader needs to set his clock on "slow" to exercise an unusual amount of self-control. Gifted people are often impatient. They may be accustomed to quick results from their efforts. They may feel impatient when they experience a lag in time from when they want something to when they get it. An effective leader is patient; he gives people time to grow. Remember, you can't push a rope, but you can gently pull a wet noodle!

Patience Is One Of The Greatest Virtues

Patience is another aspect of self-control. *Patience is a virtue. Haste makes waste.* These old clichés are more important today than ever before. Many people are looking for instant gratification. A couple of generations have grown-up with TV, fast food, credit cards, and "buy now/pay later" thinking. Many people do not exercise the self-control or self-restraint required to accept the delayed gratification normally necessary to achieve success.

True success takes time. It doesn't happen overnight. This is a *Staircase*. There's no elevator here. We climb it one-step-at-a-time. Patience is essential as we journey through life.

The Three Little Pigs

Remember the story of "The Three Little Pigs"? What does it tell us about human beings? It seems that the value of the story lies in its message that foresight, patience, and self-control may not keep the wolf away from your door. However, if he does show up, you will be better able to protect yourself.

All three pigs had the same options. The mission was the same: Build yourself a shelter, a place you can live in now and in the future. The brother who chose to build his house of straw had the easiest time finding building materials. He also put his house together the quickest of all. The brother who chose wood took more time and exerted more effort. He had trees to fell and cut, even before he could begin construction. The brother who built with bricks had a kiln to fashion, a fire to tend, and bricks to mortar. His house took the longest to build, but it was also the strongest.

All of a sudden they were all together; the three brothers now living safely in the brick house. They felt secure when the wolf came and bragged about how his huffing and puffing destroyed their straw and wood homes. They knew he couldn't do anything to the brick.

The two brothers had lost their homes because they didn't have enough self-discipline to build the best. They wanted "instant" gratification.

The brick-building brother was about to be tested. True to form, he sat beside his fire, stoking it. He knew, in his quiet, self-controlled way, that the wolf's lack of self-control would bring about his own end.

The wolf, frustrated by his inability to get results, unable to destroy the little pig's brick home, lost his self-control. In a last ditch effort to get the pigs, he plunged down the chimney into a boiling vat. It was all over for the wolf!

The fable is a tale of patience. The little pig who built with brick had patience and self-discipline. He wasn't just building a house, he was building self-control. He prepared himself to survive the showdown. Instead of the wolf eating the little pigs, they ate him. Develop enough self-control and your "enemies" may make themselves a gift to you!

Build your success with purpose, patience, and foresight. Build a solid foundation, and it could be like having a brick house. If you try to get it quickly, it rarely works. "Get-rich-quick" schemes are often like the house of straw. They're quick and they don't last very long. True success, the achievement of what is most important in your life, takes time. Look forward to the journey and give yourself time to succeed.

Anyone who plays the lottery has a greater chance of being struck by lightning than they do winning the lottery. Think about it. Playing the lottery is no way to achieve success.

There's a great opportunity for wealth and achievement. What you choose to do depends on how you define success. If being financially secure is one of your ideas of success, and you can achieve it without stepping on other people, that's fine. Sometimes people crush other people along the way to so-called success. If such a person has a self-centered attitude, they're not likely to maintain much self-control. They're probably not very concerned about other people; they don't listen, think, and assess about others' needs. They are more focused on where they want to go and what they need to do. True success, financial or otherwise, comes as a result of helping other people, and this requires patience. Practice being patient until it becomes a habit.

Sometimes I feel impatient too, and my behavior is not perfect. Nobody has perfect behavior all the time. Our attitude and self-esteem, in many cases, determines how much self-control we have. I feel more patient when my attitude is elevated and my self-esteem is intact. I feel freer to be more other-centered and flexible.

You may have heard that this is the "entertainment generation." Many people are constantly seeking instant gratification and entertainment. This requires little or no self-control. How could you be motivated to develop your mind's capacity, imagination and creativity if you're always passively involved, as with television? Television can be a wonderful way to learn about things and be entertained, but it can also be a negative influence and time waster when it's abused. It is important to use self-control here, too.

Have The Self-Control To Think

The main purpose of this book is to help you think. It's to encourage you to open your mind more and remove yourself, just a little bit, from what's going on out there. This can be a time for you to take a look inside to reflect and review some of the principles of success that can make a difference in your life. Only you know what you could lose if you choose not to participate in the adventure of "No Excuse!" living.

You Need To Have A Dream

If you get all caught-up in reaching for the stars, and you think it's going to happen overnight, you're probably going to be disappointed, and you may do nothing at all. Have dreams. Dreams are powerful because those who conquer are those who believe they can. Emerson once said, "Those who achieve, believe they can achieve." Having a dream will help you maintain self-control.

Maintain self-control and a sense of professionalism in everything you do, and you're likely to find that people will follow and respect you. To be an effective leader, you need to exercise self-control. As mentioned before, on rare occasions anger, or "losing-it" can be an effective tool, provided it's not done at the expense of other people. To be effective as a parent, a leader, and in your behavior in general, you need to maintain certain levels of consistency. If you're not consistent in your actions, people may be guarded around you and misunderstand your communication. Others may assume a defensive position. Your self-control can help you be consistent and better understood.

The greatest potential for control exists where action takes place. Internally we have great potential. When it comes to self-control, it's very important to listen to that "inner voice" (or "gut feeling") we all have. This is your intuition. Trust that voice. You'll find that experience validates it. With a sense of self-control and patience, you'll find that when you do make a decision, your intuition can have quite a favorable impact on your potential to succeed.

We Live In Acres Of Diamonds

One of Earl Nightingale's most popular programs, *Lead the Field*, has a great little story called "Acres of Diamonds." Written by Russell Conwell, founder of Temple University, it's about an African farm owner back in the late 1800's. He heard of many other farmers all across the continent who became wealthy because of the diamond mines. There was a big "diamond rush" going on.

As the story goes, the farmer was so enthusiastic about making a fortune that he actually sold his farm to another farmer and went on his merry way to find wealth and happiness. Well, after years and years of searching for diamonds and not finding any, he gave up. In fact, he became so discouraged that he finally went into a river and drowned himself.

The main point of the story began when the second farmer who bought the farm was walking around the property one day and noticed a bright, shiny object in the creek. He picked it up and was amazed at its size and brilliance. He took it into his house and set it on his mantel for display.

A few days later a friend stopped by, saw the stone, and asked the farmer where he found it. He said he found the stone in the creek, where there were many others just like it. To the amazement of the farmer, his friend told him it was a diamond.

The farm was loaded with diamonds. The original farmer who drowned himself had looked for riches on the outside, rather than looking on his own land. All the resources were there. All the wealth he could have hoped for was right there in his own backyard. Instead of taking the time to look at what he had on his own land, he looked outside.

Success is Primarily "An Inside Job"

We may fail to look inside ourselves. Instead, we may go outside searching for what we want. We might look for the external things where we can make the quick buck or get a quick fix. We could be tempted to look for where we believe it can happen the easiest and quickest, when in all honesty, true success takes time.

Some of the greatest and most fundamental resources are right there within you. Take the opportunity to tap into them. Find those wonderful principles that you know are inside you. Success is primarily an inside job. It begins with you, even though people, places, or things can be helpful as you work toward what you want. Many people mistakenly think their success depends primarily on circumstances and other external factors, rather than what's inside themselves.

Someone once said, "People quit five minutes before the miracle." Have you ever looked back sometimes and wished you had taken a little more time? Did you ever say to yourself, "If I had only exercised a little more self-control, I'd be further along"? Did you ever regret not having more patience with someone or some activity? Could you have achieved that dream, a success or accomplishment you desired, if only you had just kept going?

Success is mind-made, not man-made. What your mind creates and how you perceive it is all based on how you think. The success you will achieve in your life will be based largely on how you think. Self-control and patience are virtues that make a big difference in determining whether or not you live the life you want. Look for the diamonds inside of you. Look for what you already have inside and run with it.

Bringing It All Home

When you give yourself time to succeed, and grow personally in the process, the skills you acquire along the way help you maintain that success. If you lose your success for some reason, these skills will help enable you to build success again.

Ending your frustration with other people is a glorious thing to do for yourself and them. Anything that helps you do that frees you from the fretting that so often accompanies failure. It makes your life so much easier when you are well-prepared with a self-control mindset. You can then handle anyone or any adversity that may come your way.

Self-control is essential for a leader. Without it you'll lose credibility, and it is unlikely anyone will want to follow you. If you can't control yourself, you'll never be able to successfully lead anyone. And since you lead by example, the best way for you to teach others self-control is to practice it yourself.

Say you are a parent who comes home from work exhausted. You need to know how well-equipped you are to deal with the demands of children who are genuinely in need. They need food, comfort, playfulness, attention, and love. And remember, your spouse is likely to need some help or attention too.

Self-control is one of the most important qualities for parents to develop. Children gain many of their perceptions about life when they observe their parents. A parent in control of himself will make a positive difference in a child's life. So again, self-control becomes a matter of preparation and pacing. Come home with some reserve energy for this important time of day, this important time of life.

Use your self-control calmly; give fair warning to loved ones. When you hug someone say, "I've had a very busy day, it's good to be home. I'd love to spend a little quiet time with you." Or, you may want to tell your family that you need to take a short nap first. That's a lot different than saying, "Leave me alone. Can't you see I've had a rough day?"

If we, like the wise little pig, have done our homework in developing self-control, our home can be a secure haven where happiness abounds.

"No Excuse!" Action Plan To "Sustain Self-Control"

1. Maintain self-control at all times. In a crisis it'll enable you to operate professionally, solve it if you can, and move-on. You'll maintain credibility, and people are likely to follow and respect you. Self-control is essential for leadership.

2. Eliminate anger from your life; then exercising self-control becomes easier. Anger is an excuse to blame; it's the stance of a victim. Accept responsibility and forgive, and your anger will go away.

3. Here are three steps to help you maintain self-control. 1) Listen before you think; 2) Think before you assess, and; 3) Assess before you act. Remember these steps the next time you find yourself in a challenging situation.

4. Maintain self-control when you get home from work. It is likely that your family relationships are the most precious ones you have. Bring your kind nature home with you.

5. Listen to what people say, and ask them questions. It's a great way to recognize them and show them you care. They're likely to love you for it.

6. Find the working pace that's best for you, and respect that of others. Self-control is your willingness to patiently wait for results, while working diligently toward them. "Overnight" success generally takes about 15 years. Anything worthwhile takes time. Be patient.

THOMAS JEFFERSON'S RULES OF CONDUCT

Never put off til' tomorrow what you can do today.
Never trouble another for what you can do yourself.
Never spend money before you have it.
Never buy anything you do not
want because it is cheap.
Take care of your change;
Dollars will take care of themselves.
Pride costs us more than thirst, hunger, and cold.
We seldom repent for having eaten too little.
Nothing is troublesome that one does
of his own volition.
How much pain never-occurred evils cost us.
Take things all the time by their smooth handle.
Think as you please, and let others as well,
to prevent any disputes.
When annoyed, count 10 before you speak.
If very annoyed, count 100.

THOMAS JEFFERSON

HONESTY IS THE BEST POLICY

*I hope I shall always possess firmness and virtue
enough to maintain what I consider the most enviable
of all titles, the character of an "Honest Man."*
GEORGE WASHINGTON

*To make your children capable of honesty
is the beginning of education.*
JOHN RUSKIN

No legacy is so rich as honesty.
SHAKESPEARE

An honest man is the noblest work of God.
ALEXANDER POPE

An excuse is a thin shell of truth, stuffed with a lie.
AUTHOR UNKNOWN

*People suffer all their life long, under the foolish super-
stition that they can be cheated. But it is impossible
for a person to be cheated by anyone but himself.*
RALPH WALDO EMERSON

*Honesty is the single most important factor having
a direct bearing on the final success of an
individual, corporation, or product.*
ED MCMAHON

*There are only three things necessary to succeed: first,
normal intelligence; second, determination; and third,
absolute honesty. One cannot be a little dishonest—
it's all the way or nothing.*
WILLIAM JAMES, FOUNDER OF BOY'S TOWN

*As a father said to his son in Hamlet: This above all;
to thine ownself be true, and it must follow, as the
night the day, thou canst not then be false to any man.*
SHAKESPEARE

Chapter 9

ALWAYS BE HONEST
First Part Of The Fifth Step Of
The THESAURUS Factor

Honesty Is The Best Policy

And now we come to the "A" step: Always Be Honest/Always Dream and Set Goals. This is essential.

I could have just discussed Always Dream and Set Goals and skipped Always Be Honest, but nothing in your quest for success will matter if you are not honest. No matter what you do throughout the rest of the *Staircase,* or how many attempts you make at achieving success, do it honestly. No matter how many people you deal with, or how many jobs or businesses you have, if you operate dishonestly, you'll never feel respect for yourself or your achievements.

Emerson once said, "You can't do wrong without suffering wrong." Honest success is crucial. What are you all about? When you're honest with yourself, you'll be more likely to be honest with others. If you're dishonest with yourself, it's very difficult to be honest with others. Live honestly. *True success is honest success.*

The biggest failures that occur in life have not been in business; the real tragedies have been moral failures. People who have been at the top of their careers with everything they've ever wanted, everything society would consider success, like money, fame, prestige and power, have sometimes lost it all. How many people can you think of who have been at the "top," who got there by either lying or cheating, in some fashion or another, and then lost everything? That's why it's so important to always be honest. When you are honest with yourself and others, people are more likely to be comfortable in dealing with you because they're likely to trust you.

Have you set your goals honestly? Have you honestly acknowledged you've attained them or admitted you've failed? A satisfying life depends on honestly knowing what you want out of life for and from yourself and others. If you are unwilling to do the work of discovering that and stating it clearly, you'll probably find it difficult to be honest with yourself about other things. This implies you may live in a world of your own constantly shifting values and desires. Dishonesty, with yourself as well as with others, can cause you to take many slippery roads. Dishonesty causes inconsistency, instability, and fear.

Most all of us have dealt with people who were dishonest with us. When the truth is ultimately known, as it always is, we may feel like the "rug-has-been-pulled-out-from-under-us." Dishonest people slip and slide in many directions, avoiding the truth and evading people they are deceiving. There are no resting places for dishonest people.

This step on the *Staircase* is a resting place for people who understand the values and benefits of an honest life. I believe you will value it because you realize that the only way to stay honest is to stop and take stock from time-to-time. It is essential to honestly re-examine your goals and desired outcomes to see how close you have come to achieving them. Honest self-evaluation will tell you if you are going to "keep-on-keeping-on" in pursuit of them.

Always Act Like "Honest Abe"

Did you ever wonder how Abe Lincoln earned the nickname, "Honest Abe"? For one thing, he stuck to his values. He knew how important it was to remain true to himself, and he carried out his goals earnestly and to the letter.

In March 1833, before he decided to become a lawyer, Lincoln and William F. Berry had a grocery store and then obtained a license "to keep tavern" in New Salem, Illinois. But trade was slow on the new frontier, and Abe was pretty much a failure as a merchant.

"The business," Abe said, "did nothing but get deeper and deeper in debt." It probably didn't surprise Berry that the debt was mounting; he dipped his cup into the whiskey barrel at every opportunity. Lincoln hated drinking. He said liquor left him feeling "flabby and undone." But Berry consumed enough for both of them.

He then sold the business to William and Alexander Trent. By January 1835, Berry had drunk himself into the grave. The Trents left town, taking the merchandise and leaving the debt. Abe was then liable for these debts, as well as his own. He called the $1,100 he owed, "The National Debt." He promised those to whom the money was owed that he would pay them as quickly as he could. It took him several years to do it, but he eventually paid it off. That's how he got the name "Honest Abe." More details on this can be found in G. Fredrick Owens' book, *Abraham Lincoln—The Man and His Faith*.

Lincoln was a stickler for honesty, to be sure. That same adherence to his personal goals and value system stayed with him through his years as a lawyer and then President. Once, after listening to the case of a prospective client, he responded, "You have a pretty good case, technically. But it just isn't right in justice and equity. You'll have to find another lawyer to handle it for you, because all the time I'd be standing there talking to the jury I'd be thinking, 'Lincoln, you're a liar!' and I'm afraid I'd forget myself and say it out loud!"

Do You Live By An "Honor Code"?

At West Point, the "Honor Code" says, "A cadet will not lie, cheat, steal, or tolerate those who do." Duty, Honor, Country. Those of us who adhered to that code, as nebulous as that may sound, felt quite satisfied when we accomplished something, because we were true to ourselves. We did it ourselves. We did not look on the outside. We did it in a way that was true to who we were and what we were about.

What a difference it makes, whether in business or family life, when you are honest. Whenever you complete a task or overcome a challenge honestly, you get a wonderful feeling. If you do it insincerely, dishonestly, and without integrity, you risk losing everything you accomplished. You are unlikely to feel the same gratification. You probably won't learn nearly as much either. Also, it may not stay done. It could be questioned later. You will probably lose what you dishonestly gained.

There are two principles I hold dearest in my heart with regard to dealing with people: honesty and integrity. By operating that way, you can rest assured people will be more likely to want to deal with you. If you treat them with respect, give them a fair price, and they know they can trust you and what you say, the chances are greater that they want to do business with you. However, if they detect any dishonesty or insincerity, human nature may cause them to back away from you because they may feel uncomfortable. When you don't trust someone, how can you communicate? How can you possibly relate with those people? If you need to deal with them, you would be cautious, to say the least.

Here's an interesting little story about three high school seniors. It was during the spring, right near graduation time, when they got a serious case of "spring fever." One morning, they decided to skip school. When they returned to school, they told the teacher they had had a flat tire.

"Well," the teacher said, "you also missed a test. Therefore, I want to give it to you now. Why don't you all sit apart and take out a blank sheet of paper," she said. "The first question I have is, which tire was flat?"

See how dishonesty came back to haunt the boys? It always comes back to haunt us. As we do this, we need to forgive ourselves for any temptations to be dishonest we had in the past, whether we gave-in to them or not, and move-on.

Be assured that most of us have been tempted at one time or another to be dishonest. The challenge you and I have is to remain true to our deepest values of integrity when temptation knocks at our door.

I see things (such as TV solicitation) that point out how so many people are influenced by deception. We all need to be careful of such influences. One thing we want to be sure of before we decide to invest in or get involved with something, is that the opportunity is honest and the people behind it are of great integrity. Check things out before you invest your time and money in anything. Yes, be open-minded, but cautious at the same time.

There Is Always Hope

While many of us are hurting inside and faced with challenges, always remember, there is hope. *Webster's Dictionary* defines hope as: "To cherish a desire with expectations of fulfillment." Hope is wonderful and magnificent. It gives you something to look forward to. It keeps you going. It also can help you to be inspired. Make sure that your hope is not based on deception or lies. Be sure you're not being taken in by things that could cause internal destruction down the road. By simply watching, reading, and listening, you'll learn how people can get caught-up in falsehoods of what could be. In many cases, the resources you have inside can provide you with all the hope you'll ever need. Add commitment and diligent effort to your hope and you'll be rewarded. Your reward may be financial or something else. Your honesty will pay-off in dividends of peace-of-mind.

Always Be Humble

There's no room for false modesty on the *Staircase.* False modesty is dishonest. It's displaying an image of modesty when, in reality, that person is not modest; he's putting on a false front. It's just as dishonest to fail to acknowledge and appreciate your achievements as it is to fail to admit your shortcomings.

There's no room for bragging either. When you accomplish something worthwhile, people are likely to compliment you. That's fine. However, bragging is a sign of unintact self-esteem, immaturity, and insecurity. It is based on feelings that no one will recognize you for what you have done. Bragging is a one-upmanship, "blowing-your-own-horn," trying to make yourself look better than the next person. Bragging is different than sharing. When you share ideas and information, it is generally because you are confident that what you have to say will help someone. Sharing is great; bragging is not!

People who have made significant contributions to the world tend to be humble. "Humble" is defined by *Webster's Dictionary* as "Not proud or haughty, . . . unpretentious." They know deep in their heart that without the help of others it is unlikely that they would have accomplished what they did. If they are people of faith (and they often are), they generally give credit to their Creator as well. It is important to give credit where credit is due and to appreciate the assistance we received which supported our efforts.

Do You Know What You Want?

Let's face it. *You can never be satisfied if you don't know what you want.* Think about a two-year-old arriving in a room filled with toys. A few other children are playing there, more or less contentedly. Our new arrival studies the scene for a bit and then makes a move. Does he go toward a toy laid quietly in a corner? No! He heads toward a toy in some other child's hands; a toy that's being pushed and pulled and enjoyed. That's what attracts his attention.

Wanting what someone else has is often the first reaction of an inexperienced person. They may trust the other person's choice of the toys rather than their own untried choice. It eliminates their need to think and decide what is best for themselves.

When this little newcomer gets acquainted with all the toys in the room, he knows the potential for pleasure each offers. After the rules of the game have been explained, like "no grabbing," the toddler will then have a way of setting goals. It may mean taking turns playing with the toy, but it will pay-off in satisfaction. It is likely to put an end to wanting only what someone else has, while building respect for that other child's rights.

If you haven't found and committed yourself to your own goals, other people's pleasures will always have the potential to influence you enough to divert you from finding what is best for you. As a father said to his son in Shakespeare's *Hamlet*, "This above all; to thine own self be true, and it must follow, as the night the day, though canst not then be false to any man."

We can learn from other people by watching them achieve their goals; that's true. However, our admiration pays off best when we imitate their perseverance. We're not being honest with ourselves if we adopt *their* goals. It is, however, honest to adapt their determination to suit our own goals, which may or may not be similar to theirs.

Earl Nightingale identified being honest with ourselves as the "big thing": "The big thing," he said, "is that you know what you want."

...All Men Would Be Free

If part of being honest is knowing what you want from life, and working tirelessly toward it, then Abe Lincoln once again proves the point by his example.

Lincoln's goal for himself was something that would benefit others, namely, that "all men would be free." He spent his entire life striving to realize this outcome. His work manifested itself in two great achievements that would eventually change the course of a nation.

One was the *Emancipation Proclamation*, which offered black men and women the right to "life, liberty, and the pursuit of happiness."

The other was "keeping the Union intact," because "deference shall be paid to the will of the majority, simply because it is the will of the majority." In his famous *Gettysburg Address*, Lincoln's goal for creating a government "of the people, by the people, and for the people," was never stated more eloquently.

Today, Americans concerned about their communities, as well as citizens of the world seeking freedom, are searching for leaders with Lincoln's qualities. He was political without being corrupt; calm without being lethargic. Lincoln was open-minded, yet didn't take unfair advantage of people and situations. He was tough, yet gentle. He was determined to get things done, yet he didn't abuse his power. He was a man of faith, without being overzealous. Lincoln believed in "the ultimate justice of the people."

When you are true to yourself, you're more likely to be true to other people. What you value is what you think about most. What you think about is what you become and what you attract. Hold dear to your heart the concepts of honesty and integrity, and they'll always guide you.

No matter what failures you encounter, no matter what you accomplish, when you're honest and sincere in everything you do, you'll always feel respect for yourself and how you got there. You'll also feel more deserving.

DREAM BIG

*If there were ever a time to dare to make a difference,
to do something really worth doing, that time is
now.   Not for any grand cause, necessarily, but for
something that tugs at your heart, something
that's your aspiration, something that's your dream.
You owe it to yourself to make your days here count.
Have fun.   Dig deep.   Stretch.*
Dream big.
*Know though that things worth doing seldom come
easily.   There will be good days.   And there will
probably be bad days.   There will be times when you
want to turn around, pack it up, and call it quits.
Those times come only to tell you that you are pushing
yourself, and that you are not afraid to learn and grow.*
Persist.
*Because with an idea, determination, and the right
tools, you can do great things.   Let your instincts, your
intellect and your heart guide you.*
Trust.
*Believe in the incredible power of the human mind, in
the power of doing things that really make a difference,
of working hard, of laughing and hoping, of reaching
out, of saying "I love you," of lasting friends, of all
things that will cross your path this year.
The start of something new brings hope of something
great.   Anything is possible.   There is only one you.
And you will pass this particular way only once.*
**Live your dream!
Make a difference!**

JOYCE GIULA

Chapter 9a

ALWAYS DREAM AND SET GOALS
Second Part of the Fifth Step of the THESAURUS Factor

Where Are You Headed?

You had an opportunity to define success for yourself in the first part of this book. Now, with goal setting in mind, do you remember your definition of success? In general, remember it's the progressive realization of worthwhile dreams and goals. Without desired outcomes in mind, you don't know where you're headed. And if you don't know where you're headed, chances are you're already there!

In 1952, Florence Chadwick swam across the English Channel and back. After that, she set a new goal to cross the Catalina Channel off the coast of California, which is 21 miles long!

When she started out that morning, the weather was chilly and foggy. The men on the chase boat were even shooting sharks. The water was cold. As she neared the coast, a thick fog rolled-in. She couldn't see. She was tired and shivering. Even though her coach and her mother were vigorously encouraging her to keep on going, to not quit, she still gave up.

After she got in the boat and the reporters came over to her, they asked her, "Why did you stop?" She answered, "I couldn't see the shore. I could only see the fog." At that point, she realized that *one of the most important things in seeking something is to never lose sight of it.* This is true whether you can physically see it or not.

Florence's second attempt was successful, even though the weather was just as cold and foggy as the first time. The difference was she had already pictured in her mind what the shore would look like before she got there! Furthermore, she was so determined on her second attempt that she actually beat the men's time by about two hours. That's remarkable.

The point is, the power of the mind, the power of a vision, is amazing. Always keep in sight where you want to go. Where do you want to be a year from now, two years from now, three years from now? *Dreams and goals are essential; they literally define your success.*

Put Your Dreams In Concrete And Your Plans In Sand!

Once your desired outcomes are fixed firmly in your mind, they will assist you in reaching your dreams. Without goals, you have no direction. Dorothy, in the *Wizard of Oz*, took only one "yellow-brick-road." When you have ten "yellow-brick-roads," when you are straddling two different paths, you don't accomplish much. If you don't stay on track, if you don't have a "one-track-mind" so to speak, it's very difficult to get where you want to go. You need to be focused to achieve the results you want.

Hopefully, you have an unwavering vision of where you want to go or what you want to become. Along the way, however, you may need to change the plans you created to accomplish that outcome. You may have to deal with different forces, pressures, expectations, and challenges, depending on how things develop. Keep your focus on the outcomes you want. Be sure they complement your definition of success, your purpose, and what you want to be. You may surprise yourself and achieve outcomes beyond your wildest dreams.

Many years ago, I dreamed about being a motivational speaker and author. I didn't know if I'd ever achieve that outcome. Nevertheless, I always visualized it happening. I would think, "I want to be one of the finest motivational speakers and authors in the world." That was a dream, not necessarily a goal.

Goals are more specific. *Goals help you realize your dreams.* A goal could be something like, "I want to present to over a hundred companies during the course of a year. I want to see my book read by over one-million people during the course of a year." To realize that, I needed a plan of action. *Remember, goals define your success.* Always reach for outcomes you feel will be helpful to others and have the most importance to you. Seek to make a difference.

Goals are the most tangible of all the steps along the *Staircase.* They're like type "AB" blood. If you have "AB" blood, your system will accept "O," "A," or "B" and be "happy." Goals are the same way; they're the "universal recipient." Your level of commitment in incorporating all the steps on the *Staircase* into your life will, in many cases, determine the degree of success you have in achieving your goals.

To be an effective leader, it's essential to elevate your attitude and enthusiasm. If you have the goal of confronting your boss with a problem, self-control is necessary. If your goal is to get over what happened a year ago or just last week, you need to totally forgive. The accomplishment of these goals is emotionally related, as is the achievement of most goals. Do you see the importance of employing one or more of the "steps" in each situation?

If you want to be a more effective salesperson, you need to set goals to reach certain quotas. You'll also need to use the principles of the *THESAURUS Factor* to assist you in your presentation and communication skills. All the principles intertwine to give you a strong foundation of knowledge and understanding.

When you have achieved your goals and have realized whatever you define success to be, you are successful. In turn, hopefully, you also become fulfilled along the way. If each success supports your purpose, you are more likely to be fulfilled.

Have You Written Down What You Want?

Goal setting can be challenging at times because of the many areas of your life that call for your attention. Your personal, family, professional and financial goals all require your time and energy. Physical and mental health goals, taking care of yourself physically, emotionally and spiritually, also need attention. The key is to take some time to write all these things down and then strive to maintain a balance. Remember, it is OK to be out-of-balance temporarily, as you focus on an area that truly needs your attention. You can regain your general balance.

Lou Holtz, the famous Notre Dame coach, mentioned that one time when he was unemployed, he read *The Magic of Thinking Big* by Dr. David J. Schwartz. (It's a book I would recommend to anybody; a wonderful, motivational, inspirational book, along the lines of *Think and Grow Rich* by Napoleon Hill.) During that time, Lou took the opportunity to write down 120 things he wanted to accomplish. After he completed this list, he got so excited that he ran over to his wife and said, "Look, look, I have all these great goals!" His wife said, "Why don't you put down number 121: 'Get a job!'"

It is so important to write down your goals. It's a proven fact that you're four times more likely to achieve what you write down. The act of writing causes you to focus your attention. The process of writing causes those goals to be processed by your brain. If it's not important enough for you to write it down, it's often not important enough for you to accomplish.

The Yale School of Business conducted a survey of its 1954 graduating class. Twenty years later, it was discovered that three percent of the class had more net worth than the other ninety-seven percent combined! Those three percent had their goals written down upon graduation. Remember the enormous power of writing down what you want to see happen. Writing it down can make the difference between whether you achieve the goal or not.

Do You Use Affirmations?

An affirmation is a statement of an outcome you desire, written in the present tense, as if you have already achieved it.

Once you have your goals written down, perhaps on a "3 x 5" card, I recommend that you post them in front of you, maybe on your bathroom mirror, and read them at least twice every day; once upon arising, and once again upon retiring. These are two times when your subconscious mind is most receptive to new ideas. There's usually little or no interference from other thoughts or situations that require your attention. The subconscious also receives new input more readily when you talk to it with emotion. Read your affirmations with emotion. Reach down into the depths of your soul and pour your heart into it for best results.

Do this for 30 days straight and you will have put a new belief into your subconscious. *Repetition and emotion are how you access your subconscious.* Once the affirmation is accepted, your subconscious will then drive your conscious mind to direct you to do the things necessary for you to realize your desired outcome.

Let's assume you want to lose weight, a desire shared by most people at some time in their life. A typical scenario may go like this:

To begin, you decide to go on a diet...again! You may need to change your eating habits. You may not want to do that, because it means giving up foods you like. So, right from the start you may resist. However, you continue to strive for your goal because you're working on developing winning habits.

Let's say you want to lose ten pounds. After a bit, you notice the pounds on the scale dropping. Your initial euphoria over this accomplishment spurs you on until the ten pounds are gone. But, they may start to come back. You reached your goal, so you may now be rewarding yourself by eating, by going back to your old habits. In fact, this cycle could well be repeated time and time again, because you're constantly achieving your goal, then you may be rewarding yourself by overeating again.

The reason you may have failed is because you set an incorrect goal. Your goal was to lose 10 pounds. In order to do that, based on old habit patterns, you had to gain it back. You put yourself in a roller-coaster of pain and pleasure, suffering and reward.

The better way to approach losing weight is not focusing on losing weight, but on *being* a particular weight. First determine how much you want to weigh, i.e., define your goal. Let's say you now weigh 175 pounds, but you'd like to be 165.

The next thing you'll want to do is put a date on when you wish to realize your goal. Then write down the rewards you'll give yourself for achieving 165. You may write: "I have more energy when I'm 165; I look and feel better at 165; my clothes fit and look better when I'm 165; I am more agile and attractive to myself and others; and I like myself more than ever."

The next step is to positively spell out (don't write what you want to avoid) a plan to realize your goal. You might write something like:
a. Eat only three meals a day (This means no snacking between meals, but don't write this down.)
b. Drink eight glasses of water a day.
c. Eat only fruit and grains at breakfast.
d. Eat a salad for lunch.
e. Eat fish or poultry with vegetables at dinner.
f. Take vitamins daily.
g. Exercise aerobically 20-30 minutes daily.
h. Do toning exercises 10-15 minutes daily.
i. Read my affirmation aloud twice daily with emotion.

You could write out your affirmation to read something like this:
I now weigh 165 pounds. I drink eight glasses of water a day. I have more energy, and I look and feel better at 165. My clothes fit and look better at 165. I eat fruit and grains for breakfast, a salad for lunch, and either fish or poultry with vegetables at dinner. I exercise aerobically 20-30 minutes a day.

I do toning exercises 10-15 minutes daily. I am agile and attractive. I now weigh 165 pounds.

Like most things you wish to accomplish in life, achieving and maintaining your goal weight requires self-esteem. Do you feel enough respect for yourself to do what it takes to be at your desired weight?

Make Each Day Count

Earlier in my life, I never imagined I would be where I am today. But as I was close to achieving each goal I set for myself, I would always set a new one. As you reach the top of your current "mountain," you can see the next. This is essential to a successful, fulfilling, happy life. The first Apollo astronauts who landed on the moon, back in 1969, went into a state of depression later on, because they had no new goal to strive for. In other words, it is dangerous to rest on your laurels. You want to have something to look forward to. You'll then have the joy of accomplishment and anticipation.

Eventually, I developed a dream. I got a vision of what I wanted to do and how I wanted to contribute. I knew that every action, no matter what job I had or position I held, would contribute to the progressive realization of my goals, and eventually my dreams. That, after all, is the definition of success; it's a *progression and a journey,* not a resting place.

It's great to have a "to do" list. That is an excellent start. You have a feeling of accomplishment when you have crossed off eighteen items on a twenty-item list. However the remaining items may be the most important. Sure, you feel satisfied about crossing off eighteen things, but did you really do those things that contribute the most toward realizing your goals? Or did you just open some "junk" mail and rearrange your files?

When you have an objective, it's essential that you work toward it every day! This means prioritizing your tasks and completing them in order, as much as possible. (If it's a work-related objective, you may want to take a day or two of rest on the weekend, e.g., Sunday.)

Make each day count toward your progress. We are all affected by factors that interfere with our daily schedule and "to do" lists. However, those factors are not meant to be used as an excuse for not achieving your goals.

The things we want most in life tend to be the most difficult and take the most time to complete. As with electricity and water, it is human nature to follow the path of least resistance. If that path doesn't lead to where you want to go, you may need to change directions. Real success requires persistent, consistent, focused effort.

The "Goal Prioritizing Grid"

I want to share with you a way to help you establish and prioritize your goals. It's called the "Goal Prioritizing Grid."

URGENT

Priority #1 (Day-to-day routines)	**Priority #3** (Interruptions-Reactive)

IMPORTANT _____|_____ **NOT IMPORTANT**

Priority #2 (Goals-Proactive)	**Priority #4** (Don't Bother)

NOT URGENT

THE GOAL PRIORITIZING GRID

To use the Goal Prioritizing Grid effectively, first write down all your goals, then prioritize each one. Next, actually write in these quadrants what you want to accomplish day-to-day, week-to-week, month-to-month, and year-to-year to give yourself a larger picture or idea of what you want to accomplish.

Priority One items are both Important and Urgent. They are things you do every day to maintain the integrity, vitality, viability, and operation of an organization. Without doing them, that company's productivity could falter.

The same thing is true at home. We're focusing more on work when we talk about goals, but the same thing is true with family life. Do you have personal *and* family goals? You need to do certain things every day, week, or year to keep your home clean, organized, attractive, and in good repair. There are some basic things that need to be done. They are Priority Ones. If you don't do them, something or someone is going to suffer.

Priority Two Items Are Important But Not Urgent. This quadrant is critical. This is where your goals go. That goal of wanting to present a seminar to a hundred different companies and organizations next year; that goes here. The items listed here aren't urgent; they're not "right now," but they're so important to your success. List your goals here and invest some time in them daily, if possible. The people that "live" in the Priority Two Quadrant are primarily proactive.

Proactive is a word not found in most dictionaries, but it is common in management literature. According to Stephen R. Covey, author of *The Seven Habits of Highly Effective People*, "Proactive means more than merely taking initiative. It means that as human beings we are responsible for our own lives. Our behavior is a function of our decisions, not our conditions. We can subordinate feelings to values. We have the initiative and the responsibility to make things happen...Highly proactive people recognize that...they do not blame circumstances, conditions, or conditioning for their behavior...it's a product of their own conscious choice, based on values, rather than a product of their conditions, based on feeling."

Priority Three Items Are Urgent But Not Important. This is a quadrant in which things "just-sort-of-happen" for many people. For some reason, because of a day-to-day reaction to life's events, urgent things tend to take priority over important things. The people that "live" here are probably reactive.

Once again we look to Stephen Covey's bestseller, *The Seven Habits of Highly Effective People*. He says we are proactive by nature, however, "if our lives are a function of conditioning and conditions, it is because we have, by conscious decision or default, chosen to empower those things that control us.... Reactive people are often affected by their physical environment.... Reactive people build their emotional lives around the behavior of others, empowering the weaknesses of other people to control them."

Reactive people often exhibit an habitual robotic-like response to situations or events. For example, when the telephone rings, a reactive person automatically answers it. He's giving power to the person calling over what he's doing that instant. Remember, if it's important, they'll call back or leave a message. It's OK to let your answering machine or voice mail take calls and have them pile up. You can answer them later when the time suits *you*!

Oftentimes, the main factor that inhibits our achieving our goals is the conflict between Priorities Two and Three. It may look impressive to have a "to-do list" of 20 items and have 18 of them crossed out, but if you accomplished items that were urgent yet not important, did you spend your time wisely? As Peter Drucker, author of *The Effective Executive* said, "It is often more important to do the right things than to just do things right."

What is easier? Rearranging your desk or starting on that sales report; finding new clients or associates, or stopping by the old ones to say "hi"; working on your relationship, or giving up; changing certain behavior patterns, like drinking, smoking, and overeating, or making excuses why you "can't."

Once again, if you do not accomplish what you want most, the door of excuse-making and complaining is likely to swing wide-open. You probably have the talent and desire to accomplish your goals. However, it also requires discipline, the proper use of time, and appropriate effort to achieve them.

What's The Catch Here?

The point is, we're talking about self-responsibility. When you are self-responsible, you tend to be in control of yourself. A problem may arise, however, when you want to do everything yourself. Self-responsibility, taken to an extreme, can actually get you in trouble when it comes to prioritizing goals. If you spend time on areas that are urgent but not important (Priority Three), if you fail to delegate don't prioritize properly, it's going to be difficult to stay on track; it will take you longer to reach your goals, if you reach them at all. Once again, the major conflict is between Priorities Two and Three.

Here are some items that would fit into Priority One:
1. Making a new sales appointment. This is urgent and important, because without sales appointments you are unlikely to have any sales.
2. Planning is urgent and important. If you don't have a plan, you're unlikely to ever reach your goals.

Here are some items that would be Priority Two's:
1. Your goals, both personal and career.
2. Writing your own book.
3. Building a new house.
4. Getting tenure.
5. Retiring from your job into your own business.
6. Becoming an accomplished speaker.
7. Earning $100,000 a year, or more.
8. Doing $1,000,000 or more in sales.
9. Achieving a certain profit margin for a corporation.

In short, Priority Two's are goals. There could be a variety of things that are longer term. They're not urgent, but they're very important.

Many people certainly have things they feel are urgent (and easily done), but not important. Yet they may allow these things to get in the way of their goals. Remember, the path of least resistance may not be the path toward the outcomes we want.

To do the sometimes difficult things necessary to achieve your goals, you may need to get out of your "comfort zone." It will help you grow personally. You need to stretch. You may need to take some sort of risk. You need to step out from where you are to get somewhere else. As long as you have something to grab onto, you can leave the "comfort zone" or "familiar zone." Often this zone is more familiar than comfortable; you're just used to it.

Sometimes goals can be scary, because if they're intangible, like personal growth for instance, they're not right there in front of you. You seldom get immediate gratification and they're difficult to see. Such goals may require more imagination and faith.

What could be some goals for your children? How about setting some goals for your relationships? What might be some goals for the people who work for you or with you?

A mission statement is crucial; it's absolutely essential. If your company does not have any mission statements, there's probably no overall direction for people to follow. If you are in a position of management or supervision, it is vitally important to sit down with your people and find out what their goals and aspirations are. This enables you to work together to accomplish your company's goals, while still meeting the desires of your staff as much as possible.

Suppose you begin training seven people, all of whom you believe want to be sales managers. Suppose further, that after a year goes by, you discover that six have absolutely no desire to be managers. What have you done? You have wasted a lot of time and energy trying to train people against their will. It never works.

The best way to avoid that situation is to sit down with your people, early on, and establish goals. Something wonderful is likely to happen. In most cases, team building immediately begins to take place. Your concern and caring can help create a feeling of unity, where everybody's on the "same-sheet-of-music."

Can you imagine going to a symphony with half the orchestra playing "The 1812 Overture" and half playing "Beethoven's Fifth"? It would be a little confusing, to say the least! If an organization is not "playing-on-the-same-sheet-of-music," it's very difficult to accomplish anything.

Finally, we come to **Priority Four: Not Important and Not Urgent.** What's to be said about this quadrant? Not much, except ignore anything listed there. You would be spending time on things that are absolutely worthless to the accomplishment of where you want to be. NOTE: I would not put vacations or recreation here. They are important to your well-being and maintaining a balanced life.

It's so important to invest time in your goals. Write them down. Every motivational speaker and success consultant will tell you that all great successful people have had clearly defined goals. They've taken the time to spell them out in detail, and it would be an excellent investment of your time and energy for you to do the same.

What Can Hinder The Accomplishment Of Your Goals?

What is it that could work against our being honest with ourselves when we are trying to determine just what it is that we want out of life?

Achieving goals can be hindered by the fear of being limited to getting only what you say you want. Specifying something defines desire, and in a way, sets a limit. I recommend that you make room for increases in your goal statements. For example, you could say your goal is to "earn-$100,000-or-more" rather than limiting it to

$100,000. It is important to state what you want. If you don't, you may run the risk of wanting everything, never expressing and pursuing it, and having nothing you can call your own. This could be in the area of accomplishment and possessions you desire.

Naming something as your goal gives you a certain ownership. It is an excellent and essential beginning to getting what you want. It gives you a satisfaction that never comes to someone who gets something they didn't ask for. You've probably seen it happen. For instance, there are children who aren't given the chance to build up desire for something before it's handed to them. They could grow up unable to appreciate anything. These children may be accused of ingratitude by parents who have deprived them of a chance to know what it means to be grateful. Their parents often don't know the difference between being a big spender and being generous. Big spenders give some of their surplus to those who happen to be around. Generous people offer to be a resource for others, and allow them to determine what they need or want.

We don't want to put down the effort of well-intentioned people. Most of us do have some difficulty sorting through just what our aims are when we give. Do we just want to be liked? Do we just want to assure we'll get a gift back when it's "our turn"? Do we just want to avoid the embarrassment of being the only person who didn't give? We may have some of these reasons in mind when we give. By honestly acknowledging that, we become more aware of our intentions. We also become stronger and can come closer to being the truly generous people we want to be.

Lack of imagination is another thing that can get in the way of writing down goals. We may not even let ourselves dream of things that seem beyond our reach. This is sad. If it sounds familiar, free yourself of this limitation. A dream is a vision for something better in your life. It's people who see things as they might be and say "why not?" who bring about the changes that make life better for everyone.

A fulfilled human being is more likely to be a gift and resource to everyone around him, than is a disappointed and discouraged person. The world can benefit by your dreaming, and setting and accomplishing goals for a better life for yourself. In the process of pursuing your goals you are most likely helping others. Or, at a minimum, you are a happier person to be around. Everyone wins.

Persistence Pays Off
Once upon a time, there was a Louisville University quarterback who was obsessed with a vision. His dream was to play professional

football. Upon graduation, however, this young quarterback was not drafted. He did not give up, either. He wrote to several teams and finally got a tryout with the Steelers. He gave it his best shot but did not make even the third string.

"You got a raw deal." "It wasn't meant to be." "I guess it's time to hang-it-up," his friends told him. But the young athlete did not hang-it-up. Continuing to knock on doors and write letters, he finally received another invitation. Again, he did not make the team.

Most people would have given up long before this, but not this determined young man. He was passionately committed to his dream. From his early days of playing sandlot football, through his success in high school and college football, he had hung tight to his dream.

Patiently and persistently he continued to pursue tryouts with professional teams. He finally went to Baltimore and made the team. Training and working long hours on fitness and skill, he worked his way from third string to becoming known as the greatest quarterback in the NFL (National Football League).

Who was this persistent dreamer? You may have guessed ...Johnny Unitas!

Most People Die With Their Music Still In Them, Their Song Unsung

Honesty and goal-setting can be challenging. While they normally involve patient processing of life's experiences, there are occasional moments when we suddenly realize a truth about ourselves. The truth could be that we are not doing what we really want to do most passionately in our lives. We may not be meeting our own expectations of ourselves in several key areas.

I had an experience like that when I was the officer-in-command of a funeral detail. I was company commander in the Missouri Army National Guard, stationed in Carthage. The funeral was for a young friend of mine, my jeep driver, who had been killed in a motorcycle accident.

When I stepped forward to present the flag to my friend's mother, this is what I said:

This flag is presented on behalf of a grateful nation as a token of our appreciation for the honorable and faithful service rendered by your loved one. I could barely say the words. They were suddenly so real for me.

It was the final moment of the ceremony. The mourners had departed, the honor guard prepared to leave, and I needed to collect myself. I excused myself from my companions to spend a few solitary moments under a nearby weeping willow. It kindly lent its veil of green to hide my sorrow.

There was a bigger truth than mourning the loss of a friend. I had to honestly admit I was mourning the loss of all who die too young. I mourned the loss of all the dreams that get cut down before they blossom. I mourned the loss of people who die with their music still in them, their song unsung. I was raging against not being able to control death, not being able to prevent what I didn't want.

I realized I was as powerless at this graveside as I had been at my father's. When it came to controlling the forces of death, I was no more able to now than I had been at eleven. That boy had been unable to cry. The man I had become allowed himself to cry. Through my tears, the honesty of my grief surfaced, and the wound from my father's death began to heal.

I knew that all any of us have is the present. We can choose to be all that we are meant to be. We can choose to make a difference each day, large or small in the lives of others. We çannot change the past. We can change our lives today. We can set and achieve goals that are important to us, "one-step-at-a-time." We can embrace the present, and through our contributions to life, leave a legacy for those that follow.

"No Excuse!" Action Plan To "Always Be Honest/Always Dream And Set Goals

1. Honesty is the best policy, and it starts with you. Be honest with yourself and you're more likely to be honest with others and earn their trust. True success is honest success.

2. Live by an "honor code." Don't lie, cheat, steal, or tolerate the actions of those who do. If you achieve something dishonestly, you jeopardize the accomplishment, and you'll probably lose what you gained.

3. Imitate the perseverance of the people you admire, not their goals; that would be dishonest to you! Be honest with yourself and know what *you* want. Your goals define your success.

4. Put your dreams in concrete and your plans in sand. Once you know what you want to do and be, focus on it. Develop a "one-track-mind" passion for your vision, but be flexible enough to change your plans to overcome any obstacles you may encounter.

5. Write down five main goals and what you're willing to do to reach them. Read them out loud when you get up and before you go to sleep. Repetition and emotion are how you access your subconscious. Do this for 30 days, and you can create a new habit.

6. Reach for outcomes you feel will be helpful to others and have the most importance to you. Seek to make a difference. Serve others and you're more likely to be successful.

7. Make each day count. Do something every day toward your vision. Enjoy the trip. Remember, success is a journey, not a destination. Don't use external factors as an excuse not to go forward.

8. Develop and live by a "personal mission statement." Write down your main purpose in life. This will give you a sense of direction and help you stay "on-track."

9. Don't die with your music still in you. Persist until you accomplish your dreams and goals.

10. Leave a legacy and something that will grow when you're gone.

KNOWLEDGE

Whom then, do I call educated? First, those who
control circumstances instead of being
mastered by them; those who meet all occasions
manfully and act in accordance with intelligent
thinking; those who are honorable in all
dealings; those who treat good-naturedly persons and
things that are disagreeable; and furthermore,
those who hold their pleasure under control and are
not overcome by misfortune; finally those
who are not spoiled by success.

SOCRATES

Our knowledge is a torch of smoky pine,
That lights the pathway but one step ahead,
Across a void of mystery and dread.

GEORGE SANTAYANA

Chapter 10

UPGRADE YOUR KNOWLEDGE
First Part Of The Sixth Step Of
The THESAURUS Factor

Knowledge Is The Foundation Of Your Future

Knowledge gives you the information you need to go forward so you can grow and become. Helen Keller once said, "The most pathetic person in the world is one who has sight but has no vision." Increased knowledge can help you have a clearer vision. Always take the opportunity to learn more about things that can help you move toward your dreams.

Every time you think, you form an opinion. That process causes you to look inside, perceive better what's going on outside, and make a decision. (Your decision could even be "not-to-make-a-decision!") Every time you think deeply about something, you grow. Each time you exercise your mind, you grow. Einstein once said, "The average person uses less than ten percent of his brain power." Have you ever hired or worked with someone that's at .0001?

We've all heard the expression "mind-over-matter." It's so true. The power of the mind is phenomenal. In the area of health, for instance, it's well-known that people have recovered from illnesses that doctors said were beyond medical treatment. They made up their minds to overcome their medical condition and survived. In some cases they helped many others by sharing their experiences.

Are you spending time focusing on things that aren't necessary, applicable, or helpful to the realization of the outcomes you want? Watching the TV show "Sesame Street" is helpful to children. However, when they watch something negative or violent, is that benefitting them? When you participate in events and daily routines, ask yourself if they will contribute to your personal and professional growth. When you cease to learn positive beneficial things, you cease to grow; you're literally wasting your time.

"Push-The-Outside-Of-The-Envelope!"

Accept no limits for yourself. *The only limit we really have is our vision.* If it needs to be bigger, we can make it bigger. As test pilots say, "Push-the-outside-of-the-envelope." They're referring to taking the aircraft to the edge of its performance capabilities. They want to see what it can ultimately do without breaking it. Push at the outer edges of your knowledge, and you'll expand your vision. Did you stop doing that? Some people stop learning when they leave school. When did you first become aware of what you didn't know? When you discovered you needed knowledge in certain areas, did you take action?

Babies are born with the desire to know more. A healthy, growing child is interested in almost everything new that comes along. Kids grow by pushing at the outer limits of their knowledge, and that's how adults grow too.

Recall a child's total preoccupation with something new. When he's finished focusing, he'll often let out a sigh of satisfaction. How long has it been since you got satisfaction by learning something new? Explore the outer limits of your knowledge. Push at the edges of your interests and talents and you will grow.

Wise parents know boundaries are their children's learning frontiers. They guide each child's growth by enlarging boundaries as the child matures. Children given gentle but firm guidance can become strong adults capable of endless learning and growth.

In my travels consulting and giving seminars, I've found many people who usually act bravely are affected by *the fear of having no boundaries.* This is often a result of having lived under rigid limits in the past. Like many other obstacles in life, this too can be overcome. Once again, we need to let go of the old and embrace the new. A continuing educational program of personal and professional development books, tapes, and seminars can really make a difference in your understanding of your own boundaries. As a result, you're likely to expand your boundaries tremendously.

Knowledge is virtually useless unless you use it or share it with others. Be generous with your knowledge. There's no need to hold onto it. When you share it you still have it! Besides, there's more where that came from. Knowledge is a powerful tool to help you and others when it's used or shared. Also, sharing it reinforces and may even deepen your understanding. When you teach others, you often teach yourself something in the process.

By its very nature, the knowledge you already have is limited. On the other hand, the knowledge you don't have is virtually unlimited. Be courageous. Let go of your limits. Go to the edge and learn more. Don't settle for just what you have now. Pause on this step of the *Staircase* to *upgrade* yourself with new knowledge. "Push-the-outside-of-the-envelope" that surrounds what you already know.

Do you equate learning only with formal education? If so, you may want to consider broadening your view to include other ways of learning. Push at that edge. Thomas Edison had only three months of formal education. When he began, Henry Ford knew just a little about cars, but he knew enough to hire qualified people to design and build them. We can learn through the experiences of ourselves and others by reading, watching a presentation, observing, and listening.

Even if you have years of formal education and professional credentials, it is still important to be open and interested in the world around you. You may have been so focused on your specialty in your formal schooling, that you missed out on gaining a broad knowledge base. You may need to "lighten-up." You may have been taught to think one way. That way may not work for you any longer. You may be a perfect candidate for "pushing-the-outside-of-the-envelope" that was given to you by your schooling. Be fearless on this step. Be glad for what you know, and open up your mind to learn more.

Tap Into Your Brain's Enormous Capacity

The human brain, your brain, is incredible. About half the size of a grapefruit, it is capable of recording eight-hundred memories per second for seventy-five years without exhausting itself! It can store somewhere between ten billion and one-hundred billion pieces of information. The brain records everything it takes in and always remembers it; even though we don't recall all the information stored, it's all on permanent file.

Almost anything's possible, but I doubt that a computer will ever be built to match the brain's potential. Even if it could be done, it would probably require the space of the Empire State Building and need a billion watts to operate. The cost would be astronomical.

The mind is one of God's most amazing gifts. It separates us from the animals. The purpose of this step is to explore how you can condition your mind and yourself to use more of the tremendous potential you already have within you.

A True Warrior of Knowledge

Survival was more than just "hanging-on-for-dear-life" for Major Rhonda Scott Cornum. She's the U.S. Army flight surgeon who was in a helicopter that was shot down during the 1991 Persian Gulf War. She was then captured and held as a P.O.W. (Prisoner of War).

By the time the enemy found her, she had already been shot in the shoulder. She also suffered two broken arms, a torn knee ligament, and a fractured finger. Somehow she still managed to pull herself clear of the burning wreckage. Her captors concluded that she was in so much pain it was hard to believe she was still alive.

Cornum's survival also meant she exhibited integrity and moral courage. She couldn't risk showing cowardice during her week-long interrogation. She received no medical treatment either, while being moved eleven times! She tenaciously held onto the determination that got her through medical school and then the army.

Cornum's life reveals a continual quest for knowledge. Cornell University was her first choice for college. Unable to afford it as a freshman, she enrolled at Wilmington College in Ohio, then transferred to Cornell. In 1975, at the age of 20, she earned her Bachelor of Science in microbiology and genetics. In 1979, she earned her Doctorate degree (Ph.D.) in biochemistry and nutrition.

Cornum never dreamed of having a military career. But during her second year of graduate school, she presented a summary report abstract on amino acids metabolism at a conference in Atlantic City. There she was approached by an officer from the Letterman Army Institute of Research at the Presidio in San Francisco. He invited her to attend the Institute so she could learn a technique related to her Cornell work. Cornum accepted the invitation because she was thirsty for more knowledge and enthusiastic about their laboratory and what it could offer.

True to form, Cornum grew from her learning. Soon she developed an avid interest in military life. She was even considered a candidate for astronaut training. In 1986, she earned her medical degree.

To make greater use of her knowledge, Cornum served as a flight surgeon assigned to the 22nd Battalion, 229th Attack Helicopter Regiment. This unit was one of the first deployed to Operation Desert Shield. Her primary duty was to provide medical care to the more than 300 members of the unit.

Cornum's helicopter was shot down February 27, 1991, the fourth day of the 100-day ground war. She was on a mission to rescue the pilot of a USAF F-15 who was shot down behind enemy lines. Five of the crew of eight were killed when the helicopter was hit by intense anti-aircraft and automatic weapons fire. Fortunately Cornum survived and was released from captivity on March 6, 1991.

What Cornum learned from her experience was invaluable, not only to herself but to the entire country. It forced her to push to the edge of her own mental and physical endurance. In fact, as Cornum shares her knowledge, Americans are learning more about the role more military women could have.

"It is important that everyone be allowed to compete for all available jobs, regardless of gender," she says. Also she noted, "The qualities most important in all military jobs, like integrity, moral courage and determination, have nothing to do with gender."

About herself, Cornum says, "A long life in and of itself is not my goal. I hope I have one, but not at the expense of a great life en route." She focused on quality rather than just quantity. No one could have spoken truer words than Cornum, whose contributions come from a life invested in consistently acquiring more knowledge.

Upgrade Your Knowledge To Get More Out Of Life

If you're a nuclear physicist for instance, you could broaden your knowledge by taking-up painting. If you're a quiet gardener, you could tune into the local college FM radio station and listen to their music and what they have to say. If you're a hard rock fan, perhaps you could learn the call of a songbird and open your ears to a new world of music. Doing these things enables you to stretch and explore new horizons.

At his lectures, author Kurt Vonnegut encourages crowds of college students to open-up their minds to the surprises available to everyone. He was majoring in chemistry at Cornell when his studies were interrupted by service in World War II. After the war, he resumed his studies at the University of Michigan, this time focusing on anthropology. Later, of course, he became a writer. Now, whenever he sees an advertisement for entries in a writing contest, he sends copies to the janitors and lots of other people. He says, "You never know where the writer is."

Vonnegut has a theory why English majors don't typically become writers: they're exposed to such great writing that they may feel embarrassed and discouraged about their own early efforts. The lesson here is to courageously pursue something that you want to do, even if you stumble a bit. Most everyone, even great writers, didn't get that way overnight. Upgrade your knowledge to get more zest out of life.

How Do You Get Rid Of Self-Imposed Limits?

"Dance-up-a-storm" on this step! Your success is largely determined by your level of expectation.

Are unlimited expectations realistic? Yes, for you they could be! Whatever you believe is what's likely to be realistic for you. Your expectations of others and what they will do for or with you, needs to be limited. Believe in everyone, but count on no one other than yourself to be as committed to achieving *your* dreams and goals. *Anyone else's desire to meet your expectations will be limited by the outcomes they want.* To gain cooperation it needs to be a "win-win" situation. When it comes to what you expect of yourself, you can accelerate your success by getting rid of self-imposed limits, as well as the limits others may set for you.

Always be open to learning more. Look for an enthusiastic mentor who is teaching what he loves most. A friend who had received an excellent university education told me that was her secret. She figured she would probably be inspired most and learn best from committed educators who were passionate about their subjects. She was correct.

Inspired teachers may come to you through books, tapes, classes, seminars, people you meet, and even public television. (You might occasionally see one on commercial television as well, but it's less likely.) Follow up by obtaining additional materials to reinforce and supplement what you learned. In the great "information age" we are now in, there are plenty of resources for you to use to be on the cutting edge of your profession. If you're like most people, you probably know what you need to read, listen to and attend to keep growing in your field. The key is, do it!

Be sure you are pushing at many edges. Keep your life interesting and your learning "wheels" turning by pursuing new interests. Remember, variety makes life more exciting.

This step also has room for "the dance of self-knowledge." The sage advice, "Know Thyself," is just as true today as it was for the ancient Greeks. It is an essential part of your journey along the *Staircase.*

Find an author whose style of writing you like. Go to your local library and borrow books and audio and video tapes on stimulating subjects. Locate a store that specializes in personal development resources. You're likely to find multiple resources, including news of where courses, seminars, and workshops are given. You can even meet other people who, like you, are enthusiastic about upgrading their knowledge.

The More You Know, The More You Grow

When you cease to learn, you cease to grow. Knowledge and experience go hand-in-hand. *Experience is the validation of knowledge.* Knowledge breeds understanding, and understanding breeds wisdom. Bergin Evans, educator and writer, once said, "Wisdom is meaningless until our own experience gives it meaning."

You may read all the books in the world on scuba diving, but if you don't get into the ocean, how can you expect to see any fish swimming around? Don't you dare say "in an aquarium"! Unless you take what you learn and apply it in actual experience in the environment, it's difficult to validate what you've learned.

There is not necessarily a correlation between formal education and success! Did you know that? Just because I graduated from West Point does not necessarily mean I will be successful. Abe Lincoln was self-taught. The Wright Brothers did not go to college. Sam Walton was not well-educated either. You could go on and on. You could list many people who had little formal education, but became very successful, powerful, and accomplished. Many college graduates cannot find a job in their field of study. In fact, 90% of them eventually won't be working in the area in which they earned their degree! Formal education can be wonderful, but it provides no guarantees. Many people, in the past as well as the present, became successful without it Not having a formal education is "No Excuse!" not to be successful.

What's important is what you do with what you know. Are you adapting and applying what you learned to where you want to take your life and what you want to become? If you want to be the top salesperson, you need to invest time in learning about sales. If you want to be an excellent parent, read books and listen to tapes on how to be an effective parent. If you want to be a champion gardener, there are books and tapes that can teach you how. Get to know yourself, and learn what kinds of skills and knowledge you need and want to acquire. This is one of the keys to a more enjoyable life.

Give Yourself Time To Learn

Did you know that four years after you plant a Chinese bamboo tree, there is still no visible growth? This is true no matter how much you nourish and water it. But lo and behold, during the fifth year the Chinese bamboo grows ninety feet tall! How did that happen? For four years it established a strong root system. In fact, it has one of the most extensive root systems of any plant. To support ninety feet it needs a lot of roots. The point is, anything worthwhile, like knowledge and education, takes time.

You may not see the results of your efforts right away. You may be planting the seeds day-in and day-out. For example, when you start your own business, define success in your life, establish a purpose, and start giving to other people, you're sowing the seeds. When you take in new knowledge, you're planting seeds for even more knowledge. You may not see the results immediately; it might take three or four years or more. You are establishing a "root system." Once it's solid, nobody can topple your "tree." Your tree is you. You are your own best investment for the present and future.

No matter what you want to achieve, you need information that can assist you. Make sure the knowledge you gain can help you get where you want to go and become what you want to be.

Knowledge can help you to be more effective and can contribute to the rate of your thinking and activity. The rate at which you gain knowledge helps to determine whether you succeed or fail. It can help give you the edge over your competition.

Apply your education to serving the needs of others. You'll find that when your intention is to serve others, it can make a significant difference in your ability to provide a useful product or service.

When you increase your knowledge, you'll have more information to take care of the people you live with, work with, and serve. It can make a major difference in both your business and family life.

Associate With People Knowledgeable In Your Field

Another important aspect of upgrading your knowledge is to associate with people who are knowledgeable in your field. One of the most beneficial things you can do is to be a part of a support group. Associate with people of like-mind with whom you can share ideas, dreams and goals. It will empower you! If you're an educator, associate with other educators who are forward thinking and also want to increase their knowledge. If you own and operate your own business, mix with other business owners. If you want to market your business more effectively, make it a point to be with people who know marketing.

One mind is fine, but when you put two, three, or four minds together, what a difference it makes. It's the power of collective thinking. Two or more minds are better than one, in most cases. Associate with a group that is hungry for knowledge. You may be surprised to find there are lots of people like that who will take time to invest in themselves and you. Upgrade your knowledge. It's an investment that will last you a lifetime.

The More You Understand, The Wiser You'll Be

As you may recall, *knowledge breeds understanding, which in turn breeds wisdom.* My mother knew that, and she wanted me to know it too. Of course, it wasn't always easy for her to teach me what I needed to know to gain wisdom. However, she had confidence in me and unlimited belief in the value of education.

After my father's death, she took full responsibility for all family decisions. Guiding the growth of my sister and me, and pointing us in the right direction, were the most important things in her life. If anyone was ever a candidate for the dramatic growth of adolescence, t'was I.

My body continued to do "catch-up" for coming into the world six weeks earlier than expected. At the end of seventh grade, I was still smaller than my classmates. Furthermore, I had not yet developed the height, strength, and muscle mass I expected to inherit. Mother knew it was coming; I hoped it was. She decided to have me repeat seventh grade, even though I had passed. She was convinced it was in my best interest, and nothing I said could dissuade her. It was one of the hardest times of my life. I wanted to move-on, but I had no choice. I repeated the seventh grade and coped with the stigma.

Mom believed academic life had to be protected because it was the foundation for a future of opportunity. She didn't think mere perfunctory finishing of the primary grades was enough. She felt every student deserved to enter each grade with the possibility of *excelling*, whether he wanted to or not. If giving her son that chance meant repeating the seventh grade, then so be it.

I was transferred from the parochial school I had attended from grades one through seven and placed in the seventh grade of public school. It was a coming-of-age experience. I coped and matured, and was better prepared physically, academically, and intellectually than I would have been otherwise. I believe I was more developed emotionally too, but this was apparent later when another similar circumstance occurred.

I had confidently applied for an appointment to West Point. It wasn't easy, but I enjoyed putting all the pieces in place and jumping each hurdle. Because of my swimming ability, I had already earned a scholarship offer at an excellent school, Gettysburg College, but West Point was where I wanted to be. Before I could attend, however, West Point recommended I repeat a year of school! They even offered me a partial scholarship to the private prep school of my choice.

I said, "No." Mother said, "Think about it."

I said, "No." Mother said, "Let's visit prep schools."

I said, "Waste of time." Mother said, "I don't mind."

I said "No" to three prep schools. Mother said, "Let's go here next." Lawrenceville was the fourth prep school we visited. The moment I walked onto the campus I knew it was the place for me.

Was it wise for me to delay the starting of four intense years of college? Yes! It was as wise as it had been for me to repeat seventh grade. Even so, unless "wise" ideas "belong" to the person living them, they don't always work out.

Mother led me to the well, but there was no way she could have made me drink of the great experience Lawrenceville turned out to be. If the decision had been hers and not mine, I would have resisted; it would have been an uphill battle. Her patience and support were enough. She handled the prep school decision correctly, respecting my wishes. The "torch-was-passed" with grace.

"No Excuse!" Action Plan To "Upgrade Your Knowledge"

1.   Always be open-minded. A mind is like a parachute. It doesn't function effectively unless it's open to new ideas and more knowledge.

2.   Read 15 to 30 minutes or more a day from a personal or career development book. Leaders are readers.

3.   Listen to one or more personal or career development audio tapes every day. Turn your car into a "university-on-wheels."

4.   Attend personal and career development workshops and seminars regularly. It's exciting to be around leaders, and their enthusiasm is contagious too.

5.   Expand your knowledge-base by learning more about your favorite hobby, sport, or recreation.

6.   Keep pursuing knowledge in a new area of interest, even if you "stumble" at first. Variety makes life more exciting.

7.   Find an enthusiastic mentor who is passionate teaching what he loves most. He can guide you in your quest.

8.   Get to know yourself better. Learn where you need and want more skill and knowledge. One of the keys to a more enjoyable life is a more skillful and knowledgeable you.

9.   Experience is the validation of knowledge. Apply what you learn. Use it to serve others and things will happen.

10.   Be a part of a support group. Associate with people who have dreams and goals similar to yours. This is the single most empowering thing you can do.

HUGGING AND LAUGHTER

*It helps our body's immune system, it keeps you
healthier, it cures depression, it reduces stress,
it induces sleep, it's invigorating, it's
rejuvenating, it has no unpleasant side effects, and
it is nothing less than a miracle drug.
Hugging and laughing are all natural--all naturally
sweet and organic, no pesticides, no preservatives,
no artificial ingredients, and 100 percent
wholesome. It is practically perfect—there are no
movable parts, no batteries to wear out, no periodic
checkups, low energy consumption, high
energy yield, inflation-proof, non-fattening, no monthly
payments, theft-proof, non-taxable, non-polluting
and, of course, fully returnable.
So just have fun with people and hug and laugh every
day. Make the best of everything, think the
best of everybody, and hope the best for yourself.*

AUTHOR UNKNOWN

Chapter 10a

UNDERSTAND PEOPLE
Second Part Of The Sixth Step
Of The THESAURUS Factor

Success Depends On Communication And Language

Earl Nightingale once said, "*There is a direct correlation between communication and language and the degree of success you achieve.*" Think about it. As soon as someone begins talking, don't you immediately get a feel for where they are on the *Staircase*? You will probably get an instant impression of how educated they are by the way they pronounce their words, the effectiveness of their communication, and the extent of their vocabulary.

When you are dealing with people every day, who do you enjoy working with the most? Would you rather work with someone who expresses himself effectively or someone who doesn't? In sales, the person who can best express how the benefits of his company's product or service relates to the needs of the client will probably get the sale. Parents who can effectively express discipline to their children will be obeyed more often. The person who can communicate effectively with different types of people in his organization is likely to be more effective as a leader. Communication is the fundamental cornerstone of human relations. Without good communication skills, you cannot be an effective manager, leader, or parent.

A couple can develop true love when they understand and respect each other. You may have fallen in love and continued on to develop genuine love because you met a person who understood and respected you, no matter what you said or did, i.e., unconditionally. You communicated with each other. This type of relationship is to be treasured. I believe all of us want to feel like we're understood and respected.

Dale Carnegie, in his great book, *How To Win Friends And Influence People*, shared many ideas on how to get along with other people. The whole premise of the book is basically to show concern and respect for others; be interested in them and what they say and do.

When you show a *genuine* interest in the needs of other people, you'll be amazed at how rapidly a relationship can develop. Most people, however, tend to spend more time thinking about themselves. They would rather benefit from the interaction personally than give of themselves so others can benefit. When the person you're dealing with benefits from the interaction, the relationship is more likely to continue and grow. You'll have a better chance of communicating and developing understanding and respect.

Oftentimes people who need recognition the most get it the least, and that's many of us! Some people try to get recognition by calling attention to themselves. They are afraid no one will notice them if they don't "blow their own horn." They fail to realize that we get what we give away. If you want more recognition, understanding, and love, give it away to others first. When you meet someone, pronounce their name correctly. It's a compliment to ask someone how to pronounce their name. Reach out and do your best to understand them, and it's likely you'll increase the effectiveness of your communication. You will eventually get it back; maybe not from them, but it will come back. They or someone else will strive to understand you, and you'll feel gratified that somebody cares.

People Will Often Like You When You Listen To Them

One of the keys to effective communication is listening; it helps you understand. Remember, someone once said, "We were given two ears and only one mouth. We need to listen twice as much as we talk!" Very few people have had any formal training in listening. Yet it is important to do it every day. If you don't know how to listen, how can you expect to understand people? If you're thinking about what you're going to say while they're talking to you, how can you possibly understand them? How can you relate to them? *To be an effective communicator you need to listen.*

A wonderful colleague of mine, Jim Gallager, is one of the founders of the International Listening Association based at Ball State University, Muncie, Indiana. Once he shared with me that "we-listen-through-our-feet!" When I first heard that, it struck me as odd. What he meant was we listen based on our feelings, experiences, environment, and thoughts. Every day we have new feelings and experiences, and our environment may change. This all affects how we think, which largely determines how we listen.

When you interact with someone, your "feet" will probably have a major influence on how effectively you listen and how well you understand what someone is sharing. However, if you're focused only on your own feelings, thoughts and experiences, you're not likely to invest time listening to the other person. It is important to focus "out" of yourself and "on" the other person.

It is key that we invest our time and energy in understanding other people's feelings. Do your best to get in touch with their experiences. What are they thinking about? How are they in their environment? Do we listen through our "feet"? Sometimes we need to change "shoes." Sometimes we need to wash our "feet." In many cases then, the "feet" analogy gives us a simple way to understand how we could listen more skillfully with a stronger awareness of what we bring to the relationship.

Most speakers talk at the rate of 120-150 words-a-minute. An excited, motivated speaker talks at around 160-190 words-per-minute. We think at anywhere from 400-600 words-per-minute. For you to sit and listen while your mind is going at a different pace is a challenge. On average, you pick up only about 25% of what you hear.

To learn most effectively, it is necessary to reinforce what you've heard. This is the reason audiocassette tapes have been so successful. By repeated listening, you can learn the material much more thoroughly. Instead of always listening to music, which is nice to relax to once in a while, you could listen to something you'd like to learn or to help motivate yourself. When you don't need to relax, you could pop an audio tape in your car or home cassette deck and press "play." It can help you develop as a parent, salesperson, spouse, or something else that interests you.

It's crucial to learn how to listen with our "feet." Every time you share people's feelings and understand them and their thoughts, you'll listen better. Whenever you show respect, concern, and interest in them, you'll listen more effectively. They're likely to feel you understand them. You'll most likely have an instant relationship with them and their business. You've created a win-win situation.

When you listen, be sure to look into the person's eyes. (Ignore distractions like noises and other people walking by.) It's not just what you hear with your ears that is important, but also with your eyes. This is called empathic listening, and it shows people you care. Remember this, *people don't care how much you know until they know how much you care.*

Mother Theresa may be limited in her knowledge of science, but she's one of the world's most empathic listeners. If ever there was a person to ask, "What does it feel like to give of yourself to thousands of hurting people, day-in and day-out, showing empathy and compassion," it would be her. The lady knows how to listen.

How Do You Express Yourself?

When someone presents a talk, 58% of their impact is visual (what is seen), 35% is verbal (how it's said), and only 7% is content (what is said). In other words, we communicate primarily with feelings. Any presentation can be changed and given an entirely different meaning based on the way the speaker expresses his *feelings*, how he uses his *energy*, and how he expresses his *thoughts*. If you don't use inflection (change your voice tone and loudness), or look into the eyes of the person you're speaking to, the meaning of what you're saying may be communicated very differently than what you intended. When your voice and behavior are congruent, you communicate most effectively. For example, if you are saying you are absolutely certain about something, while looking scared and doubtful, you're incongruent; i.e., you're giving mixed messages.

How effective are you at expressing thoughts and ideas? How effective are you at sharing your products and services? If you are in sales and marketing, it is important to effectively express the benefits of your product and service and how they can satisfy your customer's needs. If you don't, you may not make many sales. You cannot be an effective manager, leader, or parent if you cannot express yourself effectively.

When you talk to others, whether you're sharing or seeking knowledge, be yourself; be real. Let people know you care about them and that you want to satisfy their needs. When you learn more about dealing with people, you'll be more able to help them.

Everyone Has A Dominant Learning Style
    We all learn and experience our environment differently. We all "see" the world through a different pair of eyes. There are three learning styles: Some of us are primarily "visual," some primarily "auditory," and some primarily "kinesthetic." So what does this mean?
    When people go to a concert, what do they focus on? Sixty percent of the people are "visual"; they tend to focus on the lights, the environment, the seating, how the orchestra or band is arranged, how the entertainers are dressed, and maybe even the colorful clothing worn by the audience. They focus on the visual aspects because that's primarily how they communicate. They best perceive the world through *seeing*. Sight is their dominant sense. A visual may say, "I see what you mean." Some people, however, are "auditory." When they go to a concert, they're not really concerned with how things look; they're more interested in the sound of the music. When auditories go to a concert, they listen for the exact notes and how precise they are. They hear the crowd and other environmental noises, like the sound of a siren sounding near the concert hall. These folks perceive the world primarily through *hearing*. An auditory may say, "I hear what you are saying."
    Can you understand how relationships are affected by the way a person perceives what's going on? When you have a "visual" and an "auditory" together, and they aren't aware of each other's dominant sense, they probably won't communicate effectively. If one person relates best by seeing and the other by hearing, they would do well to know that about each other. When they are aware of this difference, it increases their chances of relating and understanding each other.
    The "kinesthetics" perceive their world primarily by how they *feel*. What's the atmosphere like in that room? Is it exciting and friendly or unenthusiastic and cold? Does the music help to create sad or happy feelings? Do they feel comfortable in the environment? Does the program make sense? Are they feeling pleased about being there? A kinesthetic may say, "I feel the same way."
    All of us share a little of all three learning styles, unless we are unable to see or hear. We are all visual to a degree. We are all auditory and kinesthetic to a degree as well. However, we all have one dominant sense. What is yours?
    When students are learning in a classroom, the "visuals" are going to focus on the board; what it says and how it reads. The true "auditory," however, will wait until the teacher explains what he just wrote. The "kinesthetic" will ask, does it make sense? Does it feel

right? Is it conceptually correct? Can you see how this impacts the way we communicate with other people?

Would You Like To Understand People Better?

Most of us come in contact with people every day. Everyone is different and has their own style of relating to others. How can we effectively deal with these various personality types? It takes versatility. That's the ability to adapt your own personality or temperament to that of others so you can satisfy their needs. It is the key to effective communication.

Many of us have a personality and temperament different than the people with whom we associate. We all perceive the world somewhat differently. You can verify that by asking two people who saw the same event to describe what they saw. You'll almost certainly get two different answers. We all have a dominant need. Unless you understand a person's personality and need, it's difficult to have a mutually satisfying relationship, make a sale, or lead effectively.

If you make sales calls or are responsible for managing and leading others, it's essential for you to learn more about the different personalities and temperaments. If you don't, it could be very difficult to get people to work with you. You want people to work *with* you, not just *for* you. Teamwork is more likely to be productive when people feel they are a bigger part of something, not just considered a hired hand. How can you interact more effectively to satisfy the needs of specific personalities?

The idea that people have different personalities and dominant needs was developed long ago by Carl Jung in his book, *Personality Types*. To make it easier to understand these differences in people, we have adopted the approach developed by Dr. Robert A. Rohm in his book *Positive Personality Profiles*. Now let's explore what personalities are all about.

What Makes Up A Personality?

There are basically four types of personalities or temperaments, but no one is only one of them. While each of us is a unique blend of the four, we tend to favor one or two areas the most. In fact, 80% of us exhibit predominantly two temperaments. To help you better understand yourself and others, and why you think, act, and feel the way you do, let's approach this graphically with a pie chart of four quadrants.

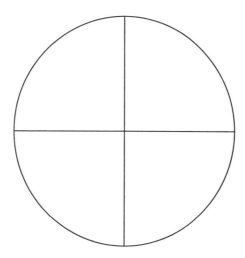

To begin with, people are primarily either "task-oriented" or "people-oriented," and either "outgoing" or "reserved." The mix of these four characteristics, and the charts that go along with them, explain the great variety of personalities that exist.

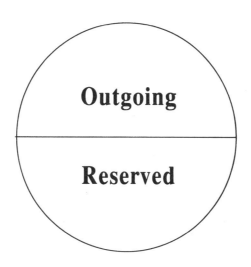

To get a handle on all of this, let's split the pie horizontally and look at the upper and lower halves. The top half represents people who are outgoing and fast-paced. The lower half represents people who are reserved and slower-paced. Active and optimistic people are outgoing, while passive and cautious, "realistic" people are more reserved. One is not better than the other, just different. When we attempt to assess someone's personality, all we are doing is observing behavior. We are not passing judgement.

Outgoing People

You know people who predominantly tell and talk. All you need to do is go to a meeting and you'll soon know who does most of the talking and telling. Some of these people do not even pause or seem to take a breath between words. They just keep talking. They go, go, go!

People who tell and talk a lot tend to be more aggressive, anxious, and enthusiastic. They are more assertive than others and express themselves more. Their expressions and how they say something are more visual. Outgoing people show their emotions more. You know immediately how they are feeling by their facial expressions, how they move their hands, their arms, and the words they use. You know if they are happy, sad, angry,or upset. They don't hide anything.

Outgoing people are self-confident and always seem to be involved in something, usually in a leadership capacity. They like to be in charge of people, programs, and events and don't mind risk. Outgoing people can "round out" their personalities by being a little more cautious and steady.

Reserved People

Then you have other people who are not nearly as talkative. They ask and listen more and tend to be more supportive, respectful, and soft-spoken. They tend to control their emotions. They don't use nearly as many facial expressions or body movements. You often can't tell if they're happy or sad, angry or upset. They internalize a lot of their emotions and are usually polite and have lots of patience.

Reserved people are cautious and don't like getting involved in very many activities. They tend to analyze things longer and can be very critical. Quality is important to them and they tend to "nit pick." They look for substance and are content to go through life with one or two close friends. They are "homebodies" and would sooner be alone rather than in a crowd. They are steady and reliable and don't care for surprises or risk.

Reserved people can "round out" their personality by "lightening-up," being more inspiring, and a little more assertive.

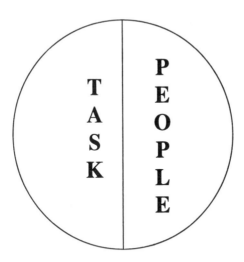

Now let's split our personality pie vertically and look at the right and left-hand sides. The right-half represents people who are primarily interested in relationships. They care most about people and how they feel and like to interact with others. The left-half represents people who are primarily interested in things. They love planning, working on projects, and getting things done.

People-Oriented People

You know people who are predominantly interested in relation-ships. They are more concerned with touching and feelings. They are empathetic, open, and love to share with and care about others.

People-oriented people are good listeners and are concerned about how other people feel. They have a strong need to be accepted and therefore are "tuned-in" to the needs of others. People are more important to them than getting things done. People-oriented people can "round-out" their personality by being more focused on their objectives.

Task-Oriented People

Task-oriented people are more focused on getting the job done. They like mechanical things to be in top running order and are very detail-oriented. They love to plan things out and make-it-happen. They are reliable and thorough.

Task-oriented people are often so hard charging and direct that they can easily offend others. Their focus is so strong that they often are not empathetic or sensitive toward others needs. They just want to get it done, no matter what. Task-oriented people can "round-out" their personality by listening and being more empathetic toward others.

Outgoing

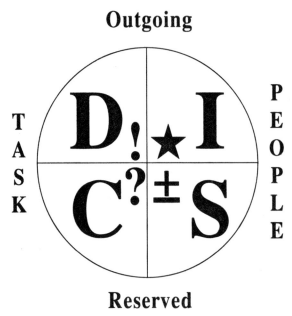

Reserved

Let's Put It All Together

Now let's put the horizontal and vertical lines on to one pie chart for a really simple and easy way to look at the four personality types. Let's also add the letters D, I, S, and C to label them, starting with the "D" and going clockwise around the pie.

The "D" (Dominant) Needs To Be In Charge

The "D" quadrant represents a person who is both outgoing and task-oriented. The letter "D" is used because this personality type tends to be a **Dominant, Driving, Demanding, Determined, Decisive Doer.** The exclamation point symbolizes this is a person with a "do-it-now" attitude! About 10% of all people are "D's."

"D's" (Choleric, according to Hippocrates) control, tell, and dictate. Their eye contact tends to be forceful and persistent. They are usually direct. Their body movements are very precise; they're in control. This is like the traditional style CEO (Chief Executive Officer) behind the desk giving orders. They need to be in control and in charge.

"D's" are always moving forward, getting things done, and looking for something better. They're task-oriented. If you're a salesperson presenting a pharmaceutical product to a physician who is a "D," he'll probably be more concerned about the effectiveness of the medication rather than its safety. Safety is important to them, but they primarily want to know that it works.

"D's" are admirable in crises; they often handle things well. They're generally accurate in dictating instructions. However, let's say you want to make a proposal or a suggestion. If you do not understand his need to be in control and you attempt to dictate to him, you'll never get what you want. You are threatening his need to be in control.

So how do you deal with a "D"? How do you communicate with someone who's dictating to you all the time, telling you what he wants? How do you deal with someone who's very efficiency-oriented and wants it done now? How do you deal with a person who only looks at what is happening in the present and who may not be concerned about what happened yesterday or what will happen tomorrow?

What is the best way to deal with someone who wants to control? Let them control! If you want to propose an idea or sell a product or service, give the "D" **options**. When you give him, say, three **options** like a, b, or c, he still feels in control. In other words, you make recommendations, but you let him make the decision. You both win. It works–even with children.

How Do You Treat Children Who Tend To Want Control?

Children, in general, tend to assert themselves, especially in their younger years. They want to be in control. They're not going to let Mom and Dad tell them what's happening. They're going to test you. I've found that by providing options to my children, I can get them to do what I want. As a matter of fact, one time my son Jared actually said, "I want options."

An excellent example is, let's say I want them to go upstairs to brush their teeth. I say three things: 1) Either go upstairs, brush your teeth, and go to bed; 2) Go upstairs, brush your teeth, and come back down to watch another ten minutes of TV; or 3) Go upstairs, brush your teeth, and come down to play your new game for ten minutes. Nine times out of ten, they'll choose one of the three.

Without any further discussion, I gave them choices and got the result I wanted.

Giving options really works. This point is important enough to repeat. Even though the example uses children, it's effective in business as well. It's amazing. Provide "D's" with options, and it's likely that you'll be delighted with what happens.

The reason for going through all this, the reason it helps to understand personalities, is so you can reach a common goal. It's a lot easier to provide options to a "D" than it is to get into a conflict and deal with the resulting anger and resentment. It's far better to give options than fighting to see who is going to push and pull to take control.

The "I" (Inspirational) Needs To Be Noticed

The "I" quadrant represents a person who is both outgoing and people-oriented. The letter "I" is used because this personality type tends to be **Inspirational, Influencing, Inducing, Impressive, Interactive, Interesting,** and **Interested** in people. The star symbolizes that this is a person who likes to "make-it-fun." About 25-30% of all people are "I's."

The "I" (Sanguine according to Hippocrates) enjoys "show-and-tell." They are enthusiastic and talk through great hand, arm, and body movement. They smile and go on-and-on. You often can't get a word in "edgewise." If you're a salesperson, they may not listen to you. When you try to provide information to them, you'll often find that as you attempt to communicate with them they're often thinking about something else.

It's often a challenge to get a decision from an "I". When you do, in many cases, it may be based on faulty reasoning. An "I's" dominant need is to be recognized. To win with them, provide an incentive. They like rewards and awards. If you provide them an incentive to do something, they'll probably do it.

When you go into an "I's" office or home, you may find quite a number of trophies on display. You may immediately know he is an excellent soccer player. It may be quite obvious how much he likes sports and how many awards he has received. He probably has an "I Love Me" room. Have you ever been in a house where everything in one room obviously belongs to the owner? You've found an "I"!

If you have someone who is more focused on the future, as "I's" are, they want to be the best at something. They also want the best equipment and the best home. Provide them with incentives and let them talk. You need to be a good listener when you're around an "I"; they love it! Whenever you can, be sure to share in their enthusiasm.

The "S" (Supportive) Has A Need To Be Accepted
The "S" quadrant represents a person who is both reserved and people-oriented. The letter "S" is used to indicate a personality that tends to be a **Supportive, Stable, Steady, Sentimental, Shy, Status-quo, Specialist.** The plus-minus sign suggests they are flexible and have a "more-or-less" attitude. About 30-35% of all people are "S's."
"S" people (Phlegmatic, according to Hippocrates) tend to show their emotion rather than hide it. How can you tell? They smile more. Their facial expressions are brighter. They tend to use their arms a little bit more. They're not nearly as restrictive in their body movements as "C's." They relate to the world through feeling; they are kinesthetic.
"S's" are people-oriented and not very assertive. They communicate how they feel by their body language. They feel, but are not necessarily taking that next step of talking with you to share what's going on. However, they are often enjoyable and pleasant to be around because of their feeling orientation. "S's" are basically relationship-oriented, and their dominant need is to be accepted.
Most of us have a certain need to be accepted. However, depending on our position or what we do at work or in our business, for instance, we may have more of a need to be in control. When the need to be in charge is greater than the need for acceptance, our "D" qualities prevail.
"S's" have soft facial expressions and tend to be more humble. Again, this is not a judgment; it's an observation. When you go into an "S's" office, there are often pictures of the family all around. You can spend time with an "S" talking about family and friends. When you share your product or service with them, they're not necessarily as concerned about its effectiveness or the statistics. They're more concerned that if they use your product or service, will they (the "S" himself) be accepted?
Today there are a lot more people with "S" characteristics moving up the corporate ladder. How come? Because when you take the time to understand and care for others, it makes a big difference in retention of people in an organization. This is one of the ways an "S" can shine.
When you have a "D" and an "S" together, who do you think "wins"? The "D." Sure. Because the true "S" is not going to sacrifice the relationship just to be in control or get his way.

How do you satisfy the "S's" with their great need for relationships? Help them feel accepted. When you visit or deal with an "S," share things about your personal and family life. They enjoy that. That's how they relate to the world. If you're in sales, for example, provide them with information. More importantly, let them know that what they're getting involved in is just fine. They need to know so the other people they deal with will still like them. By doing this you can establish a relationship.

If the "S" person you're presenting to is a physician, he wants to know if his patients accept what he is doing for them. Is the medication, for example, safe? The "S's" primary concern is that it's safe. He wants to be sure his patients accept *him*.

The "C" (Cautious) Needs To Be Accurate

The "C" quadrant represents a person who is both reserved and task-oriented. The letter "C" is used to indicate a personality that tends to be **Cautious, Competent, Calculating, Concerned, Careful,** and **Contemplative.** The question mark symbolizes a person who asks questions because he has a need to know. About 20-25% of all people are "C's."

The "C" (Melancholy, according to Hippocrates) is task-oriented and has a need to be accurate. What do you give him? How do you satisfy his needs? Give him lots of information. If you determine that a client is a "C," be sure to bring along a "truckload" of material the next time you call on him. Just put it on his desk, and chances are he'll be as happy as a lark. It may take him a "year-or-two" to make a decision, but at least you're satisfying his need. You're providing him with the information he needs to make a decision. Be sure to provide a summary sheet to give him the opportunity to move more quickly.

When an "I" salesperson deals with a "C," it can be a real challenge. Can you imagine what happens when the "I," who is primarily interested in recognition and telling, but not accuracy, tries to sell something to or relate with a "C"? It is not likely to work unless the salesperson understands the other person's needs and meets them. That's why understanding how to relate to each personality is so important. And it's true at home as well as at work.

What kind of behavior would you observe in a "C"? He asks and controls and doesn't say much. He may have a "closed" personality, and he's likely to be worried about something. An enthusiastic "I" salesperson going into a "C's" office is one of the most difficult situations you can encounter. Why? Because you often can't tell how

"C's" are feeling. You probably won't know if they're happy or sad. You may not know if they care about what you're saying, and they're often not about to tell you either. They're unlikely to express how they feel about it because that's not their need. The "C" isn't so much concerned about being assertive; he controls by exercising his need for accuracy.

If you are in sales and marketing, and you don't know what personality your prospect is, you could be headed for trouble. If he's a "C" and you come into his office enthusiastically talking about your family and friends, you'll probably turn him off. You need to provide him with the necessary information to make a decision. Otherwise, there's no relatability, and the sale is probably lost.

As an example, the "C" doctor wants to know that every study available, from "Harvard-to-Yale" supports the medication that the salesperson is showing him. He wants to know that what he is reading is statistically accurate, informative, and as foolproof as possible.

What Happens When Two Of The Same Type Are Together?

In some cases, like attracts like. We may tend to like people who are like us because our similarities often breed mutual understanding, which can lead to a relationship. As long as you are aware of the dynamics of such a relationship, you can prepare to handle it. Here are some examples:

When two "D's" are together, they may leave their discussion with anger. One may even be on the "floor" because of the "fight" that just happened! They both have a need to control. To "win" they need to give each other options.

When you have two "I's" together, just pull up a chair, sit back and watch. If they're at a party together, for instance, they are often clowning around or the center of attention. They want everybody to look at them. They both need recognition. To "win" they need to recognize and compliment each other.

Two "S's" together would likely come out of their discussion either hugging each other or crying. They are so relationship-oriented that they readily accept each other. They easily "win" with each other.

When two "C's" are together, you probably have a more "serious" situation. For instance, engineers and scientists are typically "C's." They are analytical and tend to focus on numbers and things. They both need to be accurate. To "win" they need to give each other information; they want the facts.

My Style

You may think that, as a motivational speaker, I'm an "I." But after I was tested, I was categorized as a "D/S" (Dominant/Supportive). It meant my dominant need was to be in control, while I also had a high need to be accepted.

How does this fit into the workplace? This personality combination can lead to indecision. Being interested in relationships, I need to be accepted, which can cause me to be somewhat indecisive. I don't want to jeopardize the relationship, even though I have a need to be in control. Sometimes making an unpopular decision can be a challenge to the "S" part of my personality.

How About Spouses?

In marriage it's the same way. At home I truly believe I tend to be more "D," while my wife tends to be more "S." That makes us compatible until she goes up into the "D" quadrant. I need to understand that.

At home, like Noni and I, both spouses often have different temperaments. It's less typical, for instance, to have a "C" living with another "C." Therefore it is particularly essential that both spouses learn about the personality types, so they can best deal with the one they married.

It has often been said that "opposites attract." And that certainly seems to be so in many cases. With the personality types, we often find that "D's" attract "S's," while "C's" attract "I's." Let's consider why that is.

A "D" normally attracts an "S" because "D's" like to be in charge while "S's" like to support. The "D's" confidence is reassuring to the "S" whose dominant need is to be accepted.

A "C" typically attracts an "I" because "C's" tend to be cautious, while "I's" are supportive. The serious "C" looks for the "I" whose dominant need is to be recognized. The "C" would like to have more fun.

Notice in both cases that a task-oriented person tends to attract a people-oriented person. The effect is that opposites tend to attract because they complete each other. One makes up for what the other lacks.

Putting It All Together

Yes, we're all different. People behave and express themselves differently. Take time to learn about other people. Listen to them and you can communicate more effectively. Shakespeare once said of listening, "Give every man thy ear but few thy voice." When you understand someone's personality, you can relate with them better.

We all fit in somewhere. By using the Personality Indicator, you can increase your chances for success in your relationships. This is not manipulation. It is a tremendous tool to help you communicate more effectively with people to create "win-win" results.

What Is Your Personality/Temperament?

Now you have had an opportunity to get a basic idea of what each personality type is like. What type do you think you are? What one or two quadrants best describe your personality? To help you figure it out, we've developed a "Personality Indicator."

As we said earlier, most people's personalities consist of a combination of characteristics, with one or two of the quadrants being most obvious. Keep in mind that this identification is meant to help you understand and accept yourself and others better. It is not to be used to label or value judge yourself and others. The more you know yourself, the better able you are to become more skillful in areas that are hindering you. You'll be better equipped to balance your traits.

There are two ways to approach determining your style. You could ask someone who knows you well to take the Personality/Temperament Indicator, noting the characteristics that describe you best. And, of course, you can take the Indicator yourself! When you do, be as objective and honest as possible.

Once the Indicator has been scored, you are likely to better understand why you react to people and situations as you do. I believe you'll find that it is enjoyable to share your results and give others the opportunity to take the Indicator as well.

Instructions: For each row across labelled A through Z, circle one word that best describes the way you are most of the time. Be sure to circle only one word in each lettered row. Do this for both your "Beneficial Attributes" and "Detrimental Attributes." Observe that the detrimental ones are beneficial ones taken to an extreme.

	ONE	TWO	THREE	FOUR
		Beneficial Attributes From A-Z		
A	Strong-willed	Involved	Reserved	Loyal
B	Adventurous	Talkative	Mediator	Respectful
C	Independent	Optimistic	Sentimental	Sensitive
D	Productive	Persuasive	Steady	Planner
E	Practical	Fervent	Easygoing	Idealistic
F	Resourceful	Imaginative	Calm	Deep
G	Optimistic	Outgoing	Stable	Behaved
H	Results Oriented	Cheery	Humorous	Persistent
I	Decisive	Enthusiastic	Diplomatic	Serious
J	Determined	Fun	Dependable	Competent
K	Competitive	Popular	Conservative	Orderly
L	Positive	Dramatic	Status Quo	Analytical
M	Efficient	Cute	Soft-Hearted	Thorough
N	Leader	Warm	Trustworthy	Quiet
O	Confident	Friendly	Tolerant	Self-sacrificing
P	Controlled	Playful	Single-Minded	Perfectionistic
Q	Independent	Bouncy	Friendly	Considerate
R	Direct	Personable	Specialist	Compliant
S	Bold	Refreshing	Good Listener	Cultured
T	Tenacious	Carefree	Efficient	Aesthetic
U	Persuasive	Spontaneous	Systematic	Musical
V	Self-reliant	Compassionate	Sensitive	Chartmaker
W	Mover	Interested in	Great Finisher	Gifted
X	Doer	Promoter	Cooperative	Contemplative
Y	Quick to Respond	Delightful	Helpful	Consistent
Z	Likes Challenges	Animated	Practical	Industrious
*				

*   Fill in the total number of words circled for each column.

PERSONALITY TYPE INDICATOR

Detrimental Attributes From A-Z			
ONE	**TWO**	**THREE**	**FOUR**
A	Pushy	Undisciplined	Shy	Alienated
B	Manipulative	Overly Talkative	Conforming	Critical
C	Cruel	Egocentric	Slow	Bashful
D	Domineering	Emotional	Worrisome	Self-Centered
E	Crafty	Reacting	Stingy	Calculating
F	Self-sufficient	Directionless	Unsure	Unforgiving
G	Tactless	Loud	Indecisive	Moody
H	Tough	Sloppy	Reluctant	Revengeful
I	Sarcastic	Forgetful	Spectator	Negative
J	Angry	Undependable	Dependent	Stuffy
K	Frank	Brassy	Unenthusiastic	Easily Offended
L	Demanding	Exaggerative	Mumbles	Rigid
M	Reckless	Restless	Awkward	Resentful
N	Unaffectionate	Manipulative	Blank	Depressed
O	Argumentative	Repetitious	Selfish	Theoretical
P	Intolerant	Fearful	Timid	Impossible to Satisfy
Q	Unemotional	Permissive	Doubtful	Picky
R	Inconsiderate	Unrealistic	Plain	Impractical
S	Rash	Impulsive	Self-protective	Unsociable
T	Unsympathetic	Scatterbrained	Indifferent	Insecure
U	Workaholic	Weak-willed	Aimless	Doubtful
V	Stubborn	Show-off	Inflexible	Worrisome
W	Resistant	Unstable	Fearful	"Nosey"
X	Fighter	Interrupts	Resentful	Indecisive
Y	Impatient	Wants Credit	Easily Manipu-	Compulsive
Z	Proud	Changeable	Unmotivated	Fearful
*				

* Fill-in the total number of words circled for each column.

FINAL TOTALS   (Add together your totals from Beneficial Attributes and Detrimental Attributes.)

_____   _____   _____   _____

After you've completed your circling in both the "Beneficial" and "Detrimental" tables, add up the number of circles in each column numbered one through four for each table. Add your totals from Beneficial Attributes and Detrimental Attributes together for each column. The higher the Final Total number, the more you favor the personality type represented by that column. Column One is a "**D**" (Dominant), Column Two is an "**I**" (Inspirational), Column Three is an "**S**" (Supportive), and Column Four is a "**C**" (Cautious). If you have six or seven in each column, your personality is pretty well balanced!

For more complete information on personality types and how to get a computer analysis of your personality, contact Personality Insights, Inc., at the address listed in the "Resource" section near the back of this book.

"No Excuse!" Action Plan To "Understand People"

1. Communicate with feelings; "listen-through-your-feet." Invest time and energy to understand other people's feelings. Show people that you care.

2. Take a genuine interest in people. Show concern and respect for others and take an interest in what they think, say, and do. You can build relationships faster than ever.

3. Give of yourself to others. It will come back to you. The greatest server can become the greatest leader.

4. Listen empathetically; look into the person's eyes to show them that you care. It's not just what you hear with your ears that's important, but also with your eyes. People don't care how much you know until they know how much you care.

5. Understand the three learning styles: Visual, Auditory, and Kinesthetic. This is how people perceive the world. You'll be better able to relate to and understand others.

6. Be versatile. Understand the four personality types: "D" (Dominant), "I" (Inspirational), "S" (Supportive), and "C" (Cautious). You'll then be better able to adapt yours to that of others so you can satisfy their needs and get what you want, creating "win-win" results.

7. Do the above with your friends and family as well as at work and in business. Apply them especially with your spouse and children, and I believe you'll have a happier home life.

TO MY GROWN-UP SON

My hands were busy through the day; I didn't have
much time to play the little games you
asked me to; I didn't have much time for you. I'd
wash your clothes, I'd sew and cook,
but when you'd bring your picture book and ask me to
share your fun I'd say, "A little later, son."
I'd tuck you in all safe at night; and hear your prayers,
turn out the light, then tiptoe softly to the
door—I wish I'd stayed a minute more. For life is
short, the years rush fast—a little boy grows
up so fast. No longer is he at your side, his precious
secrets to confide. The picture books are
put away, there aren't any games to play—no goodnight
kiss, no prayers to hear; that all belongs to
yesteryear. My hands once busy now lie still; the days
are long and hard to fill. I wish I might
go back and do the little things you asked me to.

ARTHUR M. SELLS

To have a friend, you need to
first be a friend.

EMERSON

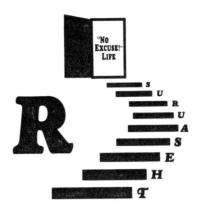

Chapter 11

REMEMBER TO HONOR FAMILY AND FRIENDS

Seventh Step Of The THESAURUS Factor

What Matters Most To You?

If I could spell "thesaurus" by making the first letter "R" I would, because it stands for Remember to Honor Family and Friends.

How many people do you know who, in their search for glory, fame, and wealth, aren't rich at all? They've stepped on everybody important in their life along the way. You can have all the money in the world, but if you don't honor those who supported and assisted you, you will not be truly successful or happy.

A house without caring inhabitants is not a home. Life can be much more satisfying when you enjoy it together with loved ones. And the extent to which you love, honor, and respect others is based on how much you love, honor, and respect yourself. To honor someone is to value them. If you don't have those feelings toward yourself, how can you expect to have it for others? As mentioned before, you can only give something you already possess. A house becomes a home when the inhabitants honor each other.

Your family and friends define your success in life. Once you leave this earth, what can you take with you? You're born with nothing material, and you can't take anything material with you when you pass away. Your material possessions are not important. Life is an opportunity to create a legacy of who you are and what you are about to the people around you and others you influenced along the way. As Bill McGrane, II, said, "Leave something to grow."

Aren't your children and friends a reflection of who you are? Of course! They know both your weaknesses and strengths. It's likely they know almost everything about you, which is one thing that makes them so special. When they comment on your unskillful behavior, or show an interest in you as a person, sometimes it can be difficult. Perhaps they are helping you confront issues instead of hiding or running away. As you grow personally, they may too. Or, they may not grow, which can present even greater challenges. As they become more knowledgeable, they may understand more about who you are and appreciate you more.

Honor one another. That's the key for excellent relationships. Henry Wadsworth Longfellow said, "The best portion of a good man's life is his little, nameless, unremembered acts of kindness and love." When we give to each other unconditionally (expecting nothing in return), that's when family and friends truly become a part of our lives. It is then that we can be truly successful and happy.

When you leave this earth, all you leave behind is what you've contributed. Yet many people, on their climb toward success, squash those around them. Unfortunately, it just doesn't seem to make any difference to them.

As I watch my children grow, I see a little more of my wife and me in them. It's rewarding. Every time I share with them, or experience them, it means more to me than earning any amount of money. If my children grow up feeling a loving respect for and value who they are and where they came from, I will consider myself successful. It doesn't matter whether they live under the same roof with me or not. As they become older, I expect them to leave our home. In today's society it may be difficult, and even undesirable, to remain living with the same people with whom you started your life. And it doesn't matter. The strength of the loving bond can reach beyond the boundaries of what they once called home.

What matters most is what you give of yourself to your children; this reaps the greatest rewards. It's what you take for granted that can create the greatest losses in your life. When I see my children grow, and I realize that over the years they have gotten to know who I am, that's just as important as what I did for anyone else.

After I lost my dad, I was hurting for awhile. Not having him to lean on was tough. It was difficult not having a father I could ask, "Hey, am I doing OK?" Let's remember forgiveness; we all need to forgive and let go. It is important to let go of the excess "baggage" if we really want to move-on. Most of us are going to lose some of the people we care about as we grow older. That's why it's so important to treasure the time you have with them now, rather than waiting five or ten years!

Honor Your Family And Friends Today

When Eric Clapton, the great guitarist, lost his little boy in a tragic accident; he wrote a song, *Tears in Heaven*, to honor him. Part of the lyrics went like this: "Would you know my name, if I saw you in heaven?" If you lost a loved one today, would they have known who you are? Would they have known what you're about? Take time to share who you are with them, and honor them today. Tomorrow may be too late.

What could be more special than honoring someone you care about? For example, there was a little girl who was in the hospital to have her tonsils removed. While she was in the operating room, a gift from her aunt arrived. It was a pretty little planter that looked like a Hummel figure of a little girl holding a small animal. As she lifted the girl from the rolling cart to her bed, the nurse told her about the gift. When she opened her eyes and saw it, the little girl said, "It's just what I always wanted!"

It would have been even more special if her aunt had been in the room. Nonetheless, her aunt had touched her heart by giving her something she wanted. No doubt, that honored little girl has remembered her aunt's kindness over and over again. Now that she's a grown woman, she is a gift-giving, honor-bestowing person herself.

This step of the *Staircase* is an excellent place for you to discover the gift most worth giving and receiving; the gift of honoring people. Remembering to honor family and friends is, for me, the most serious step of all. This is what St. Paul meant when he warned that, "If you have not charity, all else is as a ringing emptiness."

Native Americans (Indians) measured a leader's greatness by his generosity of mind and spirit. Their culture did not "keep score" on getting just for the sake of getting. Everything was meant to be shared. In other words, what and how much you *gave away* determined your reputation as an honorable, admirable person. The person of distinction was the one whose talents brought them rewards, yes, but also whose generosity prompted them to share their rewards with others. A hunter bringing back food for the tribe is an excellent example. The American Indians knew the value of giving.

When we live a life of sharing, we are naturally led to gain another piece of wisdom; giving thanks and honoring people is the most excellent gift of all. The greatest gift of thanks is to remember to honor someone with gratitude; to appreciate what they have done for you.

Many of us have family and friends who deserve to be honored for the love and support they have given us. Remembering the kind things they have done has another benefit. Martial, the Roman poet, said, "To be able to enjoy one's past life is to live twice!" Memories of honoring those closest to us can be a real joy.

When my daughter Nicole was seven, I invited her (for the first time) to hear me speak. It was at Union College in Schenectady, New York, where I presented to about ninety sorority sisters. Of all the seminars my daughter could experience first, this would be the greatest for her. She would be in the audience with the sisters and hopefully enjoy herself tremendously.

To my surprise, she managed to sit through the whole thing. She may not have listened to all of it, but she was there. She watched what I did and gained an appreciation for what I was about.

As I drove home with her, she turned to me and said, "Dad, don't stop what you're doing. It seems to help a lot of people." I felt incredibly honored.

How can you put a price tag on kind words of appreciation, especially from a child? When you see your child developing and maturing, reflecting your values and skillful behavior, isn't that success? Then she turned to me and said, "How about that 'Happy Meal' from McDonald's you promised me?" I felt happier than I had in a long, long time. Whether or not I got paid for speaking that night didn't matter. Nicole's gift of appreciation was so much more important to me.

Robert Louis Stevenson once said, "A friend is a present you give yourself." True friendship is rare. Unconditional love and honoring people for who they are is also rare. Giving to other people without expecting anything in return may be a challenge at first. However, it is the essence of friendship and kindness in general. Learn to give for the joy of giving. It is fun! Smile without expecting one back. Share who you are with other people without expecting them to share themselves with you. Honor others without expecting honor in return. I believe you'll be happier because of it.

When you honor others outside your circle of family and friends, do you get a warm and loving feeling inside? When you give to a homeless or needy person, you can also feel warm inside. So how come it is so difficult sometimes for us to do that? Could it be that some of us lived in homes where we weren't honored? Maybe we were criticized or belittled. It is a learning process to honor family and friends, and others as well. Be patient with yourself as you do.

How we treat our family and friends often determines our happiness. Happiness, with your family and life in general, is something you cannot buy. No matter how many material things you may buy, they can't create happiness. Yet look at the families that are destroyed by searching for happiness in all the "wrong" places. They need to look inside themselves and at the actions they take. When more people honor each other, many arguments that are detrimental to living a successful life can be avoided.

The "No Excuse!" philosophy is meant to help people understand that the principles of success can be used not only in your business life, but to enhance your personal life as well. When you employ techniques and skills in communications, and a more positive attitude, your life will gain new meaning. How can you justify throwing self-control out the window when you get home, after maintaining it all day at work? Aren't your family and friends most deserving of your honor and patience?

"No Excuse!" is a philosophy for everyone. When you employ its principles, you'll feel more respect for who and what you are. You can only contribute significantly to your family and friends when you feel respect for yourself. Living by the principles of "No Excuse!" will help you do that as you develop your vast potential.

A Story About Foes Who Became Friends

No event in the United States Civil War breathes life into this part of the *Staircase* more than the historic surrender of Robert E. Lee to Ulysses S. Grant at Appomattox.

This account of Lee's surrender, as Grant himself recalled it, demonstrates how powerful friendship can be in the face of a foe:

When I left camp that morning, I had not expected so soon the result that was then taking place, and consequently was in rough garb. I was without a sword, as I usually was when on horseback in the field, and wore a soldier's blouse for a coat, with the shoulder straps of my rank to indicate to the army who I was. When I went into the Appomattox Court House, I found General Lee. We greeted each other, and after shaking hands, took our seats. I had my staff with me, a good portion of whom were in the room during the whole of the interview.

What General Lee's feelings were, I do not know. As he was a man of much dignity, with an impassable face, it was impossible to say whether he felt inwardly glad that the end had finally come, or felt sad over the result and was too manly to show it. Whatever his feelings, they were entirely concealed from my observation; but my own feelings, which had been quite jubilant on the receipt of his letter of surrender, were sad and depressed. I felt like anything rather than rejoicing at the downfall of a foe who had fought so long and valiantly, and had suffered so much for a cause, though that cause was, I believe, one of the worst for which people ever fought, and one for which there was the least excuse. I do not question, however, the sincerity of the great mass of people who were opposed to us.

The two men then hammered out the terms of the surrender. Like a true friend, Grant worked to avoid humiliating the Confederates. He allowed them to return to their homes, undisturbed by United States authority. He also let them keep their personal effects, including private horses, baggage, and sidearms. This was his way of honoring them. For this, Lee was grateful.

Grant's account of the historic event continues:

When news of the surrender first reached our lines, our men commenced firing a salute of a hundred guns in honor of the victory. I at once sent word, however, to have it stopped. The Confederates were now our prisoners, and we did not want to exult over their downfall.

I determined to return to Washington at once, with a view to putting a stop to the purchase of supplies, and what I now deemed other useless outlays of money. Before leaving, however, I thought I would like to see General Lee again; so next morning I rode out beyond our lines toward his headquarters, preceded by a bugler and a staff officer carrying a white flag.

Lee soon mounted his horse, seeing who it was, and met me. We had there between the lines, sitting on horseback, a very pleasant conversation of over half an hour, in the course of which Lee said to me that the South was a big country and that we might have to march over it three or four times before the war was entirely ended, but that we would now be able to do it, as they could no longer resist us. He expressed it as his earnest hope, however, that we would not be called upon to cause more loss and sacrifice of life; but he could not foretell the result. I then suggested to General Lee that there was not a man in the Confederacy whose influence with the soldiery and the whole people was as great as his, and that if he would now advise the surrender of all the armies, I had no doubt his advice would be eagerly followed....

I was accompanied by my staff and other officers, some of whom seemed to have a great desire to go inside the Confederate lines. They finally asked permission of Lee to do so for the purpose of seeing some of their old friends, and the permission was granted. They went over, had a very pleasant time with their old friends, and brought some of them back with them when they returned.

When Lee and I separated, he went back to his lines and I returned to the Court House. Here the officers of both armies came in great numbers, and seemed to enjoy the meeting as much as though they had been friends separated for a long time while fighting battles under the same flag. For the time being, it looked very much as if all thought of the war had escaped their minds....

William Penn once said, "Friendship is a union of spirits," and nowhere is his statement more appropriate than here. The model of friendship and respect shown between Grant and Lee served to help the opposing armies unite in friendship. It also restored a true Union of spirit for the American people.

Gratitude–A Gift Of Attention You Can Give

Many people long to be honored or appreciated for the contributions they make as they go through life. It's a pleasure to return to a place and find someone glad to see you again. Most people appreciate such kind attention. We give that gift to others when we honor and greet them with obvious pleasure. Honoring others for the gifts they give us, whether the gift is years of devotion by a loving spouse, or the innocent smile of a child, increases our capacity for a fulfilling life.

We enrich both ourselves and others when we give thanks. We lift ourselves and others when we honor family and friends. We can be so happy that we feel encouraged to continue honoring people. Our memories of these times are so sweet.

To have gratitude for the things, opportunities, and people in our lives requires a certain level of maturity. As we grow, we are more likely to realize we have been enriched by them. Like that child in the hospital, it would honor the giver if we can honestly say, "It's just what I've always wanted," even for the most surprising gift. We may need to open our eyes and recognize the gifts we received. We may not have been paying attention. Or perhaps we took the gifts for granted. Appreciate all gifts, large and small, for they represent the fullness of life, both in the giving and receiving.

Appreciate "Tough" Love

By honoring others, we "fill" ourselves again with the gifts they gave us. "Give" is a powerful word. I suggest you add "to give" to your list of desires, and be specific about what and to whom you'd like to give something.

If giving is the mark of the truly rich, showing appreciation is the mark of the rich and wise. Richness, in this case, may not be related to money or possessions. These people have appreciation for everyone and everything around them. Most of all, they have a deep appreciation for those they love most.

Stay close to those you love. Appreciate them. This is how you can keep love fresh. Express how much you love your family and friends through words and deeds. You'll want to do this now, for later on they may no longer be able to receive it.

Sometimes we need to show gratitude for having learned a difficult but valuable lesson. Always appreciate what a challenge it can be for a loving person to correct you when they feel in their heart they need to do so. The greatest value a friend or family member can give us is to respect us enough to risk our rejection or anger. This is called "tough" love. Sometimes we need to be told what we may not want to hear so we can move-on.

How To Make Friends

Dale Carnegie, who wrote *How to Win Friends and Influence People*, once said, "You can make more friends in two months by becoming interested in other people than you can in two years by trying to get other people interested in you." To drive home his point, Carnegie tells how dogs make friends: "When you get within ten feet of a friendly dog, he will wag his tail. If you pet him, he may lick and jump all over you. The dog became man's best friend by *being genuinely interested in people.*"

Be Courageous And Honor Someone By Telling Them The Truth About Their Behavior

I want to share with you a little note my daughter wrote to me. It is one of my greatest treasures, and it taught me more about being a parent than any book or expert ever did.

One morning I got angry with her. And because I'm part "D," I pointed a finger at her while I was disciplining her. Here is what she wrote:

Dear Dad,

I'm sorry if I get you upset, but please don't poke your

finger at me when you are angry. I will try to do better, but you must try and understand I am only eight years old, and that I am trying to learn from your example, but sometimes it is hard.

I love you,

Nicole

I've been told before about my behavior and how others felt about some actions I took in the past. However, no one ever left a more lasting impression on me than my daughter, not even my superiors at West Point! You can feel truly loved when you know that someone cares about you enough that they'll tell you the truth about your behavior towards them. They'll let you know what's acceptable to them.

Recollections Of A True Friend

This brings me to a painful memory of a friend's unacceptable behavior and its consequences. It was one of my deepest struggles.

The Honor Code at West Point is essential to character development, with an emphasis on integrity. It says, "A cadet will not lie, cheat or steal, or tolerate those who do."

During my second year I discovered my roommate had copied a paper I had written, which he submitted as his own. I had considerable mental anguish as I made my decision about what to do about his actions. I reported his violation, and he was transferred to another company.

I remember him with some distress. Duty called me to honor the code, while my loyalty to our friendship made it almost impossible. Not only was respect for the corps and myself at stake, but also respect for my friend. This included expecting him to honor me for honoring the code, despite his breech of it. I had to believe that, in his heart, he also wanted to honor it. I also had to believe that he did not cherish the hollow victory of getting a passing grade on another man's work. If I had failed to keep my promise to honor the standards of the institution, I would have dishonored West Point, myself, and my friend.

Develop A Family Or A Personal Mission Statement

In Steven R. Covey's *The Seven Habits Of Highly Effective People*, he shared that he has a family mission statement. We've all heard of corporate mission statements. A company owner gives direction to employees not only to meet quotas, but hopefully to encourage a sense of values, purpose, and contribution to society. Have you ever thought about having a family mission statement, or a personal one if you live alone? Would you consider incuding some language that encourages your family to honor each other as well as friends and other people? To give you an idea of how to do a family mission statement, I'll share ours with you in a moment.

First though, I want to interject something about humor. Some of the funniest times we have had as a family are when we are sitting around the dinner table. All of a sudden the children start laughing. And it's contagious. It could start with my son or wife making a funny face. Soon everybody starts laughing, and it goes on for several minutes. It's a time when we forget all the stresses of the day. It's fun and relaxing.

Some of the special things your children do can be so inspiring. For instance, my son Jared loves to sing Michael Bolton's "When A Man Loves A Woman," at the top of his lungs. He doesn't know how to sing, but he loves doing it. What can you learn from that? Life doesn't need to be so serious, so heavy. Most of us could probably stand to lighten-up a bit, or maybe even a lot.

So there we were, sitting around the dinner table, all laughing. After we got settled, we decided to come up with a family mission statement, the "Rifenbary Family Mission Statement." Each of us thought of something we felt was most important for our family, and then we wrote it down. (If you're alone, what's important to you?)

The first thing we wrote was "to demonstrate courtesy to each other and other people." If my children can grow up being courteous and kind to others, I'll feel I succeeded as a parent. It's easy to be kind to a king. It takes a truly caring person to be kind to a beggar. If my children are courteous and thoughtful of other people; regardless of who they are, the color of their skin, or what their occupation is, they have given a gift to them. This would be a gift of honor.

If we communicate our feelings in an open, loving relationship with one another, the children are more likely to come to us when they get into trouble. They are less likely to want to hide anything from us.

The second statement of our mission is "to do the very best in everything we do, no matter what. It doesn't matter if you fail, as long as you give it your all." That can help you feel respect for yourself (self-esteem), regardless of your outcomes.

The final statement is "be truthful in all you say and do. Be honest with one another so that if something is bothering you, you won't "beat-around-the-bush. Don't try to deceive." *If you deceive, you'll never truly achieve.* Be open and direct. Communicate your feelings. Be honest.

Our family mission statement is on our refrigerator door, like other important things we want to remember, including our dreams. We are honoring our family by making our mission statement a priority.

Respect In The Workplace Can Lead To Greater Productivity

It is also important to remember to honor the relationships with people at our place of work. The United States is no longer a "melting pot"; it's really more like a "salad bowl." We all come from many backgrounds and cultures, often with different ideas. Many of us need to learn to appreciate and respect each other, as everyone is a person of worth and has something of value to contribute.

What do I mean by "salad bowl"? A salad may be made with ripe red tomatoes, fresh green peppers, fresh lettuce, maybe some crisp spinach, onions, and mushrooms. When they're all mixed together, they make a delicious salad. Each vegetable has something to offer.

We need to understand this in the workplace. We live in a multi-cultural world. We cannot afford to be biased, prejudiced, or judgmental of other people.

I have taught my children to always respect people for who they are. I never want them passing judgment. Who are we to pass judgment of others? We need to observe behavior, as we do when we are assessing personality type; but we don't need to, nor is it recommended, that we pass judgment.

Families, businesses, and other organizations are systems. This country is a very complex system, much like a car. If the transmission goes out, the car won't go. If one element of the family, business, or other organization is out of balance or missing (like a lack of communication, respect or courtesy), the system doesn't work correctly.

In the workplace, if there's resentment, people are blaming each other, rumors are circulating, and some people are power-hungry, how can they work together? If people are always trying to look good, be right and cover themselves, how can much of anything get done? If people don't show respect for each other, how can they be an effective team? It cannot happen. What's happening in your workplace? What can you do about it? Are you willing to address these issues?

Let's talk about courtesy. We're all from many different cultures and races, that's true. But the sooner we can accept that we're all in the *human* race, the better off we'll be. Remember, we all have something to offer. Most of us want to be honored and contribute something to the world; we want to make a difference. We need to honor others and encourage them to contribute to the world as well.

In an organization, in most cases, each person wants to contribute in some way to the other people. Most people have a specific talent or skill and a need to be productive, to at least some degree. They may not be at the same level of proficiency as someone else, but that doesn't matter. As long as they have an opportunity to contribute, we can all learn from them. We live in a society of systems; a salad bowl. Each of us has a part to play. The happiest people, I believe, are those that play their part from their heart and in line with their purpose. This would be someone who loves what he does.

Do You Appreciate Others?

When was the last time you showed those closest to you that you really care about them? How do you do that? It could be through a phone call, a letter, a gift, saying "thank-you," a greeting card, or perhaps treating them to a meal at their favorite restaurant. It doesn't need to be fancy. Something as simple as giving an unexpected hug, coupled with a few kind words, can make all the difference in the world.

I wrote my sister a letter one time when she was struggling with her career. She didn't know what to do or where to go. In my letter I said, "Look, whatever you do, I'm behind you. You have the experience and knowledge. You've done so much in your life that, no matter what you do, it's OK." I supported her, affirmed her experience, knowledge, and what she had done, as well as gave her unconditional love.

To this day the letter is still hanging, framed, on the wall in front of her desk. She treasures it more than anything else I ever gave her. This shows that appreciation doesn't need to be expensive. What's important is that it comes from the heart.

Most parents would treasure a letter. They might read it a hundred times if you wrote them a letter saying, "Thanks for just being there."

How come some families are in such disharmony when they get together, especially during the holidays? It's simple; the people closest to you think they know you and your behavior. They probably don't realize how much you may have developed, while they may not have, since the last time you were together. Therefore, they tend to treat you as they knew you before, and this can cause friction.

Fortunately, the more you personally develop, the more accepting you are likely to be of the people closest to you. Growing up, I can remember my mom disciplining me. I would say, "Oh no, I don't have a bad temper. I have lots of patience. I'm not dependent on you." I would resent any constructive comments she made about my behavior. As I grew, however, I discovered most of what she said was true. Did you ever come to the conclusion that the older you get, the more you appreciate your parents' wisdom? That's a sign of your personal development.

The more you show appreciation for other people, the happier you're likely to be. It's important to show it at home, as well as at work, and to the people you encounter outside of home and work. Your personal growth is the key. The more you grow, the more you are likely to be appreciative as your understanding increases.

Be Open And Shed The "Make-Up" On The Inside

If we allow ourselves to get caught-up in what society dictates success to be for us, we may begin to lose touch with who we really are. Facial make-up may be acceptable for a performer, or a woman striving to enhance her appearance, but what about using "make-up" on the inside? How much "make-up" are we using to cover (i.e., not reveal to others) our true thoughts and feelings? Are we dishonoring ourselves?

Are we willing to remove the emotional make-up that's inside to let those people closest to us see who we really are and what we're really about? When we do, we're better able to share with others everything that we are. It takes concentration, confidence, and self-esteem. It takes a positive mental attitude and self-control. It takes the understanding that we are all different and we grow differently. Therefore, we need to know that we are all OK so that we can accept ourselves and others unconditionally. Honor people with who you really are. It is one of your greatest gifts.

You also need to know that people have specific needs that may be different from yours. You may choose to sacrifice what you want for the wants of others if it's for results that benefit all! That can be a challenge, but it's essential if you want to be a leader who honors others.

"No Excuse!" Action Plan To "Remember To Honor Family And Friends"

1. Give unconditionally to the people you care about. None of us knows how long we'll live, so treasure the time you have with others right now. Tomorrow may be too late.

2. Discover the gift most worth giving and receiving: honoring people we care about. Learn to give for the joy of giving. Smile without expecting one back. Honor others without expecting to be honored in return.

3. Enrich yourself and others by giving thanks. Write a list of the people, things, and opportunities for which you are thankful. Maintain an attitude of gratitude; be thankful for what you have, and realize you have a lot when you have people who you care about and who care about you.

4. Stay close to those you love. Appreciate them. This is how you can keep love fresh. Express how much you love them through words and deeds.

5. Make friends by becoming interested in other people. Listen to them and meet them at their need.

6. Develop a family mission statement, involving your spouse and children (or a personal one if you live alone). By communicating in an open, loving way with each other, the children are more likely to go to the parents when they get into trouble.

7. Respect and appreciate your co-workers, as everyone has something to offer. Let go of bias, prejudice, and judgment of other people if you haven't already done so.

8. Be open and real with other people. Honor them with who you really are. Don't try to present a false image of what you're about. Base your relationships on self-esteem.

9. Honor people, but don't do things because you think it will please them if it requires sacrificing who you are. Sacrifice what you want for the wants of others if the results will benefit all.

HONOR OTHERS AS GEESE DO!

*Next fall, when you see geese heading south for the
winter...flying along in a "V" formation...
you might consider what science has discovered as to
why they fly that way. As each bird flaps
its wings, it creates an uplift for the bird immediately
following. By flying in "V" formation,
the whole flock adds 71 percent greater flying range
than if each bird flew on its own.
People who share a common direction and sense of
community can get where they are going
more quickly and easily because they are traveling on
the thrust of one another. When a goose falls
out of formation, it suddenly feels the drag and resistance of trying to go it alone...and quickly
gets back into formation to take advantage of the "lifting power" of the bird in front. If we have as
much sense as a goose, we will stay in formation with
those who are headed the same way we are
(and willing to accept their help as well as give ours to
others). When the lead goose gets tired, it
rotates back into the formation and another goose flies
point. It is sensible to take turns doing demanding
jobs. With people, as with geese, we are interdependent
on each other. Geese honk from behind to
encourage those up front to keep up their speed. We
need to make sure our honking from behind
is encouraging, and not something else. Finally...and
this is important...when a goose gets sick,
or is wounded by gunshots and falls out of formation,
two other geese fall out with that goose and
follow it down to lend help and protection. They stay
with the fallen goose until it is able to fly again
or dies. Only then do they launch out on their own, or
with another formation, to catch up with
their group. If we have the sense of a goose, we will
stand by each other in difficult times
as well as when we are strong.*

MILTON OLSON

PRESS ON

Nothing in the world can take the place of persistence. Talent will not; nothing is more common than unsuccessful men with talent. Genius will not; unrewarded genius is almost a proverb. Education alone will not; the world is full of educated derelicts. Persistence and determination alone are omnipotent.

PRESIDENT CALVIN COOLIDGE

If we were to do all we are capable of doing, we would astonish ourselves.

THOMAS EDISON

Chapter 12

UPRAISE YOUR DETERMINATION
Eighth Step Of The THESAURUS Factor

Are You Determined?

Does the word "determination" scare you? That's OK! With seven steps behind you, you're ready; you've got a strong footing.

How you feel about determination depends on your attitude. When I first opened my retail business, I can't tell you how many times I wanted to "throw-in-the-towel." My desire was tested every day by people telling me, "You'll never make it." My determination was challenged by the media saying it was a difficult time economically for the business world. Desire comes from within, and I had a strong desire to succeed, despite the obstacles. Without this desire, it would have been difficult, if not impossible, to establish the determination to succeed.

"Don't Flinch, Don't Foul, Hit The Line Hard."

Theodore Roosevelt was an excellent spokesman for determination. From very early in life, he committed to achieving everything he set out to accomplish.

As a young boy, he suffered from heavy asthma. Doctors said the mere act of breathing put a strain on his heart. His father, who also was a man of determination, told his son, "Theodore, you have the mind but you have not the body, and without the help of the body the mind cannot go as far as it could otherwise. You need to *make* your body perform."

Young Teddy accepted the challenge. He began exercising. He spent long hours alone in the gym, working harder and harder toward the goal of supreme physical fitness. He launched a vigorous routine of tennis, hiking, boating, and swimming. Though doctors continued to believe he could not expect to live a long life, Teddy was proving them wrong.

The same determination Teddy Roosevelt applied to building his strength and endurance, he applied to his studies and career. At the age of fifteen, for instance, he began studying for the Harvard entrance exams. His father hired a tutor to help him with math, Latin and Greek. Teddy set up a study schedule for himself of six to eight hours daily, five days a week. Sure enough, Harvard accepted him the following fall.

Teddy Roosevelt devoted his career to upholding the ideals he learned from his father. He believed that each person needs to create his own future. The state was responsible for ensuring equal opportunity. Citizens were responsible for accepting the challenge. Therefore, he was staunchly determined to eliminate corruption and bring about reform.

With his ideals to guide him and determination to give him strength, Colonel Roosevelt formed his "Rough Riders" to battle the Spanish in Cuba. His cause was freedom. As Governor of New York, he fought against corruption in big business and battled for the rights of immigrant workers. As President of the United States, he waged war on the "real and grave evils" of large industry so that both workers and management won, in what he called "a square deal."

Roosevelt's determination was brought full-circle in the way he raised his children. He wanted each of his sons to "use his fighting instincts on the side of righteousness." Speaking to his brood of six, he often sounded like a coach; "Don't flinch, don't foul, hit the line hard."

When he took his children on what he called "obstacle walks," the rule was to always go "over-and-through," never around an obstacle. This is the way he said he wanted to live his life, cutting straight through problems, never avoiding them. *Determination often leads to success.*

"Never, Never, Never Give In...."

The opposite of determination is discouragement. It pays to be aware of our options and to periodically reconsider certain aspects of our lives. Changing circumstances often demand changed perspectives in order for us to keep our determination. You could feel compelled to reconsider your goals because someone else's action or something else impacted your life. Maybe your partner leaves the relationship, or your company shuts down. Maybe as a child you wanted to be a jockey, but you grew to be 6'2"! At times like these, we need to know the difference between changing goals and quitting. We need to be flexible. Flexibility is one of the most important keys to maintaining your determination and leading a less stressful life.

Staying with a realistic goal that can be attained with perseverance is the objective of "No Excuse!" living. Some people quit "five-minutes-before-the-miracle." They may live with regret. Some keep going until they win. They can say, "No excuses, no regrets." Grab hold of your dream and go-for-it!

Sir Winston Churchill's determination made him a leader of unusual distinction. He spoke against appeasement when it was his nation's policy with the Nazis. If he had been in power at that time, perhaps the horrors of World War II would not have been so great. It was when Germany went to war with its neighbors and England that Churchill's party was elected to power. He assumed leadership of a nation as Prime Minister of Great Britain.

He offered the English his determination to continue the fight. That, and the inspiration of the "blood, sweat and tears" of his famous speech, was all he could offer. Churchill's early life had taught him some valuable lessons in not quitting.

Churchill had his share of "strike-outs," as most successful people do. His nine years of boarding school were marked by extreme academic difficulty, including repeated failures. But through those years he kept his determination intact. He was not satisfied to just be an observer of history. He chose to be a participant and leader. He sat for the entrance exams for Sandhurst, the West Point of Britain, three times before he was admitted.

Years later, he returned to the Harrow School, his prep-school alma mater, to speak to a graduating class. It is one of the shortest commencement speeches in history: "Never give in! Never give in! Never, Never, Never, Never–in nothing great or small, large or petty– never give in except to convictions of honor and good sense."

Now, as that speech demonstrates, never quitting doesn't mean never resting. There are times to rest, and excellent reasons for interrupting and re-evaluating any course of action that isn't bringing you the desired results. The difference between quitting and resting is this: With quitting the dream often dies; with resting the dream can be more easily rekindled, if necessary. Never quitting means keeping your dreams alive, even if you need to regroup and increase your determination.

Overcoming Challenges Makes You Stronger

If you feel you don't have options, in most cases you are just a prisoner of your own thinking. Or you may not have a dream.

A teenage boy who believes he can't go to school unless he wears the "correct" clothes or sneakers to "fit-in" makes a big mistake. If he spends time and money buying them, instead of investing in his future, it may be because he has no dream. He may be caught-up in trying to please others in an attempt to be accepted. He may be living out a "dream" or "image" fashioned by others (probably the clothing and shoe manufacturers that seek to sell their products). He may have let them manipulate his behavior, at the sacrifice of both his own dream and of being his own unique self.

Parents may suffer while watching their children try to find their own dreams. And sometimes it's the parents' dreams that threaten to have an entrapping influence on their children. Parents may try to achieve their own dreams vicariously through their children. This is harmful unless the children truly share the same dream. Guiding your children to find what is best for them is very different from insisting, for instance, that they fulfill *your* dream to be a super athlete, scholar, or something else.

Difficulties most often trigger the temptation to quit, to give up on a dream. Yet difficulties are as much a normal part of life as a butterfly breaking out of its cocoon. Overcoming difficulty builds strength. If we were to cut the cocoon open instead of letting the butterfly break out on its own, it would emerge with wings too weak to fly, and it would soon die. Much the same can be said for a chick in an eggshell; it gets strong by hatching on its own!

Successful people often welcome difficulty. For example, a math whiz may get very excited tackling a challenging problem. Difficulties can stimulate our creative instincts. We can experience tremendous growth in the process of overcoming challenges. And remember this, behind every adversity is a seed of an equal or greater benefit. It may not be immediately obvious, but the benefit will become evident at some point.

What's The Relationship Between Desire And Risk?

Living a "No Excuse!" life requires responsible behavior. It means you may need to take some calculated risks. This does not mean doing something foolish or dangerous, mind you. It's just that calculated risks are often necessary when we're faced with difficulties, or when we pursue a goal based on a big dream. Lindbergh took a calculated risk when he flew solo across the Atlantic; the potential reward was too great not to do so.

His daring not only changed his life, but also the lives of millions. His accomplishment brought him more notoriety than any human being has ever had, which led to his writing books and pioneering the airways. His achievement excited the people of the world because he bridged nations together like no one had ever done. The world was forever changed because one man had a dream and was willing to take a calculated risk to make it come true.

Let's consider the relationship between desire and risk, quitting and change. Have you ever quit something and within a year regretted it? Did you quit because you didn't have enough patience? How come you didn't stick-it-out just one more day?

Sometimes people quit just as they are about to achieve the outcome they want. It may look a little bleak, so they give up. People who win go the extra mile, take the extra step, take that calculated risk. There's a direct correlation between risk and success. How can you grow if you don't take risks? This is true for many aspects of life.

You take a risk every time you try to understand who you are. You are risking when you try to close a sale. It is a risk every time you meet a new person. You take a risk every time you attempt to resolve a conflict. Every time you risk, you have an opportunity to learn and expand your horizons. Every time you take a risk, although you may increase your possibility of failure, you also increase your potential for success. The "failure" is actually a learning experience; it's not a negative. Without risk there is little chance to achieve the success you've always wanted.

If you believe something is *too* risky to "break through," maybe you could go around it. Danger and drudgery are enemies of accomplishment. You may need to cut back on the risk some to lessen your fear. Then you can let go of much or all of your fear, renew your strength, and let your strong desire carry you through the rest of the way.

Remember the child learning to ride a two-wheeler? If all he hears are cries of, "You're going to fall," he'll probably hear, "You're going to fail," when he tries something new later in life. If he hears instead, "You're going to love this when you've learned how," his determination to ride is likely to outweigh the risk of falling.

Take swimming, for example. Telling a child to stay in shallow water is wise if he doesn't know how to swim. You can cut the risk of him going into deep water with a life jacket and swimming lessons, while assuring him of the joys of swimming. Now you've brought the risk to a manageable level and the child can get on with developing the determination to succeed.

Your Life Is Structured By Your Will

Back in the 1800's, a philosopher named Arthur Shopenhower wrote a book entitled, *The World As Will And Idea*. Initially, his philosophy was not widely accepted. He believed that *your life is structured by your will*. God's greatest gift to man is free will; the gift of choice.

Let's think about that for a minute. Your desire to succeed, your desire to grow, and your life, in most cases, is structured by your will. If you don't have a will to achieve, risk, and grow, you won't grow; you won't move forward.

Reflect back on your life for a minute. Who made your decisions? Ultimately, wasn't it you? Aren't you the one with the choice, the final say? Aren't you responsible for almost everything that has structured your life? *Everything you've done in the past, whether you've succeeded or failed, has been like a story. You've basically created your own story. There's no one to blame. You are wiser not to make excuses because, for the most part, you have created your own plot in life, your own circumstances. Your will, your desire to grow and succeed, has largely determined what that story is all about.* Your will primarily determines the pattern, format, and structure of your life.

My desire to grow and share these ideas with others is very important to me. Whether they succeed or fail, they influence how I view and express myself to others. Whenever I reflect back, I always ask myself what, where, and how have I contributed to other people; and how can I improve my skills? The power of my will, my internal desire to serve and make a difference, is an important part of who I am.

If Your Desire Is Great Enough, The Risk Doesn't Matter

The conflict between quitting and change is the conflict between desire and risk. When desire outweighs risk, you continue on. As long as the dream is viewed as bigger than the price, you'll be more likely to pursue it. You may consider quitting but you won't; you will persist. If you love what you're doing and what it can do for you and others, quitting could be eliminated from your vocabulary. If this is not true for you, you may want to do something you love. If risk outweighs desire, maybe a change is necessary. You may think it through with the help of a mentor, but ultimately it is your decision.

Shakespeare once said, "We are such stuff as dreams are made on." History is full of people who believed in their dreams and persevered to see them come true. Will you be one of those people? You can, you know.

Plato labored intensely over his *Republic* masterpiece. In fact, he rewrote the first sentence nine different ways before he was satisfied. As famous author Mario Puzo once said, "Rewriting is the whole secret to writing."

As a young boy, Jesse Owens went to hear the speedster Charlie Paddock speak. Young Jesse approached Paddock after the speech and said, "Sir, I've got a dream! I want to be the fastest human being alive." Developing his scrawny legs, Jesse Owens persevered to become the fastest man ever to run the 100-meter dash, as well as the 200-meter dash. He won four gold medals. His name was inscribed in the charter list of the American Hall of Athletic Fame.

Franklin D. Roosevelt was struck down by polio, but he persevered. Even though he was unable to walk, he proved to people across the world he could lead as President of the United States. FDR never made excuses because of his disability. He just kept pressing on.

Adam Clark labored forty years writing his commentary on the Holy Scriptures. Milton rose every morning at 4:00 a.m. to write *Paradise Lost*. *The Decline and Fall of the Roman Empire* took Gibbon twenty-six painstaking years to complete. Ernest Hemingway is said to have reviewed *The Old Man and the Sea* manuscript eighty times before submitting it for publication. It took Noah Webster thirty-six years to compile *Webster's Dictionary*.

As a boy, he dreamed of drawing comic strips. As a young man, he was advised by an editor in Kansas City to give up drawing. He kept knocking on doors, only to be rejected. He persevered until finally a church hired him to draw publicity material. Working out of an old garage, he befriended a little mouse who ultimately became famous. The man was Walt Disney, and his friend became Mickey Mouse. A nervous breakdown in 1931, and many rejections and setbacks, could not steal Disney's dreams. Walt Disney once said,

"All of our dreams can come true if we have the courage to pursue them."

Totally deaf and blind, Helen Keller became a famous author and lecturer. Instead of wallowing in grief, she lived life fully, in spite of her handicaps. She even graduated *cum laude* (with distinction) from Radcliffe College. Helen Keller had perseverance.

Leonardo Da Vinci spent ten years perfecting "The Last Supper." He reportedly became so engrossed in his work he would forget to eat for several days.

"The Last Judgment," considered one of the twelve master paintings of all time, consumed eight years of Michelangelo's life.

The Chicago fire of 1871 inspired Dwight L. Moody to build a school that would train young people to know the *Bible* and spread its teachings.

Then there was Fritz Kreisler. As a young boy, he wanted to play the violin. His parents encouraged his interest by paying for his lessons. Kreisler didn't progress as he had hoped and finally quit. He tried to study medicine and failed, then joined the army and wasn't successful there either. He tried and quit many other pursuits. Desperate for a successful experience, Kreisler went back to his violin instructor. "I want to play," he told her. "Fine," his instructor responded. "But you must acquire one irreplaceable quality. You must exhibit undefeatable determination." Fritz Kreisler persevered until his music filled Carnegie Hall.

Finally, here's a couple of people whose desire was so strong they overcame great risks; they put their lives on the line!

Imagine Neil Armstrong, in the middle of his astronaut training saying, "Well, this could be one small step for mankind, but I'm not taking it. I'm too scared. I'm too nervous. It's not for me." Instead, he said that "No matter what the risk, no matter what the sacrifice, I'm going to take that first step. I'm going to be the first man on the moon."

What if Martin Luther King had said in the middle of his "I Have A Dream" speech, "I'm getting out of here. I better not say any more. I could get hurt." Of course he knew the risks involved, but his desire to make a difference, his desire for world peace, his desire for equality, surpassed his fear of failure and even death.

And how about the Wright Brothers' courage and commitment to invent the airplane? They designed, built, tested, and experimented for four years under almost unbearable conditions; enduring high winds, hordes of mosquitoes, and numerous accidents. What if they had said, "This is too tough; let's go home and forget it"? They jeopardized and lost their bicycle business while risking their lives to follow their dream. What if they had said, "It's not worth losing the business"? Their willingness to risk everything changed the world, bringing us all closer together.

Desire. Risk. How strong is your desire to make a difference? Is it worth the risk? How much do you want to improve your family life? What sacrifices are you willing to make? What price are you willing to pay?

How much do you want to improve your business skills, your selling skills? How much do you want to improve your leadership skills, your communication skills?

What risks are you going to take to get what you want? Are you going to change jobs? Will you change careers? Do you plan to start your own business? Or do you plan to build the business you already have to make it bigger and more productive? Are you going to leap off your current path onto another? What risks are involved? Whether you'll take action depends on your desire to grow and become the best you can be, and to serve others in the best way you possibly can.

A Determined Man's First Sales Call

My transition from military to corporate life called for upraised determination. I had a whole new culture to learn, and a whole new set of skills to develop. Sure, I was building on transferable life skills, but I still needed to face the risk and let desire take over in order to succeed.

Risk and excitement go hand-in-hand and can contribute to determination when they are in proper balance. My beginning forays into sales had both of these elements. My first sales call as a pharmaceutical representative was amusing. The firm I represented offered a spectrum of medications that ranged from non-steroidal anti-inflammatory agents for treating arthritis, to calcium channel blockers for treating heart or anginal conditions.

I was geared up for my first appointment. Accompanied by my district manager, I made the presentation with all the energy and persuasiveness I could muster. The doctor was thoughtfully attentive, and when I finished and requested his response, he agreed to try our products. Much to my chagrin, he reminded me that his specialty was orthopedics. He pointed out that I had presented the benefits of three medications he'd be unlikely to prescribe because they were for heart patients.

It wasn't an easy moment for me. It seemed my determination had been focused on the wrong cause. But in reality, it had paid off. The doctor and I became friends. He appreciated my knowledge and was willing to hear about other products that could benefit his patients. After that experience, you can be sure I cut down on the risk by first reviewing the specialty of the doctor before making the visit.

As for my manager, he supported me first with his silence. He let me go down the path I had chosen. He never embarrassed me with his superior knowledge in front of the doctor. Later, his constructive comments were affirming and encouraging. My manager's confidence in me was critical at that point in my career. He gave me a gift I could pass on to others.

Stay Motivated By Taking The V.I.P. Approach

Some of us get hit with negatives nearly all the time. How do we maintain our motivation if we're constantly bombarded by other people and the environment saying, "You can't do that"? How do we handle people who say the steps we're taking will not give us the results we want? First we need to examine whether they're qualified to give us recommendations. If they are well qualified, we need to consider whether they are correct. If they are poorly qualified, we can choose to prove them incorrect. If they are not being helpful and are consistently "dumping" on us, it might be wise not to associate with them. We can choose, instead, to be around people who support us. We can find a mentor who offers us wise choices to consider.

Some people say motivation is shallow, and they're correct. That's why you need it every day, much like a shower or a bath. Furthermore, real motivation comes from within. If you are not self-motivated, you'll probably have little desire to sustain the determination you need to succeed. Motivation can be stimulated externally, but it's your internal drive that keeps you going.

How do you enhance self-motivation? I've structured something called V.I.P., "Very Important Person." *Unless you believe in who you are and what you're doing, it's difficult to be self-motivated. How can you have any desire if you don't feel you are important?*

I've also filled the acronym with a few other words that can enhance your ability to stay self-motivated. The "V" stands for *value*. You need to put value on yourself and your goals. When in your heart and mind you feel you are a valuable person, and that your goals are valuable, you'll have a greater desire to achieve them. When you feel worthless or undeserving of your dreams, your desire to achieve them diminishes. Value yourself, the people around you, and your goals. You'll find it makes a big difference in your self-motivation.

"I" is for *integrate*. Integrate with people who have dreams similar to yours. Allow those who share in what you want to achieve to be incorporated into your life, your business, and your family. When you associate with a group of people with common dreams and goals, you're likely to be more self-motivated because their energy will affect yours. You can support one another. This is one of the greatest secrets of success. When you find those people, it can make a tremendous difference in how you feel about life; because you realize you're not alone in your quest and you have support

In a lot of ways, we're all basically in the same boat. Sure, some of us are more challenged in certain areas. Yet all of us have many of the same situations just by the fact that we are people. When you find people who understand you, your difficulties, and what you want, it can be uplifting and rewarding to be associated with them. Today there are many networking organizations and support groups that offer this kind of camaraderie.

The "P" means *participate*. Participate in events and seminars that support and reinforce your desires. If you have a desire to be one of the top salespeople in your company, participate in events that can teach you how. Get involved in activities that can help trigger your motivation.

If you want to be a more skillful and loving parent, participate in workshops, read books and listen to tapes that can help you enhance your parenting skills. This approach works across the board, regardless of your area of interest. The more you dream and do the correct things, the quicker you're likely to accomplish what you want.

You become and attract what you think about most. (Remember to think about what you want rather than what you don't want!) All of this will occur when you *value* what you think about, *integrate* with other people, and *participate* in appropriate activities. Remember to V.I.P.

The other step on the *Staircase* that dramatically affects your desire and self-motivation is your self-esteem, the Second Step. If you don't feel respect for yourself, if you don't believe in who you are, your determination to succeed will be severely affected. You need to feel enough respect for yourself to do whatever it takes to give yourself what you want, within the mission of your life.

Time Management And Desire Destroyers

What does time management have to do with desire? What is time management anyway? Can anyone manage time? No, not really! You can only manage activities. In other words, you manage yourself. Time never stops. It's managing activities within a certain time frame that enables you to move forward. When you ineffectively manage activities, your desire is severely hampered. How come? Because it causes disorganization and problems. When you're disorganized, it's difficult to stay on your path of success. We'll cover more on that later.

Here are some key factors associated with time/activity management that can interrupt and actually destroy your desire. I call them "Desire Destroyers."

The first Desire Destroyer is procrastination. Why does putting things off have such a significant impact? If you procrastinate, how can you possibly get where you want to go? Procrastination hinders your determination to succeed. Procrastination is generally the result of lazy behavior or fear of failure and the unknown. Lazy behavior usually means that there is a lack of a dream or goal, and thus a lack of desire. The cure for this, of course, is to find a dream big enough so that you are motivated to do whatever it takes to get the outcome you want. If you're feeling unsure, you may put off doing what you need to do. If you need to take a risk, and you fear failure and the unknown, you may procrastinate to the degree of your fear.

There are four solutions to procrastination. *Number one; find your dream, or at least something you want very much. Number two; begin.* Just get started. Someone once said, "Getting started is half done." *Number three is called "the cold cut technique."* Say you've got a big salami. Obviously you can't eat the whole thing at once, so you cut it up into small slices. In other words, break a task into small, manageable chunks. If things are perceived as too big or too difficult, we may tend to procrastinate. This is similar to the fears of risk, failure, and the unknown. The key is to complete one small piece at a time. You'll feel encouraged, and eventually you'll get the whole job done. Inch-by-inch, anything's a cinch! The key is to get out of your inertia and set things in motion to gain momentum. Once momentum is gained, it's easier to do than not to do your task.

Once, while I was on a radio talk show, I got a call from a woman who wanted to clean her basement. She said it had been bothering her for the last eight months; it was filled with all kinds of old stuff. I responded, "Well, why don't you rope off just a small corner of the basement and clean that first?" Two weeks later, I got a note from her saying she did that and it worked. I don't know if she moved everything into that corner or just cleaned it out, section by section. However, tackling a small chunk first enabled her to get the job done. It didn't seem so overwhelming. Instead, it seemed like a more possible task.

One day you may decide to paint a room, but you may keep procrastinating because of all the preparation required before you can even begin painting. The solution is to take it one-step-at-a-time. Develop an action plan. The first week go ahead and pick the color. The second week buy the paint and the brushes. The third week paint one wall. Eventually what happens? Before you know it, the room is painted. You may have been so excited that you went ahead of your own schedule!

The "cold cut" technique works with getting almost anything done. The things we want most in life may take the most time and/or may be the most difficult. Just break the task down into small chunks, and you are less likely to procrastinate; your desire will remain.

You may be familiar with the 80/20 rule; the Preado Principle. In retail, for example, I made eighty percent of my profit from twenty percent of my product. In sales, you're likely to make eighty percent of your quota based on twenty percent of your clients. It applies to almost everything, especially in time/activity management. You'll find that you'll spend eighty percent of your time and energy on about twenty percent of your tasks. That twenty percent is the most difficult and takes the most time.

The fourth technique to overcome procrastination is to provide yourself with incentives. Reward yourself along the way. Don't work just to work. After you eat that small piece of salami, give yourself a pat on the back. Say, "Hey, I did it!" When you provide a little bit of positive reinforcement, you'll find it inspires you to eat that next piece of salami, paint another wall, or clean out another corner of the basement. After you've finished a challenging task, it's important to reward yourself with something like a movie, a new outfit, a book you've wanted, or something else you would enjoy. In other words, enjoy the trip.

The second Desire Destroyer is disorganization. This occurs predominantly in meetings, with paperwork, and your environment. When you walk into an office and it's a complete mess, with papers all over the place, doesn't that have a negative impact on you? It makes it more difficult for you to focus on the task at hand.

How about meetings? When you don't have an agenda, you have disorganization, which leads to an ineffective meeting. It has a significant negative impact on your desire, especially once you leave the meeting; you may feel disheartened, having gotten little or nothing from it. Disorganized meetings inhibit activity almost more than anything else. Generally, meetings can enhance your desire only when they're conducted effectively.

How do you handle disorganization? What is the relationship between that and activity management? *First, you assess the situation.* For example, if your office is a mess, look at it and assess it. What do you have to do to get it organized? *Secondly, you prioritize. Third, you implement.* Look at your office, prioritize the things you have to do, then do them. It'll have a major impact on your degree of organization and allow you to be more productive.

Success-oriented people don't like to be disorganized. If you're disorganized when you work with and express yourself to other people, you won't get much done. If the organization or company where you work is disorganized, it can have a major negative impact on your desire to be self-motivated to accomplish the tasks at hand.

You might want to think of yourself as your own business. No matter what your environment is or what you do, you are, in fact, your own business. For best results, you need to be organized. You might even think of yourself as "Me, Inc." Conduct yourself and your life in a businesslike, organized manner.

The third Desire Destroyer is interruptions. And, of course, the major interruption for most people is unscheduled visits from others. The second interruption is telephone calls. The third is crisis situations.

Did you ever consider that it's actually valuable to be interrupted? If you were never interrupted, that would probably mean no one needed you. If your phone didn't ring or you didn't have any memos coming across your desk, you might get the idea you weren't needed. You may ask, "Am I valuable to this organization?"; "Am I valuable to this family?" If you're not interrupted, you're probably not needed.

Interruptions are a fact of life. How do you deal with them? *First, manage your people, your environment, and your office. Second, instruct people on when you may be interrupted. Third, delegate activities that would take you from your main focus and that someone else could do.* It takes self-esteem to do this, and it's well worth the results.

You can spend more or less time on time/activity management; it's completely up to you. Even a little management of your activities can go a long way and can be an excellent start. No matter what's going on around you, it's your responsibility to deal with it so you can be most effective with the time, energy, and resources at your disposal. Upraise your determination. The more you organize and manage your activities, the greater desire you'll have to continue your quest because of the clarity of mind you will have achieved. It is important to eliminate clutter in your life. The greater your desire to accomplish your dreams, the more self-motivated you are likely to be in general; and specifically, to control how much you'll allow yourself to be interrupted.

Determination Is The Key To Realizing Your Dreams

The relationships you have with your teachers, mentors, and leaders impacts the strength of your determination to accomplish what you want. Are they encouraging or discouraging your determination? Consider shying away from relationships with people who discourage your precious determination. Choose these key people carefully.

The dream of democratic self-rule, that began with the signing of the Magna Carta in 1215, was finally realized by the 20th Century. However, it was threatened in England, as well as in Europe, with the rise of Fascism in the 1930's. It was Churchill who sparked the British people's determination to keep on going so they could maintain their freedom.

When you dream, have the determination, and take the appropriate action to go where your dream leads you, you'll know one of life's greatest joys. If you give up too easily on your dream, your purpose, you'll never have a fulfilling life. You can choose to become whatever you desire to be. If you're filled with determination, you'll attract friends who share your dream; you'll find people who will support you.

By now I believe you are wise enough to understand that what you have means nothing next to who you are. (Unfortunately, in this world where material goods are often the focus, many people don't realize this important fact.) Who you are is with you wherever you go. Your determination can lead you to take the necessary action to take you to your dream. What you become along the way is what it's all about!

Here's an interesting poem I want to share with you. It's called "Mr. Meant To":

Mr. Meant To had a comrade, and his name was Mr. Didn't Do.
Have you ever had the chance to meet them? Did they ever call on

you? Well these two I hear they live together, in a house called never win. And I hear this house is haunted by the ghost of might have been.

Author Unknown

Always think about what you can do, rather than what you could have done. Remember, the desire from within can enable you to do what is necessary to realize your dream.

Think of your life as a giant 1,000 piece jigsaw puzzle of a beautiful landscape. One of the first things you would do is take the lid off and turn the box over to empty the pieces. This is like being born. One of the earliest major accomplishments is when you turn the pieces over. It's like an infant going from its stomach to its back. Then, like the foundation of your life, you begin to put the frame of this puzzle together. You put that together first because it's easier, fundamental, and important. It's like when you first walked, talked, and graduated from high school.

As life goes on, you reach the half-way point, say 500 pieces, and all that's left is blue sky. You look at all those similar-looking pieces and you ask, how in the world am I going to get that puzzle together? How am I going to become what I was created to be and live the life I imagine? The answer is you just keep going. Never quit. Success is a journey, not a destination. Some pieces are put in place easier than others, but you need to persevere. You may never get all the pieces of your puzzle of life together; but as long as you "keep-on-keeping-on," giving of yourself, your feelings, ideas, talents, and skills, you'll grow and become; you'll make a difference.

Walt Disney failed in business five times before he saw his dream come true. He just wouldn't quit. Once during a student tour of Disney World, one of the children raised his hand and said to the tour guide, "Wouldn't it have been great if Walt Disney was here to see this?" The tour guide responded by saying, "He already has. That why it's here." Disney had the vision before it became reality. He believed it before he could see it.

Always keep sight of what you want to become and where you want to take your life. When you have the desire to achieve, everything you do can have value. You know you will make a difference in this world if you just keep moving-on toward your dreams. Be strong and stay determined. You can do it!

"No Excuse!" Action Plan To "Upraise Your Determination"

1. Grab hold of your dream and go-for-it! "Never, never, never give-in...except to convictions of honor and good sense." (Winston Churchill) Success comes to those who persevere.

2. Welcome challenges. They nourish your creative instincts and cause you to grow in the process of overcoming them. Behind every adversity is the seed of an equal or greater benefit.

3. Take a chance. The more you risk, the greater your potential for success. Without risk there is little chance to achieve the success you want.

4. View the dream as bigger than the price. When your desire outweighs the risk, you'll continue.   You may consider quitting, but you won't; you'll keep on going toward your dream.

5. Don't make excuses for your inabilities or disabilities. When the dream is big enough, you figure out how. You'll overcome your obstacles along the line.

6. Stay motivated all the time by taking the V.I.P. approach. Value, Integrate, and Participate. *Value* yourself and your goals. *Integrate* with people who have dreams similar to yours. *Participate* in events and seminars that support your desires. Know that you are a Very Important Person!

7. Overcome procrastination by doing four things: a. Find your dream, or at least something you want very much. b. Begin; just get started. c. Use the "cold cut" technique; complete one small piece at a time. d. Provide yourself with incentives. Reward yourself when you achieve certain goals. This helps you realize the meaning of your work and can motivate you along the way.

8. Get organized by doing three things: Assess, Prioritize, and Implement. Look at the situation you're in and assess it. Prioritize the things you need to do; then implement them. Organization is a key quality of successful people.

9. Handle interruptions by doing three things: Manage, Instruct, and Delegate. Manage your people, your environment, and your office. Instruct people on when you may be interrupted. Delegate activities that would take you from your main focus. Don't waste time doing mundane tasks that are OK for someone else to do.

10. Always think about what you can do, rather than what you could have done. You become and attract what you think about most. Your inner desire can enable you to realize your dream.

JUST FOR TODAY

*Just for today I am happy. Happiness is from within;
it is not a matter of eternal circumstances.
Happiness is a choice. Just for today I work with what
I have and don't complain of lack. I do
whatever it takes to find or create the circumstances I
need to achieve my goals. Just for today I
take care of my body. I exercise it, care for it, nourish
it, not abuse it nor neglect it, so that it will
be a perfect machine for my bidding. Just for today I
strengthen my mind. I learn something
useful. I am not a mental loafer. I read something
that requires effort, thought, and concentration.
Just for today I exercise my soul in three ways; I do
somebody a good turn and not get found out.
I do at least two things I don't want to do, as William
James suggests, just for exercise. Just for
today I am agreeable. I look as well as I can, dress as
becomingly as possible, talk softly, act
courteously, I am liberal with compliments, criticize not
at all, nor find fault with anything and not
try to regulate nor improve anyone. Just for today I
live through this day only and don't tackle
all my problems at once. I can do things for twelve
hours that would appall me if I had to
keep them up for a lifetime. Just for today I have a
program. I write down what I expect to
do every hour. I may not follow it exactly, but I have
it. It eliminates two pests, hurrying and
indecision. Just for today I have a quiet half-hour all
by myself and relax. In this half-hour
sometimes I think of God, to get more perspective into
my life. Just for today I am unafraid, especially
I am not afraid to be happy, to enjoy what is beautiful,
to love, and to believe that those I love, love me.*

AUTHOR UNKNOWN

Chapter 13

SUCCEED AND BALANCE YOUR LIFE

Ninth Step Of The THESAURUS Factor

The Fruits Of "No Excuse!"

With this final step, we want to "tie-it-all-together" so it is really clear that success is a journey, not a destination. All the principles of the *Staircase* are interwoven and interdependent. To be truly successful, you need balance in your activities. They all affect each other in determining how successful and balanced your life is or can be. Also, you can go up and down the *Staircase*, dwelling on one step if necessary, depending on your needs at that point in time. It is a back-and-forth process. You may want to refer back to this book as many times as you seek new understanding in any area covered.

Your thoughts are the only things you can have absolute, total control over. Once you understand that, you can become liberated. Unlike animals, which live by instinct, God gave us a free will so we can make choices. The power to choose releases you from idle hope and lets you open your life to healthy expectation. It enables you to rely on your inborn resources and abilities, as well as on the skills you have developed.

Your journey along the *Staircase* sets the stage for a life of great adventure and achievement. By reading and studying this book, you have had an opportunity to open your mind to ideas and principles that can help you create a successful, happy, and fulfilling life. Keep them fresh by daily application, and you can eliminate any habits and excuses that could prevent you from fulfilling your destiny.

Mark Twain once said, "Habit is habit and is not to be flung out the window but coaxed down the stairs, one-step-at-a-time." You can avoid new excuses just as you can eliminate old ones. With "No Excuse!" living, you can guard against the negative thinking that may threaten to undermine your efforts.

One of the first things we addressed was how to define success. Remember, whatever it is you define success to be, as you achieve it you're successful! Then you can come up with something brand new and exciting to achieve. This is all part of your journey. It's a progressive realization. Again, my definition of success may be different than yours. That's OK! Also, you and I may experience happiness in different ways. That's OK, too! Happiness comes from within. What is happiness to one person may not be to the next.

You may go to work in the morning, and if so, you probably come back home at night. Or maybe you work later hours or travel out of town. If you are a parent, student, or retiree, and you don't work outside your home, it is still likely you have a daily routine. Life is very much a "full circle." "No Excuse!," as a philosophy for success, is also a full circle. Without the integration of all the other steps, your chances of being happy, fulfilled, and purposeful are reduced. If you keep making excuses, how can you expect to have a rich life experience? Is there any excuse not to achieve success? How can you blame lack of time for not accomplishing things when it's probably your inability to effectively manage activities? How can you blame other people for misunderstanding and not giving you the outcomes you want, when it may be your inability to communicate effectively with them that caused the situation?

Whenever you have a task or situation that you need to handle, and you have an excuse, think again. Remind yourself that you are responsible for your decisions, and you're likely to find these excuses irrelevant. *As a result of being a student of the "No Excuse!" philosophy, I recommend that one of your major goals be to eliminate excuses from your life.*

"Succeed And Balance Your Life" is the integration of all the other steps. Without self-esteem it's very difficult to believe in yourself. Without purpose, without having any idea of why you are here, it's very difficult to define success for yourself. They're all interconnected and interdependent.

Are you willing to take responsibility for the decisions you are going to make now and in the future, regardless of their outcomes? They are all going to make at least some impact on your life and the people around you. When you take responsibility for your decisions, you'll grow from the experience whether you receive the outcome you want or not!

You Need Your Own "Declaration Of Independence"

Back in 1776, the *Declaration of Independence* proclaimed the beginning of a great Republic. Fifty-six men put their lives on the line to be free. They didn't make any excuses and they were ready to take responsibility for their actions. Today, "No Excuse!" living prepares *you* to sign your own "declaration of independence" for a life of personal freedom and enterprise.

Why did our forefathers create the *Declaration of Independence*? They had reached such maturity and self-reliance by the end of Britain's successful struggle against France that they were no longer willing to tolerate England's control. The Americans had become self-responsible to the point where they no longer needed outside influence for support.

May I suggest that you consider this text from the *Declaration of Independence* as your own personal declaration of freedom:

> *We hold these truths to be self-evident, that all men are created equal, that they are endowed by their Creator with certain unalienable rights, that among these are life, liberty, and the pursuit of happiness. That to secure these rights, governments are instituted among men, deriving their just powers from the consent of the governed. That whenever any form of government becomes destructive to these ends, it is the right of the people to alter or to abolish it, and to institute new government, laying its foundation on such principles and organizing its power in such form as to them shall seem most likely to affect their safety and happiness.*

When you are empowered by "No Excuse!" living, you are, in effect, your own "independent state." You have the right to make peace, establish alliances, conduct business, and do all those things that independent states do. On July 4, 1776, fifty-six men secured a future of self-determination and changed the course of history.

Right now you can boldly pledge your own independence. I suggest you write the date and this affirmation in your personal diary, planning book, or on a calendar: "From here on out, I'm more self-responsible and self-assured than ever. I am exercising my own inalienable right to life, liberty and the pursuit of happiness."

Where Does Success Come From?

Recently, I went to the dictionary to see what it said about success. Much to my surprise, one of the definitions was, "Success is the outcome of an event whether positive or negative." Does that intrigue you like it did me? It means that even a "negative" (unwanted) outcome can be viewed as a success because, hopefully, you *learned* something from it. Ideally, you gained understanding and wisdom; you grew. Your perception and attitude has a lot to do with how you interpret the event. Remember, *behind every adversity is the seed of an equal or greater benefit.* In effect, you could say *there's no such thing as failure! There is only the opportunity to learn.*

How do you deal with failure? Life is always up-and-down, ebb-and-flow. If you worry about failure, it's more difficult to overcome; a lot of your energy is wasted worrying. Einstein said, "Men worry more about what they can't see than what they can see." If you're always concerned about your outcomes being negative, you're setting yourself up for failure. A constant negative focus makes it difficult to overcome failure and look beyond it. *You get what you focus on.*

Totally Forgive

Forgiveness is a vital aspect of success. If you blame yourself and your past, and use that as an excuse for not achieving, you'll never move forward. If you use others at home, at work, or elsewhere as an excuse for your failure or potential not to succeed, you'll never move ahead. If you use your environment, i.e., your circumstances as an excuse, you'll be stuck. When you forgive, you'll feel more respect for yourself because you are taking responsibility. You'll also feel relieved because you have released all that resentment.

Can you honestly use what's going on around you as an excuse not to develop personally? Can you use it to avoid becoming what you desire to be? *No matter how many excuses you develop, you are still responsible for your life.* No matter what factors are out there, you are still the ultimate manager of your career and personal life. Once you deal with failure and once you forgive, a transition begins. When you have a purpose and a path to follow, you'll feel more confident about who you are; you are more likely to know that you are "in the driver's seat" of your life. As a result, when you make decisions you accept full responsibility for them.

Have Self-Esteem

How can you possibly achieve success if you don't feel respect for yourself? How can you succeed if you don't believe in who you are and what you are about? How can you succeed if you doubt yourself?

Your self-esteem and any fears of rejection and failure you may have, in all likelihood, stem from your childhood. Throughout life, in most cases, we all want to be accepted by others and succeed. Your self-esteem is always fluctuating, depending on the respect you feel for yourself. This, in turn, determines how you feel about the world around you.

What you see in the world around you is a reflection of your thoughts and feelings. For example, if you are happy, you are likely to see the happiness in the world; you are likely to see sadness in the world if you are sad. How we feel about the people with whom we live and work, in many cases, determines how much we let the fears of failure and rejection influence our performance. If we feel accepted and comfortable with these people, we are more likely to take greater risks around them.

You can enhance your self-esteem by being committed to respecting your talents and desires and doing what you love. The only way you can injure your self-esteem is by value judging. It is also important to treat people the way they want to be treated. Respect them and where they're coming from without putting them on a pedestal. Lou Holtz said this excellently in his "Do Right" philosophy. When you do these things, you'll feel more respect for yourself and where you're going. You'll smile more and give more to other people. You'll want to share your happy feelings with others too, as well as what you've learned along the way. When you assist others, you reinforce what you have learned. You will also gain a deeper understanding through the process of teaching others.

Elevate Your Attitude And Enthusiasm

When you feel pleased about yourself, it's easier to give and share with others. This is done primarily through your attitude and enthusiasm. An elevated, enthusiastic attitude brings "magic" to the workplace as well as the home. It's the first impression you give to other people. *It's your attitude and not your aptitude that determines your altitude!*

The best way to measure your attitude is to see how others respond to you. If your attitude is negative and unenthusiastic, people most likely won't want to be around you. Your attitude and enthusiasm are reflected in the way you dress and groom yourself. They show in the way you speak and how you express yourself. People can see it in your eyes and the way you carry yourself. Your facial expressions and hand gestures indicate where you are. Your attitude and enthusiasm come out through every little bit of you. Positive or negative, they affect your performance.

If the leadership of a company is negative and unenthusiastic, the employees are likely to be the same way! The positive employees may choose to go elsewhere. An organization cannot be effective if its people are negative and unenthusiastic.

Like the leadership of a company, if parents are complaining, blaming, whining and angry, it will have a negative impact on the children. It is especially important to maintain an elevated attitude and enthusiasm with your family. By doing so, you can uplift them and show them how important they are to you. Norman Vincent Peale's great book, *Enthusiasm Makes The Difference*, says it all. I recommend you read it.

Sustain Self-Control

Your first "test" on the *Staircase* is "S"–Sustain Self-Control in everything you do. Self-control is a measure of your professionalism and how much you believe in and respect yourself, as well as your respect for others. It's a measure of who you are and tells other people about your self-esteem and attitude.

Self-control is also related to patience; true success takes time. There is no such thing as "get-rich-quick." You may hear of so-called "overnight" successes, but if you investigate you'll probably find that "overnight" took years. Occasionally someone will come up with something like the "Pet Rock," but those are few and far between. You hear about them because they *are* so rare. Anything worthwhile takes time. Sustain self-control in all your thoughts, words, and deeds. Be professional with others at work and patient in all arenas.

Always Be Honest

True success is honest success. If you don't adhere to the principles of honesty and integrity, no matter what you do, no matter how much money you earn, no matter how many buildings you may build, you're unlikely to be happy and at peace inside.

I believe most people want to do the "right" thing. If you jeopardize your honesty and integrity, your conscience will eventually bother you. You may feel guilty because you are angry with yourself. If you have not been honest with yourself and others, it's likely you'll carry it around with you and it'll drain energy from you until you resolve the situation. The only possible resolution may be forgiving yourself and righting whatever is wrong. If others *perceive* that your dishonesty does not affect you, and that you have no intention of "coming clean," they may be refusing to admit the truth. They may not even talk to you about it, which is called denial. They could be rationalizing their *own* dishonesty. They may be afraid to take the risk of discussing the matter with you because they might be fearful of your reaction.

No one can achieve true success if they don't base their life on values and morals. What you think about all the time shows what you value. You become and attract what you think about most. Stand up for what you believe in. *If you don't stand for something, you'll probably fall for anything.* Stand up for who you are, at home, at work, and wherever else you may go. Have integrity and be honest with others. When you do, they're more likely to trust you, communicate with you, work with you, and even have fun with you. As a result, your business and family can grow and prosper.

As someone once said, "An excuse is a thin shell of truth, stuffed with a lie." So to always be honest, never make excuses. Just tell the truth. Honesty is the best policy.

Always Dream and Set Goals

Success is a journey. As author and businessman Glenn Bland puts it, "Success is the progressive realization of predetermined, worthwhile goals, stabilized with balance and purified by belief." Goals define your success. If your definition of success is a happy family and a stable career, your goals need to reflect that. To realize that outcome, you'll need to have a plan and take the necessary steps.

A big key to achievement is to put your goals on paper. You're four times more likely to achieve something when you write it down! If it's important enough to you, you'll write it down. It it's not important to you, you won't write it down. Writing ensures the information was processed through your mind. Seeing your goals in writing gives you visual reinforcement.

I have my dreams and goals posted on my desk where I can see them every day. I know exactly what I want to accomplish and what I want to be. I also know how much money I want to earn. Once they are embedded in my subconscious through daily viewing and self-talk, I don't need to see them as often. Those thoughts have become a part of me. The ideas have become so ingrained that I feel like I'm on "automatic pilot." The subconscious directs my conscious mind, which drives me to do what needs to be done to realize the outcomes I want. I suggest you keep your goals posted in front of you, too. Remember, it's the internal and not the external that structures what you become and how far you'll go in life.

Without dreams and goals, you have no direction. You could have twenty different roads to follow, as in the movie *The Wizard of Oz*, but you'll never get to the "Land of Oz" unless you're on "The Yellow Brick Road." There are so many variables in life that we may not reach our goals when we want to. No matter what the outcome, there's always a lesson. *You may want to adopt the idea of setting your dreams and goals in concrete and your plans in sand.* Be open and flexible; modify your plans to reach your desired outcome.

Upgrade Your Knowledge

Knowledge in the area of your dreams and goals is your refueling mechanism. It's a major resource that you need in order to achieve. To "know" and not "do," however, is often no more beneficial than not knowing at all. Always strive for more information that can help you achieve what you want. There are so many resources, like books, audiotapes, and videotapes, that there's "No Excuse!" for not knowing what you need to know to succeed. Attend seminars regularly. Many professionals go to seminars to seek knowledge to develop themselves and improve their performance.

If you want to be the best salesperson you can be, study sales. If you want to be the best parent you can be, study parenting. If you want to be the best businessperson you can be, study business. Listen to audiotapes, especially in your car. Why *spend* hours just listening to music when you can *invest* a large part of that time listening to an educational or motivational cassette tape? Knowledge helps to provide the understanding, which can lead to wisdom. Unless you read and listen, it's virtually impossible to grow, other than learning from one difficult experience after another.

Understand People

People have different personalities and temperaments. It is important to keep in mind that the "D" (Dominant) needs to be in charge, the "C" (Cautious) wants information, the "S" (Supportive) needs acceptance, and the "I" (Inspirational) wants recognition.

When we communicate with others, both in our personal and career life, we need to observe, without judgment, their personality traits. With an understanding of our own personality, we need to consider "how we can best interact with others." If you are married, it is especially important to understand your spouse's personality so you can communicate more effectively. Much of your success will depend on your ability to understand and relate with people, so investing your time and energy in this area is key.

Remember To Honor Family And Friends
Without strong, loving relationships with your family and friends, what do you have? Who really cares if you gain all kinds of material things at the expense of your relationships? People want and need to be honored. *When you give to other people, you reap the greatest rewards.* What you take for granted can result in the greatest losses. I believe how you honor the people you are close to defines how successful you ultimately become.

While reading through a book of letters from the Civil War, I came across one from a soldier to his family. It said, "I never knew how to value my home until I went into the Army." I sure related to that, and it touched me. If you've ever been in the military, went away to school, or left home for an extended period, you probably know how the soldier felt. As the song goes, "Be it ever so humble, there's no place like home."

Take care of the people in your family. Like a tree, if one main branch dies, the tree will probably survive. But if four or five main branches die, the tree may die. Be sure to stay close to the most important people in your life. Put them in your mind and heart.

Upraise Your Determination
Look at all the people who have overcome tremendous obstacles. There have been untold numbers of athletes who have beat the odds. Look at Wilma Rudolph and Jesse Owens. Because they believed in themselves, had determination, and a burning desire to make it, they did. They achieved and succeeded. No matter what challenges laid before them, they focused on their vision, not on the obstacles. They were thinking beyond the present. They were always headed in the direction they wanted to go, even if an occasional detour was necessary.

Determination is synonymous with courage. As Amelia Earhart once wrote in a poem, "Courage is the price life exacts for granting peace. The souls that know it not, know no release from little things."

Think about that for awhile, and you'll probably come to the conclusion that determination is a key ingredient in your becoming happy, as well as successful.

Democracy And Free Enterprise Provide The Environment For A Happy, Productive, Fulfilling Life.
You now have the tools to help yourself and those around you lead a better life. There's "No Excuse!" not to do so. When you integrate forgiveness, self-esteem, attitude, enthusiasm, self-control, honesty, dreams, goal setting, knowledge, understanding people, honoring family and friends, and determination so you can grow and become, you'll have a wonderful life. The combination makes it almost inevitable that you'll succeed, live a balanced life, and be happy and fulfilled.

We live in a time of magnificent change. There is no major conflict in the world, and Russia, the superpower that was a self-proclaimed enemy of democracy and capitalism, has sought our help. We're teaching them how to satisfy the universal human needs of their people, as well as their socioeconomic needs.

A few years ago, Mikail Gorbachev, Premier of the former Soviet Union, addressed the crowd at Founder's Day ceremonies at the University of Virginia. Ironically, the campus was founded by Thomas Jefferson, chief architect of the *Declaration of Independence*. Jefferson's thoughts about democracy continue to have a profound effect on American life. In fact, his ideas are inspiring leaders all over the world who are still working to instill democratic reforms. Jefferson left a legacy that opened the human spirit to change. It would no longer be confined to the hopelessness and disrespect of unacceptable situations. Part of this change was reflected in the fact that Gorbachev spoke at this campus.

A government needs to provide its citizens with an environment to support life, liberty, and the pursuit of happiness. We personally have a responsibility to embrace life, cherish liberty and free enterprise, and to pursue our dreams while encouraging others to do the same. Happiness is a byproduct of pursuing our dream, i.e., going toward our vision. In the process, we can learn to know ourselves better while giving of our skills and talents to contribute to the world.

One of my favorite quotes of all time, by Ralph Waldo Emerson, describes a life of success and balance:

To laugh often and much; to win the respect of intelligent people and the affection of children; to earn the appreciation of honest critics and endure the betrayal of false friends; to appreciate beauty; to find the best in others; to leave the world a little better place than we found it, whether by a healthy child, a garden patch or a redeemed social condition; to know even one life breathed easier because you lived. This is to have succeeded.

How can success be more special than that? We all have the opportunity and potential to make a difference in the lives of other people. *It's easy to make a dollar, but it's more important to make a difference.* There is truly "No Excuse!" not to be successful.

Get Ready To "Fly" And Live Your Dreams

Like *The Knight In Rusty Armor* at the end of his journey, are you ready to embrace life and its opportunities? Your training on the *Staircase-of-Success* has given you an opportunity to be more aware of the simple joys of daily life. There's a poster that shows a butterfly in flight; soaring from his cocoon. The caption says, "You can fly, but that cocoon has to go." May I suggest that you let go of your cocoon, and get ready to "fly"!

People who *receive* without effort often end up *having* without appreciating. When you work for something, you are more likely to realize its value and be grateful for it.

Those not content to rest on their laurels (just be satisfied with what they've done so far) are inspired to know they can live the life they want. They just need to define what success means to them.

We will not scoff at people who don't know what they want; we can help them find it. We can show them the satisfaction that comes from deciding on a dream and going for it. This is critical because, as it says in the Scriptures, "Where there is no vision, the people perish." As a bonus, happiness comes as you pursue your dream.

As you live the "No Excuse!" life, you can experience success with balance. Just as West Point produces leaders, "No Excuse!" living helps you to become successful. You can achieve the outcomes you want because you now have the principles you need to develop your skills and help other people.

"No Excuse!" living is exciting! Your mind has now been exposed to the opportunity for positive living, and the healthy accumulation of "wealth" in *all* areas of your life. You now know that you can open your life to the adventure of living your dream. As you apply these principles, your life can become more exhilarating than you ever imagined.

"No Excuse!" Action Plan "To Succeed And Balance Your Life"

1. Your thoughts are the only things over which you can have absolute control. Choose them wisely. You attract what you focus on and become what you think about most.

2. Boldly declare your own independence. Write it down, put a date on it, and post it where you see and read it every day. Deciding is "half-done."

3. Don't be concerned about failing; it's unwise use of your time and energy. Failure is actually meant to be a learning experience. You can literally fail your way to success.

4. Forgive yourself, others, and your environment. Let go of all resentment and hatred. You can't get to second base with one foot on first. Use your newfound energy to move-on.

5. Have self-esteem; feel respect for yourself. Eliminate the destructiveness of self-image thinking and behavior, which is based on value judging and comparison. Your fears of failure and rejection will disappear.

6. Your attitude, not your aptitude, determines your altitude. Maintain an attitude of enthusiasm and good cheer. More people will want to be around you, and you'll be able to accomplish more.

7. Sustain self-control in thought, word, and deed. It's a measure of your professionalism and how much you believe in and respect yourself, as well as others. Be patient with yourself and others as you go forward. "Overnight" successes require years of dedication.

8. Be honest in all you do. True success requires correct values and morals. Maintain your integrity at all costs. This will help you gain people's trust. You'll be able to communicate with them better, and they'll be more likely to want to associate with you.

9. Find something you're really passionate about, and pour your heart and soul into achieving it. Dream dreams and set goals

to give your life purpose and direction.   Happiness is a byproduct of working toward your vision and other things of interest to you.

10.   Learn everything you can about your chosen field.   Read books, listen to tapes, and attend seminars and training sessions. Success becomes easier the more you know.

11.   Be determined to achieve your dreams and goals.   Do whatever it takes to make it happen. Success comes to those who "never, never, never quit...." (the famous words of Sir Winston Churchill).

12.   Honor your family and friends. When "push-comes-to-shove," who really cares about you? Stay close to the most important people in your life. There is no true success without them.

13.   Learn about the various personality types.   Understand yourself and others, and you can communicate more effectively. Relating with people is essential for success.

14.   Balance your life in the seven key areas: Physical, Mental, Spiritual, Family, Career, Financial, and Social. Stop and smell the roses. Success is truly a journey, not a destination. Savor each day like the precious gem it is, and make each one count.

EQUIPMENT

*Figure it out for yourself, my lad, you've all that the
greatest of men have had, two arms, two
hands, two legs, two eyes, and a brain to use if you
would be wise. With this equipment they
all began, do start from the top and say, "I can." Look
them over, the wise and the great, they take
their food from a common plate, and similar knives
and forks they use, with similar laces
they tie their shoes, the world considers them brave and
smart, but you've all they had when they
made their start. You can triumph and come to skill,
you can be great if you only will. You're
well equipped for what fight you choose, you have arms
and legs and a brain to use, and the man
who has risen great deeds to do, began his life with no
more than you. You are the handicap you
must face, you are the one who must choose his place,
you must say where you want to go, how
much you will study, the truth to know. God has
equipped you for life, but He lets you
decide what you want to be. Courage must come from
the soul within, the man must furnish
the will to win. So figure it out for yourself, my lad,
you were born with all that the great
have had, with your equipment they all began. Get
hold of yourself, and say: "I can."*

EDGAR GUEST

Chapter 14

INCORPORATING "NO EXCUSE!" INTO YOUR LIFE

To "top-off" your journey along the *Staircase-of-Success*, we're going to share some more ideas on how you can actually incorporate the "No Excuse!" philosophy and the principles of the *THESAURUS Factor* into your daily life.

For instance, how do you practice forgiveness every day? Have you ever thought about that? Probably not. When you have allowed yourself to feel as though someone has hurt you, you may choose not to like that person for awhile rather than forgive them. Let's practice forgiving them more quickly. You'll find it to be a relief to let go of the anger and resentment. You'll have more energy to move-on.

Do you think about how you feel about yourself every day? Do you wake up and look in the mirror and say, "I'm excited"? Or do you say, "It's just another day, same old, same old"? It depends on how you feel. How is your attitude? Do you think about and work on your attitude and enthusiasm on a daily basis? Do you think about being positive? How can you be positive with other people every day? Just practice the principles of the *THESAURUS Factor*. You will notice a positive change in your attitude.

Do you believe *you*, as an individual, have the ability to make a difference in the lives of other people? Among the millions of people in the world, can you *really* make a difference? The answer is definitely "yes"!

There's a story about an old man walking on the beach. In the distance, he noticed a younger woman who seemed to be dancing at the edge of the surf. As he approached her, he saw she was actually picking up starfish, running to the ocean, and throwing them in. The old man asked, "What are you doing? Why are you spending your time like that?" She said, "If the starfish remain on the beach, they'll be killed by the heat of the sun." And the old man said, "There are thousands of starfish on the beach and hundreds of miles of beach. Why are you taking your time with them? Does it really make a difference?" The young lady picked up a starfish, looked at it, threw it into the ocean and said, "It made a difference to that one!"

We all have the ability to make a difference. No matter how many millions of people there are around us, there's still the potential to make a difference in at least one person's life. How? The key is practice; repetition of what has been shared on these pages. Think about and work on your attitude every day. Think about the differences you can make by living a "No Excuse!" life. How can you incorporate these principles? Repetition. Continue to learn, put in place what you've learned, practice it, and grow.

Affirmations–A Tool To "No Excuse!" Living

One thing that can assist you in reinforcing your ideas about "No Excuse!" living is affirmations. Wouldn't it be great to wake up in the morning and read something taped to the mirror that could help you grow? Wouldn't it be nice to have a statement posted in your office that says, "I have a positive, cheery attitude with all the people I encounter today"? Wouldn't it be wonderful to see an affirmation that says, "I have the potential, willpower, belief, and determination to accomplish everything I want to do"?

By using affirmations every day, you can make major changes in your life. Simply write the affirmations on 3" x 5" cards and post them where they can be easily seen; like on the dash of your car, bathroom mirror, or office lamp. You could call them your "No Excuse!" affirmations. They'll make it easier for you to reinforce your mind with positive suggestions every day.

An affirmation is, in essence, positive self-talk. When you consider that, on the average, seventy-five to eighty percent of what people say to themselves is negative, wouldn't it be nice to see a message that says "I like myself" each day? Or how about seeing a message that says, "I can make a difference"? Or perhaps your message could say "I am self-responsible." Or you could have a card that says, "I am responsible for the decisions I make every day."

Some other affirmations could include: "I honor my family and friends; I exercise self-control in thought, word and deed; I possess the knowledge I need for my career; I'm always learning more about my profession; I have excellent people skills; I'm continually developing my professional skills and talents; or I am a slender, healthy ____ pounds." They all start with "I," are in the present tense, are as specific as possible, and have an action verb that pertains to you.

Make a two-column list. On one side are your affirmations, and on the other, statements objecting to your affirmation; so you can "flush" out your disbelieving ideas. Eventually you'll be able to write the affirmation without the objections coming up. Read them day-in-and-day-out, and you'll be delighted at the changes they'll help you make.

Some Application Ideas From The "No Excuse!" Workbook

The "No Excuse!" workbook contains many different exercises you can use to assist you in adopting the idea of being self-responsible. Here are some key examples:

How Do You Define Success?

Defining your success is one exercise that can get you off-and-running with "No Excuse!" and self-responsibility. Begin by listening to some of the people you admire. Who do you believe is successful? Who do you aspire to be like? There may be many people you may admire, with talents in various professions. Take a look at who they are. Biographies are a wonderful source. You can learn a lot by reading about people like Abe Lincoln, Charles Lindbergh, Ben Franklin, Amelia Earhart, Thomas Edison, Mother Theresa, Teddy Roosevelt, Lee Iacocca, Martin Luther King, Jr., Eleanor Roosevelt, the Wright Brothers and many others. Learning about them can help you define how you want to be and what you want to do and accomplish.

After you do that, ask yourself, what does life have to offer me that I feel is important for me to achieve? Is it a beautiful home, travel with your family, helping your church, helping your children through college, contributing to your favorite charity, building a large business, inventing something, writing a book, or something else that excites you? What do you believe you can do to make a difference? How can you contribute more and thus create more happiness for yourself? Is it a harmonious family life, a rewarding career, or the opportunity to share with others that fulfills you?

Once you know what you want to contribute to the world, you can write your own definition of success. My definition of success is to provide for my family, have a happy home life and share "No Excuse!" with the world. Success to me is much more than material things; they come and go. It's shallow and empty to do things just for money. Don't get me wrong. We all need money to live and money is the only thing that does what it does. It is important not to focus on money, however. We need to focus on a cause, a dream, or a mission. *Success is a result of service, and money is a result of success.*

Giving Is One Of The Secrets Of Successful, Happy Living

I've found that when you discover who you are and do what you love most in serving others, you'll be happy. Life is really about giving and serving. Find what that is for you and you can have a great life; you can succeed. Again, you become and attract what you think about most.

I'd also like to reinforce the fact that, as it says in the Scriptures, "As you sow, so shall you reap." If you want to be successful, if you want to create and satisfy your definition of success, it's going to be up to you to give to other people. What you give will come back multiplied. If you're always taking from others, you may be draining them. When you need their support in the future, you may find that they are tired of giving to you without receiving anything in return.. Those you take from may have nothing left to give back to you when you need it. We all have times when we need help. When we do, we need to be humble enough to graciously receive it.

Always ask yourself if you are making enough daily deposits in your emotional bank account. Will you have a balance when you need support, or is your account overdrawn? Make deposits every day by showing kindness, fairness, honor, and respect to other people. When you do this, you will find that you are more likely to achieve whatever success is for you.

Exercise Your Power To Decide

Make a list of decisions you plan to consider in the next week, month, and year. Do you want to start a family? Do you want to be promoted? Do you want to change jobs or careers? Do you want to start your own business or make the one you have more profitable? Listing them will help reinforce what success means to you.

Will the decisions you are getting ready to make contribute to your definition of success? If you plan to make decisions that are not relevant to where you want to go, you may need to reconsider. At a minimum, be sure your decisions do not distract you from your chosen path. The key is to make decisions that are in line with your definition of success, and then do whatever it takes to make them work out. When you make a decision, realize that whatever the outcome may be, whether it's positive or negative, you are responsible for it. "No Excuse!" please!

How do you wipe out an excuse? Just say, "No Excuse!" It's a wonderfully easy, but powerful, thing to do. Catch yourself in the act! Make a list of your personal excuses. What's your favorite excuse? "I don't have enough time"? "I'm too tired"? "I don't have any money"? "My wife or husband won't let me"? "My co-workers did it"? "My boss won't let me"? "The dog ate it"? The list could go on-and-on. The point is, most of us have some favorite excuses we have used in the past because we were afraid to admit the real reason. For example, maybe the truth is that we don't want to do something rather than we don't have the time. Be honest.

We may get down on ourselves and use certain excuses to relinquish responsibility. That's exactly what excuses are used for; to avoid doing something or to "pass-the-buck." **I dare you to make a list.** Then when you hear yourself or others making an excuse, simply say, "No Excuse!" Imagine how others will respond to you when you say "No Excuse!" rather than whining and complaining. They will probably be surprised, but they'll know you're in charge of the situation.

I think whining is one of my favorite words because it has such impact. I go nuts when I hear someone whine. Does it bother you too? A person who whines tells you they are not being responsible! They are not taking charge, they are not in control, and they are not moving ahead.

Make a list of excuses, then wipe them out. Crumple-up the paper they are written on and throw them away! If you have a fireplace, light a fire and throw them into it! It can be a powerful experience.

Attitude And Self-Control Make The Difference
Take time to examine where you can have a more positive attitude and exercise more self-control. At one point we discussed how home,

of all places, is where you could use the most self-control. I believe our family members are the most important people in our lives. Sometimes, however, we may come home tired, and self-control might go "right-out-the-window." Maybe home is a place where you can assess things and say, "I could be more patient and more tolerant."

As tired as you may be after a full day of work, be sure to have some energy left to be kind and to have self-control for your family, if you have one. Before you get out of the car, tell yourself, "I'm a kind, loving, and understanding spouse and/or parent." Mentally prepare yourself to be the most skillful and caring person you can be for the ones you love the most. It can be very gratifying.

Setting Goals Defines Your Success

When you set goals, it's essential to write them down. They directly support your definition of success. Even if it's just four or five, write them down. Where do you want to be a year from now? Three years from now? Five years from now? What job do you want? Where do you want to take your business or company? Where do you want to take your family?

You'll Feel Special When You Honor Family And Friends

With family and friends, honor is the exercise here. Make a list of people you would like to show appreciation to, and send them a card or a letter. I believe they'll treasure whatever you write to them for a long time. People love to be remembered. We're not talking necessarily remembering people with something material, either. We're talking about the heart. Let those precious people, who have given of themselves to you, know that you appreciate them. As a result, you're likely to feel a warmth from them that you may have never felt before.

It is difficult to describe the impact this philosophy has had on my life. I've discovered that honoring the people I care about most has affected me in a beautiful way. I realized it was the determining factor affecting whether I would be successful or not. It has given my life greater meaning, focus, and purpose. Honor those you care about. It's the "No Excuse!" way.

Can you see how what you give out comes back to you? "No Excuse!" is not just for you; it's to be shared with others. You'll find "No Excuse!" is a way to assist and support other people. Every time you do that you'll find it helps you! Sharing "No Excuse!" principles with others helps reinforce them for you. As Ralph Waldo Emerson has said, "One of life's greatest compensations is that no man can help another without helping himself." I love that because it's so true. When you live a "No Excuse!" life, you set a wonderful example for others. It doesn't matter whether you're a parent, salesperson, manager, clerk, secretary, business owner, or do something else, some people may look to you as an example. Every day we are around others, we teach them just by the example we set. "Actions speak louder than words," someone once said.

Taking an interest in other people is the theme of Dale Carnegie's book *How To Win Friends And Influence People*. Showing respect is not to be reserved just for people who look like you either. We live in a multi-cultural environment. It is important to show respect and appreciation for everyone of every race, creed, color, or religion; no matter what. We're all in the *human* race. It is also important to respect and appreciate those with physical and mental challenges. We're all part of the world, and we all have a chance to make a difference, large or small. No one is an island unto himself; we all affect each other.

Respect is the key. How come? Because everyone has something to offer and most people want to offer it. When we discourage or prevent someone from offering their gifts, talents, and skills, we may not only negatively affect them, but also ourselves and others.

How do you show respect for other people? By being self-responsible. By providing support. When you see people who are hurting, suffering, negative, have unintact self-esteem, or little self-control, go ahead and take a step. Take a chance and say, "Look, I have some ideas that may help you. I've noticed some things about you that tell me you're hurting." Provide them with emotional support. Show them you care.

It's likely you know best what you can do for others. When you're self-responsible, I believe you'll find you want to give support to others. Share your knowledge and understanding. Share the "No Excuse!" concept with other people.

Begin incorporating not just "No Excuse!" into your life, but all the resources that are available for you to grow. If you've enjoyed this book, there are lots of other materials on the market that can reinforce and supplement what you've learned here. You will find some excellent titles listed at the back of this book. Share those and other resources you find with others too. Help people get on the path of self-responsibility. Encourage them to know that they are the decision-makers for their own life. There are many people using excuses who are not taking responsibility for their families, careers, or personal lives. When you can at least share the knowledge with them, even if they don't agree with everything you say, it may make a difference. If you can only help them open their minds just a little, you've made a difference!

The "bottom line" in helping others, in making a difference, can be found in this little phrase: *People don't care how much you know, until they know how much you care.* We all have the ability to give to other people, and at least one person has a need for what you can give.

Why Is It Necessary To Live A Balanced Life?

To live a happy, fulfilling life, we need balance. What good would it be to achieve success, while totally disregarding how you treat other people? You probably wouldn't enjoy your success much, not to mention all the enemies you'd make! Of all the ideas discussed, balance is critical. The environment, the eco-system we live in, is in a state of balance. Do you know what happens when something gets out of balance? Something else is negatively impacted.

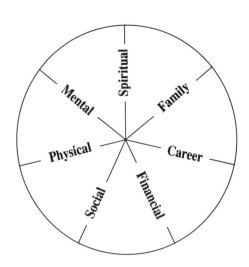

THE WHEEL OF LIFE

All "spokes" need to be of equal length for your life to be balanced.

The world was not created "out-of-balance," and neither were you. Take a look at all seven areas of your life: Social, Physical, Mental, Spiritual, Family, Career, and Financial. Ask yourself if you're spending too much time in any one particular area. Is your life in balance? Or is your life like a car with an out-of-balance tire—a little shaky? For example, are you spending too much time at work and leaving your family or your spiritual well-being behind? Are you spending too much time on household or other responsibilities while letting your health deteriorate? Are you doing too much volunteering, while your income suffers? It may be necessary to be out-of-balance for awhile to accomplish something. Remember though, "All things in moderation" is an excellent rule to live by in general. You may want to consider examining your life and balancing things out, if necessary.

Take some time for recreation. If all you do is work, and you never play, you may create a pretty dull life. Pace yourself. You can accomplish more in the long run.

It is helpful to sit down and analyze exactly where you're spending time and energy. Eventually you can get a clearer picture of what's happening in your life, and you'll be better able to make appropriate adjustments. If you discover that you spend too much time at work and are "almost never" home for your family, you could lose your most precious relationships. You could take action to perhaps delegate some work to your staff and go home earlier. Or you could explain to your boss that you need an assistant.

If you don't take care of your health, your body will have to work that much harder to maintain itself. You may get away with it for awhile and not notice a decline, but eventually it'll catch up with you and your body may say, "No more." That's where physical and mental breakdowns can come from; too much stress and not enough regard for your health. Whatever you don't take care of eventually goes away. This dentist joke explains it so well: The dentist said, "Don't take care of your teeth, and they'll go away!" Your health can "go away" too.

You may not think much about your spiritual life either, but it's so important. It gives you that "something extra." It helps give you a vision and an understanding of why you're here to begin with. Why were you put here on this earth? The spiritual aspect of your life is vitally important in helping you determine your purpose. Life is really about serving. Find out how you can best serve, then do it. When you serve, success will follow.

You've probably heard the expression "money is the root of all evil." Is that true? Of course not! The actual words are, "The love of money is a root of evil." Money pays for food, shelter, clothing, heat, transportation, education, schools, churches, and many other things. Without money, it would be almost impossible to live and participate in today's society. If you neglect the financial aspect of your life, it's probably out of balance. Did you know that arguments and situations that arise from lack of (or mismanaged) money are a major cause of family challenges?

After most of us finish school, some people may have a tendency to neglect the mental aspect of life. They may stop reading, learning, and growing. There are so many excellent books and other resources available today, there is "No Excuse!" for not growing. If you want a richer, fuller, more rewarding life, you need to learn and grow. The mind is like a muscle. If it's not exercised, it will atrophy. Einstein once said that we use less than 10% of our brain! Just think of the untapped resource that resides in your head. You probably eat three times a day to nourish your body. Could you read 15 to 30 minutes a day from a personal development or educational book to enrich your mind?

Self-Responsibility To The Rescue

I remember one night when I learned just how exciting "No Excuse!" living can be.

We were seniors at West Point. One weekend, three of us traveled to visit a women's college in Saratoga Springs, New York. Even though we knew an early start back to the Academy would have been an excellent idea (considering winter travel conditions in upstate New York), we delayed our departure. When we finally left, we knew we were cutting our two-and-a-half hour trip pretty close.

Two hours from West Point, just outside of Albany, the car broke down and the snowstorm picked up. That was not an ideal situation; cadets who return late face disciplinary action.

In the silent car surrounded by swirling snow, we began to feel a bit queasy thinking about what we were about to face. We saw ourselves saying, "No Excuse, Sir!" to an officer as we accepted the discipline. We would be an example to all of the price to be paid for returning late. Our fear of that outcome was enough for us to come up with a plan that propelled me into "No Excuse!" action. Out of the car and away from the road I bolted, jumping guard rails, crashing through frozen fields, over a fence, dashing through a parking lot, and into a nearby church. I ran like a cartoon character. My mission: bring Mother to the rescue.

I called her at home, less than an hour away in Kingston, New York, and she promised to come. We then began a journey against time and the elements that none of us will ever forget.

Until you've driven the highway that wraps around Storm King Mountain near West Point, racing against time, in a blizzard, in your mother's car, with your mother a passenger in it, with two friends you think are thinking you really could go faster, you may not quite understand the excitement that "No Excuse!" living can bring.

When we arrived at West Point, we were ecstatic as we leapt from the car, gave Mom a hurried but grateful farewell, and suggested she drive slowly back to Kingston. (Mom deserves a lot of credit for being a "No Excuse!" person.) We then dashed to the doorway of the Orderly room and caught our breath before going in to sign our names and time of return in the "cadet sign-in book." We did not need to even consider making any excuses! Our self-responsibility, along with Mom's help, saved us.

Now that's a story that could have been included in "Remember To Honor Family and Friends." Mom honored her family (me) by helping us out. The principles and pleasures of the *THESAURUS Factor* overlap.

That story, even though it's a light-hearted retelling of a high-spirited predicament and rescue, demonstrates a lot of what "No Excuse!" living is all about. It's about family and friends and enjoyment of life. It's about exceeding ordinary limits when circumstances demand it. It's about enlisting the aid of allies who believe in the cause. It's about experiencing great satisfaction when the goal has been met by doing whatever it takes. It's about building success.

Our desire to be back on time said something about the kind of officers we wanted to be. Honoring the expected standards says something about the kind of officers we became.

The Little Boy In The Park
I will leave you with one final story. A little boy was walking through the park. He looked down and found a shiny penny in the grass. He picked it up and was very excited and pleased. He was so turned-on by finding the "free" money, that every time he went outside his head would be down as he looked for more. Over the course of his lifetime he found many nickels, dimes, quarters, and even a few dollar bills. They totalled $12.96.

That money hadn't "cost" him anything, or so he thought.   In reality, however, the true cost was in what he missed: about 30,000 sunsets and over 300 rainbows, his children growing up, birds singing and flying in the sky, sunshine, laughter, and so many other beautiful things. The lesson here is to remember to look beyond day-to-day activities; pick your head up and look at the true riches and splendor life has to offer. Live fully and enjoy your journey.

The Rewards Of "No Excuse!" Living

West Point and the Army were magnificent experiences—"No Excuse!" experiences! They taught me to live a "No Excuse!" life, which led to developing this program and writing this book.

The Army did many great things for me. I'm especially thankful for learning the value of family, friends, God, country, and myself. The greatest gift the Army gave me, however, was teaching me to accept responsibility for my own life. The Army also taught me to move-on to a new challenge when my purpose indicated it was necessary; when it was the "No Excuse!" thing to do.

I hope you embrace the "No Excuse!" lifestyle, practice self-responsibility, and take care of your family and yourself. Follow the dream in your heart and become the best *you* you can be. When the going gets tough, just say, "No Excuse!" It can help you to overcome obstacles and achieve personal excellence.

THE "NO EXCUSE!" CREED

*I am a "No Excuse!" person. I live self-responsibly and
I am accountable for everything I say and do.
I know what it means to be alive, and my direction is
clear. I understand my purpose in life, and
do things with a sense of mission. I act with integrity,
own all my decisions, and always do the best
I can. I forgive myself and others for what was or was
not done that may have caused heartache
and failure in the past. I forgive my environment and
I overcome obstacles. I let go of the past
and move-on to achieve excellence. I have intact self-
esteem and maintain it by value judging no one.
I give everyone total unconditional acceptance, because
we are all equal in the eyes of God. I am
no better than anyone else, and no one is better than
me. However, as a "No Excuse!" person, I am
always confident of my talents and skills. I maintain
excellent health, feel energetic, and carry a
cheerful countenance. I maintain self-control in
thought, word, and deed, and I have the patience to
see things through. I am always honest
with myself and others, and set goals which are true for
me. I have a dream big enough to overcome
my fears, handle risks, and live the life I choose. I am
always learning and growing; ever expanding
my mind and learning new skills. I care about people,
and encourage them to be all they can be. I understand and communicate effectively with
others. I honor my family and friends and realize how
important they are to me. I respect others,
appreciate their talents and skills, and have love and
compassion for everyone. I have a strong
desire to serve others and make a difference. I balance
my activities among the seven key areas of life:
Physical, Mental, Spiritual, Family, Career, Financial,
and Social. My life is a product of the decisions
I make, and I am in charge of it. I have "No Excuse!"
All my excuses are gone. "No Excuse!" living is for me.
I am a "No Excuse!" person.*

EPILOGUE

At the beginning of this book, I was twelve-hundred-and-fifty feet above the earth and falling fast. My parachute lines had twisted and the parachute would not open.

As the ground came "rushing up" to meet me, I realized I had two choices. I could either hit the earth and die, or I could accept responsibility for my life and take the steps necessary to live.

Gathering all the courage I could muster, and with the knowledge I had learned in training to assist me, I took charge. My survival was at stake. The "No Excuse!" philosophy rang in my ears. It forced my feet, in heavy combat boots, to move in a circular motion and loosen the lines that threatened to "hang" me.

Success!

I called on the best I had in me and survived. Like magic, my parachute fluttered open and I floated gently to the ground.

That parachute jump is an illustration of the "No Excuse!" philosophy in action. By learning the skills needed to jump, and accepting responsibility for my own survival, I overcame an obstacle as big as the sky.

As you embrace the teachings of this book and put them to use in your life, you too can find ways to float safely and successfully to the destinations of your choice.

May I suggest that you consider the "No Excuse!" philosophy and the steps of the *THESAURUS Factor* as the basic training for your jump into a new life.   Remember, there's no need to "fall-in-a-tangled-mess." The lessons you have had an opportunity to learn can, like a parachute, carry you gently over any thresholds you want to cross.

Then comes the greatest thrill of all. When you finally land in the place you want to be, you can "hit-the-ground-running." You can shrug off the parachute that once buoyed you up, set your sights on a new challenge, and charge off toward the bright horizon to achieve your dreams and goals with boundless optimism and energy.

Best wishes, "No Excuse!" cadets. Go for it and be an example of excellence for others to follow. This is not "The End." It's "The Beginning" of your "No Excuse!" life; a life based on self-responsibility, purpose, and integrity. God bless you. March forth and make a difference....

HIGH FLIGHT

*Oh, I have slipped the surly bonds of earth and danced
the skies on laughter's silver wings. Sunward
I have climbed and joined the tumbling mirth of sun-
split clouds, and done a hundred things you
have not dreamed of. Wheeled and soared and swung
high in the sunlit silence. Hovering there, I
have chased the shouting wind alone and flown my
eagle craft through footless halls of air. Up,
up the long, delirious burning blue, I have topped the
wind-swept heights with easy grace where
never lark or even eagle flew. And then, with silent
lifting mind, I have trod the high,
untrespassed sanctity of faith, put out my hand, and
touched the face of God.*

JOHN GILLESPIE MAGEE, JR.

APPENDIX

Acknowledgements (continued)

We have a wonderful feeling of gratitude for the development and production of the book, which would have been impossible without you:

To our parents, Catherine (in loving memory) and Mark Markowski, and Roy (in loving memory) and Alice Roth who taught us our work ethic, to strive for excellence, and to live self-responsibly with purpose and integrity. We are eternally grateful for the way you raised us and always saying "you can do it!"

To our teachers, professors, and pastors, especially Dr. Robert Schuller, for what we learned from them and the values they instilled in us.

To Toni, Rose, and Bob for all their love and support.

To Rich DeVos and Jay Van Andel for encouraging free enterprise and compassionate capitalism, and giving us an opportunity to develop and succeed.

To Fred and Linda Harteis for their most excellent training and development programs, example, love, and support.

To our mentors and friends, Greg and Lin Johnson, for their leadership, encouragement, and love.

To our friends and business associates Kerry and Helen Brooks, Ko Lindeboom, Dave and Ellen Beauclaire, and Doug and Kay Haldeman for your love and encouragement.

To Miriam Burkart for her love, mentorship, and belief in us, as well as for her raising our understanding of self-esteem and allowing us to incorporate her ideas into the text.

To Dr. Robert Rohm for his remarkable teachings on personality types, raising our understanding of people, and allowing us to incorporate his ideas into the text.

To Gary Smalley for his wonderful teachings on honoring people.

To Rudy Ruettiger for his inspiring movie, *Rudy*, and book *Rudy's Rules*.

To Charlie "Tremendous" Jones for his love, mentorship, encouragement, and example.

To thank God for blessing us with the talents and skills needed to publish this book and for leading us to our true mission in life. We also thank Him for our precious relationship and how we complement each other so well. We are truly blessed.

To Jay Rifenbary, special friend and business associate, for developing the "No Excuse!" philosophy and honoring us by choosing us as his publisher. It is truly a joy working with you.

To Kathy Mahony for her Herculean efforts in deciphering our handwriting, and typing and re-typing the manuscript so many times we lost track!

To Adrianne Kihm and Richard Rossiter for great cover design work.

To our dear friend and editorial consultant, Michelle Taylor Zdankiewicz, for her loving support and encouragement, and for "tearing-the-manuscript-apart" and bringing clarity to several key issues.

To Dan Poynter and Tony Curtis for their mentoring in the publishing business. Thanks for sharing your knowledge, wisdom, understanding, encouragement, and most of all, your friendship.

To John Zuknick, our super sales rep, and Craig Meeson and the gang at Fairfield Graphics for their great work in manufacturing the book.

To all those whose wisdom developed the inspirational quotes used throughout the book. We are all richer for your contributions.

And finally, to all the individuals who reviewed the book and provided their heartfelt testimony.

-Mike & Marjie Markowski

BIBLIOGRAPHY
AND SUGGESTED READING

Allen, James, *As A Man Thinketh*, Grosset and Dunlap, New York, 1959.
Ambrose, Stephen E., *The Supreme Commander: War Years of General Dwight D. Eisenhower*, Doubleday, Garden City, NY, 1970.
Andrews, Andy, *Storms of Perfection*, Lightning Crown, Nashville, TN, 1991.
Bassham, Lanny, *With Winning In Mind*, Press Publications, San Antonio, TX, 1989.
Begg, John, *The Story of The Declaration of Independence*, Oxford University Press, New York, NY, 1954.
Bland, Glenn, *Success! The Glenn Bland Method*, Tyndale House, Wheaton, IL, 1972.
Blumenson, Martin, *Patton—The Man Behind The Legend 1885-1945*, William Morrow & Co., Inc., New York, NY, 1985.
Bradley, Omar N., *A General's Life*, Simon & Schuster, New York, NY, 1983.
Bradley, Omar N., *A Soldiers Story*, Henry Holt and Co., New York, NY, 1951.
Brown, Les, *Live Your Dreams*, William Morrow, New York, NY, 1992.
Bugle Notes 1976-1980, Volume 68, United States Military Academy, West Point, NY, 1976.
Carnegie, Dale, *How To Win Friends And Influence People*, Pocket Books, New York, NY, 1981.
Carnegie, Dale, *How To Stop Worrying And Start Living*, Pocket Books, New York, NY, 1984.
Churchill, Winston, *A Churchill Reader*, Houghton Mifflin Co., Boston, MA, 1954.
Cohen, Roger and Claudio Gatti, *In the Eye of the Storm: The Life of General H. Norman Schwartzkopf*, Farrar, Straus and Giroux, New York, NY, 1991.
"Cornell Today," *Alumni Profiles*, Winter, 1993, p. 3.
Covey, Stephen R., *Seven Habits of Highly Effective People*, Simon & Schuster, New York, NY, 1989.
DeVos, Rich, *Compassionate Capitalism*, Penguin, New York, NY, 1993.
Farago, Ladislas, *Patton Ordeal and Triumph*, Ivan Obolensky, Inc., New York, NY, 1964.
Finkelstein, Norman H., *The Emperor General: A Biography of Douglas MacArthur*, Dillon Press, Minneapolis, MN, 1989.
Fisher, Robert, *The Knight in Rusty Armor*, Melvin Powers, N. Hollywood, CA, 1990.
Flexner, James Thomas, *George Washington in the American Revolution 1775-1783*, Little, Brown and Co., Boston, MA, 1967.
Frankl, Viktor, *Man's Search For Meaning*, Pocket Books, New York, NY, 1984.
Gabor, Don, *How To Start a Conversation and Make Friends*, Simon and Schuster, New York, NY, 1983.
Giblin, Les, *How To Have Power And Confidence In Dealing With People*, Prentice-Hall, Englewood Cliffs, NJ, 1956.
Gilbert, Martin, *Churchill: A Life*, Henry Holt & Co., New York, NY, 1991.
Grant, Ulysses, *Personal Memoirs of U.S. Grant—Selected Letters 1839-1865*, Southern Illinois University Press, 1967-1985.
Griffith, Joe, *Speaker's Library of Business Stories, Anecdotes and Humor*, Prentice-Hall, Inc., New Jersey, 1990.
Hill, Napoleon, *Think & Grow Rich*, Ballantine Books, New York, NY, 1937.

Jeffers, Susan, Ph.D., *Feel The Fear And Do It Anyway*, Fawcett Columbine Book, New York, NY, 1987.
Jones, Charlie, *"Tremendous," Life Is Tremendous*, Tyndale House, Wheaton, IL, 1968.
Just, Ward, *Military Men*, Alfred A. Knopf, New York, NY, 1970.
Littauer, Florence, *Dare To Dream*, Word Publishing, Dallas, TX, 1991.
Littauer, Florence, *Personality Plus*, Power Books, Old Tappen, NJ, 1983.
Manchester, William, *American Caesar: Douglas MacArthur 1880-1964*. Little, Brown, & Co., Boston, MA, 1978.
Mandino, O.G., *The Greatest Miracle In The World*, Bantam, New York, NY, 1975.
McGinnis, Alan Loy, *Bringing Out The Best In People*, Augsburg, Minneapolis, MN, 1985.
McGrane, William, CPAE, *Brighten Your Day With Self-Esteem*, Markowski International (Success Publishers), Hummelstown, PA, 1995.
Miers, Earl Schenck, *Abraham Lincoln in Peace and War*, American Heritage Publishing Co., Inc., New York, NY, 1964.
Mumford, Lewis, *Ralph Waldo Emerson: Essays & Journals*, The Programmed Classics, Nelson Doubleday, Inc., 1968.
O'Brien, Robert and Morris Chafetz, M.D., *The Encyclopedia of Alcoholism, 2nd Edition*, Facts on File and Greenspring, Inc., New York, NY, 1991.
O'Brien, Robert; Sidney Cohen, M.D.; Glen Evans; and James Fine, M.D., *The Encyclopedia of Drug Abuse, 2nd Edition*, Facts on File and Greenspring, Inc., New York, NY, 1991.
Owen, G. Frederick, *Abraham Lincoln—The Man and His Faith*, Tyndale House Publishers, Inc., Wheaton, IL, 1967.
Parks, Rosa, and Elaine Steele, *Quiet Strength*, Zondervan Publishing House, Grand Rapids, MI, 1995.
Peale, Dr. Norman Vincent, *The Power of Positive Thinking*, Ballantine Books, New York, NY, 1982.
Peale, Dr. Norman Vincent, *You Can If You Think You Can*, Prentice-Hall, New York, NY, 1974.
Peale, Dr. Norman Vincent, *Enthusiasm Makes The Difference*, Prentice-Hall, New York, NY, 1967.
Peck, M. Scott, M.D., *The Road Less Traveled*, Simon and Schuster, New York, NY, 1978.
Peifer, Charles Jr., *Soldier of Destiny: A Biography of George Patton*, Dillon Press, Minneapolis, MN, 1989.
Peterson, Merril D., *Thomas Jefferson & The New Nation*, Oxford University Press, New York, NY, 1970.
"Review & Outlook, Responsibility's Return," *The Wall Street Journal*, New York, January 21, 1993, p. A14.
Rohm, Robert A., Ph.D., *Positive Personality Profiles*, Personality Insights, Inc., Atlanta, GA 1994.
Ruettiger, Rudy and Mike Celizic, *Rudy's Rules*, WRS Publishing, Waco, TX, 1995.
Rutledge, Leigh, *Excuses, Excuses*, Penguin Books USA, Inc., New York, NY, 1992.
Satir, Virginia, *My Declaration of Self-Esteem*, The Avanta Network, Issaquah, WA.
Schatt, Stanley, *Kurt Vonnegut Jr.*, Twayne Publishers, Boston, MA, 1976.
Schloegel, Irmgard, *Wisdom of the Zen Masters*, New Directions Publishing Corp.
Schuller, Dr. Robert H., *The Be Happy Attitudes*, Bantam, New York, NY 1987.
Schuller, Dr. Robert H., *Self-Love*, Hawthorn Books, New York, NY, 1978.
Schuller, Dr. Robert H., *Tough Times Never Last, But Tough People Do!*, Thomas Nelson, Nashville, TN, 1983.

Schwartz, Dr. David J., *The Magic of Thinking Success*, Wilshire Book Co., N. Hollywood, CA, 1987.

Schwartz, Dr. David J., *The Magic of Thinking Big*, Simon and Schuster, New York, NY, 1987.

Schwartzkopf, H. Norman, *It Doesn't Take A Hero*, Bantam Books, New York, NY, 1992.

Seuss, Dr., *Oh The Places You'll Go*, Random House, Inc., New York, NY, 1990.

Shakespeare, William, *King Henry V*, Cambridge University Press, New York, NY, 1947.

Smalley, Gary, *For Better or Best*, Harper Collins, New York, NY, 1988.

Smalley, Gary, *Homes of Honor*, Today's Family, Missouri, 1994.

Timberlake, Lewis, *Born To Win*, Tyndale House, Illinois, 1986.

"Training Notes: The Ranger Course," *Infantry Magazine*, May-June, 1991, p. 37.

Van Ekeren, Glenn, *The Speakers Sourcebook*, Prentice-Hall, Inc., New Jersey, 1988.

"We Are All Responsible," *Parade Magazine*, April 11, 1993, p. 4-7.

Whitelaw, Nancy, *Theodore Roosevelt Takes Charge*, Albert Whitman & Co., Morton Grove, IL, 1992.

Wilson, Larry, *Changing The Game: The New Way To Sell*, Simon & Schuster, New York, NY, 1987.

ABOUT THE AUTHOR

Jay Rifenbary, husband and father, is a professional speaker, consultant, and trainer, and founder and president of the Rifenbary Training & Development Center. He is a graduate of the United States Military Academy at West Point and was a qualified Airborne/Ranger and Military Commander. He was also a top ranking Sales Professional, Corporate Manager, and Entrepreneur. He is a member of the National Speakers Association, and in 1995 was officially recognized as New York State's "Most Outstanding Citizen" in the field of business.

Jay brings a unique background of interpersonal skills, military experience, and business acumen to each of his speaking and training engagements. He is sought after as a speaker and author on success, motivation, leadership, communication, team building, and family and interpersonal relationships. He lives with his wife, Noni, and their two children, Nicole and Jared, in Saratoga Springs, New York.

ABOUT THE RIFENBARY TRAINING & DEVELOPMENT CENTER

This organization is dedicated to assisting individuals in their personal and professional development, and to improving organizations in their quest to be more productive and profitable. Their mission statement reads:

Our mission is to provide individuals and organizations with the finest resources and training for the accomplishment of their goals, through the teaching and application of "No Excuse!" principles, and the integration of self-responsible behavior.

The Rifenbary Training & Development Center accomplishes this mission by conducting on-site development seminars and workshops that empower leading corporations, including: financial, medical, real estate, and manufacturing industries. It also works with military, government, educational, and network marketing organizations. RT&DC provides a variety of "No Excuse!" subject areas.

- *No Excuse!* - **An Action Plan For Success**
- *No Excuse!* **Leadership–Today's Manager, Tomorrow's Leader**
- *No Excuse!* **Communicating–Overcoming The Communication Barriers With Others**
- *No Excuse!* **Teaming–Implementing Self-Responsible Work Teams**

(NOTE: *No Excuse! - An Action Plan For Success* is available as a keynote, half-day, full-day, or multiple-day training session. All other "No Excuse!" topic areas are available as full-day or multiple-day training sessions.)

"No Excuse!" training programs and seminars have positively affected lives from young adults to CEO's. They provide insights and techniques to ignite an organization's productivity. They also help individuals recognize and utilize principles to create a richer, happier, more fulfilling and rewarding life experience.

Other resources include:

- The *No Excuse!* introductory video/audio/workbook set.
- The *No Excuse!* audiocassette training set.

For more detailed information on on-site seminars and available resources contact:

The Rifenbary Training & Development Center
12 Bog Meadow Run
Saratoga Springs, NY 12866
1-(800)-724-0845; 1-(518)-587-6411; Fax: (518)-587-6417

Resources

The following organizations contributed to this book in a special way, and they have a lot to offer. You may contact them for further information about their products, services, seminars, and workshops.

- Avanta—The Virginia Satir Network, 310 3rd Avenue NE, Suite 126, Issaquah, WA 98027; (206) 391-7310. Personal development and relationship issues. Virginia Satir's *My Declaration of Self-Esteem* is used with permission of Avanta. All rights reserved. A poster is available.
- McGrane Self-Esteem Institute, 2055 Dixie Highway, Suite 114, Ft. Mitchell, KY 41011; (800) 341-3304; (606) 341-2216; Fax: (606) 341-9634. Self-esteem issues, *The Tree* poster, and *Brighten Your Day With Self-Esteem—How To Empower, Energize, and Motivate Yourself to a Richer, Fuller, More Rewarding Life*, is available in book and audiocassette tape album. Contact the Institute for individual sales and the Publisher for quantity sales.
- Personality Insights, Inc., P.O. Box 26592. Atlanta, GA 30358-0592; (404) 509-7113; Fax: (404) 509-1484. Personality issues, including computer analysis. The book *Positive Personality Profiles*, by Dr. Robert A. Rohm, is available directly from Personality Insights.
- Today's Family/Homes of Honor, 1483 Lakeside Drive, Branson, MO 65616; (800) 848-6329; Fax: (417) 336-3515. Family and relationship issues.

Quantity Sales of *No Excuse!* in book and audiocassette album are available at special quantity discounts when purchased in bulk by corporations, organizations, and special interest groups. Custom imprinting can also be done to meet specific needs. For details contact:

Success Publishers/Markowski Int'l
One Oakglade Circle
Hummelstown, PA 17036
(717) 566-0468; Fax: (717) 566-6423

Leaders Comments (continued from page 4)

"No Excuse! provides the necessary philosophy to allow people to grow and become better people. As a secondary classroom teacher, this philosophy of "No Excuse!" is a welcome alternative to adolescent blaming and lack of ownership in the educational process. What a great philosophy for life!"

-Charles A. Kuenzel, M.S.
Former Vice President, Saratoga Teacher's Association

"Every entrepreneur would be thrilled to have his key management exercising the principles in this book. One cannot but wonder why they (key management) do not understand this."

-Greg Sutliff
Owner, Sutliff Chevrolet/Sutliff Saturn, Inc.

"In his warm, easy to read, and down to earth style, Jay presents proven methods for achieving success in your business and personal life. He encourages you to take responsibility for your life and make healthy and practical choices. *No Excuse!* is highly motivating and leaves you bursting with optimism and enthusiasm."

-Bernard J. Sullivan, Ph.D.
Clinical Psychologist

"The "No Excuse!" philosophy is an excellent business success tool, and it was my first exposure to you. However, the "No Excuse" presentation you made to my whole family served its highest and best purpose. Your passion for your message and the intensely personal delivery evoked tears and laughter from the ten-year-old to the octogenarians. Most importantly, months later, you are still the frequent subject of our conversations. This book is full of gems that work for families and businesses."

-Geff Yancey
President, Perry's Ice Cream
Past President, Heluva Good Cheese
Former Candidate for Lieutenant Governor, State of NY, 1990

"An enthusiastic and positive approach to taking responsibility for oneself! Mr. Rifenbary seems to have put a lot of himself into this book. His personality and powers of persuasion are evident on every page. The book is filled with encouragement and inspiring stories of success. His description of the components of self-responsibility is very helpful. The visual representation of the *THESAURUS Factor* helps people carry shorthand reminders in their memories. The book doesn't say 'Just do it!' and tell superficial stories about other people's experiences; it offers practical advice on how to achieve fulfillment by taking responsibility for one's life. It was enlightening to me, and I believe it will be a great help to many others."

-Edward B. Carskadon
Former Chief of Staff to the Secretary
Pennsylvania State Department of Public Welfare

"*No Excuse!* provides a practical and purposeful game plan to help you make your dreams come true. This book reflects the notion that 'It is important to value what you do...and to do what you value.' *No Excuse!* guides you through the 12 principles of the *THESAURUS Factor* and at the same time increases your response-ability."

-Dr. Joel Goodman
Director, The HUMOR Project
Author of *Laffirmations: 1001 Ways To Add Humor To Your Life and Work*

"*No Excuse!* is a terrific book. I was very impressed with the motivational thoughts and fascinating examples. It will help anyone who reads it. I strongly recommend it."

-Pat Williams
General Manager, The Orlando Magic

"*No Excuse!* will fill a void in the personal and professional lives of everyone who reads it. Through Jay's insight and the principles presented, *No Excuse!* provides the essence for developing more effective leaders and higher levels of organizational productivity. *No Excuse!* will have an enduring, positive impact at home and at work."

-John Brekke
President, Brekke International Consulting, Inc.
Minneapolis, MN

"Jay has taken a timeless message and turned it into a working tool that facilitates success."

-Matt Oechsli
President, Oechsli Institute
Author of *Mind Power For Students*

GIVING AND RECEIVING

I launched a smile; far out it sailed
On life's wide, troubled sea.
And many more than I could count
Came sailing back to me.
I clasped a hand while whispering,
"The clouds will melt away."
I felt my life was very blessed
All through the hours that day.
I sent a thought of happiness
Where it was needed sore,
And very soon thereafter, found
Joy adding to my store.
I wisely shared my slender hoard,
Toil-earned coins of gold;
But presently it flowed right back.
Increased a hundredfold.
I helped another climb a hill,
A little thing to do;
And yet it brought a rich reward,
A friendship that was new.
I think each morning when I rise,
Of how I may achieve,
I know by serving I advance,
By giving I receive.

THOMAS GAINES